MUHAMMAD ALI

THE LIFE OF A LEGEND

FIAZ RAFIQ

This edition first published in Great Britain in 2020 by

ARENA SPORT
An imprint of Birlinn Limited
West Newington House
10 Newington Road
Edinburgh
EH9 1QS

www.arenasportbooks.co.uk

First published in 2010 as *Muhammad Ali: Conversations* by HNL Publishing
Copyright © Fiaz Rafiq, 2010 & 2020

ISBN: 9781909715936
eBook ISBN: 9781788853293

British Library Cataloguing-in-Publication Data
A catalogue record for this book is available on request from the British Library.

Designed and typeset by Polaris Publishing, Edinburgh
www.polarispublishing.com

Printed in Great Britain by CPI Group

CONTENTS

ACKNOWLEDGMENTS

A big thank you to the staff of *M.A.I.* and *Impact* magazines: Moira, Martin, Neal, John, Roy and especially editor Bob Sykes for giving me the opportunity and embracing me earlier on my writing career. The fifteen years working relationship was fun. To all my editors at the magazines and national newspapers whose help and support have contributed to my success in my professional writing career. Also, I would like to thank the personalities I have interviewed over the years from the sports and entertainment worlds – you are an integral part of the reason behind my success.

I would like to thank my personal long-time friends Diana Lee Inosanto; Royce Gracie; Rasheda Ali; Ron Balicki; Bob Sykes; Ronnie Green, Lance Lewis, Seyfi Shevket and Peter Consterdine for their countless years of support and encouragement.

I would like to thank Muhammad Ali's brother Rahaman Ali, and Ron Brashear for their friendship and working relationship. I would like to thank my agent Charlie Brotherstone.

Thank you to my editor Joel Snape for editing the manuscript. A special thank you must go to Neville Moir and my editor Pete Burns at my publishers, Arena, for believing in me and for all their hard work.

I would like to thank my friends in the industry, both in the USA and United Kingdom, who have enriched my life and supported me.

Last but not least, thanks to the man himself, Muhammad Ali, and also Bruce Lee, for without you both my dreams may never have manifested into a reality.

FOREWORD

I was deeply honored when my dear friend Fiaz Rafiq asked me to write the foreword to his book *Muhammad Ali: The Life of a Legend.* It was refreshing to read all of the beautiful encounters from prominent figures that made a huge impact in my father's career. Figures such as Angelo Dundee, Jim Brown, Sugar Ray Leonard, George Foreman, Chuck Wepner, Larry Holmes, Dr. Harry Edwards, Lou Gossett Jr, Jose Sulaiman, Butch Lewis, and many others. These stories encompass the diversity of my father: the sportsman, friend, father, family man, humanitarian and icon.

What made my dad the greatest was his inexplicable talents in the ring, but most of all the love he had for his people. It was incredibly spiritual how he made others, especially minorities and African-Americans, feel about themselves. What he stood for and how he inspired the world to be great and do great things will continue to impact the very foundation of our hearts. I hope this oral biography helps to inspire others to not only love themselves, but make a difference in others' lives and encourage us to be the best version of ourselves.

Thank you for the memories.

God bless.

Rasheda Ali

PREFACE

One of the most remarkable personalities of our time and perhaps the greatest sportsman to emerge in the modern era is Muhammad Ali. A figure of mythic proportions who was perhaps the most recognizable man alive in his time, at the height of his career The Greatest made it into the *Guinness Book of Records* for being the most written about human being on the planet. Ali himself, of course, was characteristically humble about his own stature. "I'm the most recognized and loved man that ever lived because there weren't no satellites when Jesus and Moses were around," he told one interviewer, not long after John Lennon proclaimed The Beatles bigger than Jesus. "So people far away in the villages didn't know about them."

Almost four decades after his last fight, Ali is still remembered for both his boxing and his principles – for the daring lean-away style and hummingbird jab that flummoxed Sonny Liston and the stand he took against the Vietnam War, for his battles with Frazier and Foreman and his willingness to spend time with almost anyone. He was a fighter with a great love for the world, and a figure who carried his bravery far beyond the ring. He might be more beloved today than he was as the heavyweight champ, appealing to men and women, young and old.

For me, Ali has been one of the two great influences in my life. Muhammad Ali and Bruce Lee both impacted pop culture and the world in different ways, two fighters who changed the meaning of the word and had a profound effect on me personally. Both men stood up for what they believed in. Both men fought against racist stereotypes, overcame insurmountable odds and left legacies that are still in evidence today. Lee's spectacular life was cut short as he was reaching him prime – his early death cemented his legendary status. Ali lived to the ripe age of 74, and his influence is arguably greater.

Having already interviewed dozens of Bruce Lee's friends, relatives and associates to write an oral history of the Little Dragon, I knew from experience that such an endeavor was one of the best ways to shed new light on a beloved icon. I also knew from the beginning of writing this book that attempting to capture the life of an individual of the caliber of Ali would be an arduous task – to say nothing of trying to say something new about a man who has had so many column inches, books, films and TV shows devoted to him. Nevertheless, The Greatest endeared himself to me as I pursued him – with every revelation from his friends and family revealing more about a man that so many people know something about. I was intrigued as I immersed myself in Ali's life, finding new depths to a man already famous for his charitable work and giving nature. There were also complexities to the three-time heavyweight champion that I had never considered, strengths and weaknesses that humanized the legend as I learned about them. Gradually, I began to piece together the jigsaw puzzle of a complex man – his political, social and religious leanings, his sensibilities and habits, and the things that made him so beloved.

I have gone to some lengths to make this tome a balanced read as well as a compelling one. I believe, and I'm sure many may share this thought, that it is incumbent to broach the facets of Ali's life that go beyond his boxing career. Ali was a catalyst for social change, which resonated with and endeared him to many people. Of course, the humanistic side to the man and the public persona are both appealing and profoundly define the essence of Ali's true character.

This book has been a tremendous task to put together. In researching it, I reached out to dozens of Ali's family members, friends and colleagues, collaborators, coaches and acquaintances. I spoke to old sparring partners about days in the gym, to former opponents about how it felt to face the greatest of all time, and to some of his closest friends about how Ali acted when the cameras were off. What I hope emerges is a more intimate sort of biography, an unvarnished version of events that allows everyone to tell their own story. I feel with great conviction that this unconventional approach is one of the best ways to tell a story, as it allows the reader to make up their own minds about a complex individual and build up their own picture of who he was as a man. In these pages, you'll discover a vibrant, humorous, intuitive man who was a warm, caring and approachable person – an astonishing fighter who was as gentle outside the ring as he was ferocious inside it.

Furthermore, through personal accounts of family members, close friends, associates and adversaries, this book showcases the thoughts, memories and anecdotes of a remarkable public figure who refused to let fame go to his head. Talking to those who were close to Ali, I found new reasons to admire him. His importance as an historical figure is well documented, but dozens of tiny moments came to light in the course of my interviews that showed just why he was admired.

Muhammad Ali is many things to many people. Many view him as the greatest heavyweight boxing champion and sportsman to emerge in modern times. Others are inspired by his courage and humanitarian work. People from all walks of life are aware of this symbolic figure and celebrity, whose mass appeal and awareness is still evident despite his demise. I hope that in these pages, devoted fans of The Greatest, as well as those who only know him from grainy YouTube clips and news footage, will discover something new about a modern-day legend.

Fiaz Rafiq

INTRODUCTION

In the 1960s, two sportsmen emerged on the global stage who would eventually reach such heights of fame that each would be recognizable from one name alone. Both were black men from unpromising backgrounds; both won vast fortunes and became synonymous with success in their respective fields. Soccer's Edson Arantes do Nascimento, of Brazil, became the world's greatest player and an iconic figure of the most played game on the planet – known to his fans as Pele. Parallel to this Ali garnered mass appeal as he elevated the sport of boxing to something like art. But while Pele and Ali both helped their sports to truly become, respectively, the beautiful game and the sweet science, Ali went on to transcend his sport and become something greater.

The essentials of his life, of course, are well-established. Born Cassius Marcellus Clay Jr., on January 17, 1942, Ali grew up in what, for the time, was a relatively middle-class African-American family in Louisville, Kentucky. He changed his name to Muhammad Ali in 1964 after joining the controversial religious group the Nation of Islam, just days after claiming the heavyweight crown, arguably the most important title in sports, from the hard-slugging Sonny Liston. Subsequently he was catapulted to fame like no sportsman before; rising from the obscurity of small-town life to global prominence.

Every great sporting figure, of course, is a product of their era, and the 1960s was a time when two of the principal preoccupations for the American population were equality of rights for African-Americans and war. The civil rights movement that came to national prominence during the mid-1950s was a huge influence on Ali, as he became more aware that African-Americans were the people whose blood and sweat helped build America yet they faced discrimination, poverty and were treated with disdain as second-class citizens. During Ali's upbringing, African-Americans were harassed, beaten and even murdered by whites regularly, and the case of Emmett Till could not have escaped his notice. The Ku Klux Klan used violence against blacks and attacked and murdered them and burned down houses – behavior which was particularly rife in the Southern States. The struggle was about more than merely civil rights under law; the people who had played a pivotal role in building the greatest country in the world wanted to be treated like any other white citizen.

So, during the 1960s the stage was set for stepping up the movement to achieve freedom, justice and equality for the African-American population. In this battle, leaders like Malcolm X (also known as El-Hajj Malik El-Shabazz), and Martin Luther King took a stand against racism as they fought for dignity and respect as well as social and economic equality. Dr King was inspired by Gandhi's non-violent activism, but Malcolm X and the Nation of Islam were less inclined to take the moral high road. Muhammad Ali would soon step into this struggle, defying the establishment and risking his career in the process. He stood up for what he believed in and transformed the image of African-Americans.

Meanwhile, the civil rights movement in the United States attracted attention globally and became a lodestone for the human rights revolution worldwide. Most of the campaign for civil rights took place in the Southern part of the United States, where marches, boycotts and 'sit-ins' were the primary forms of protest. Although Ali didn't come from the ghetto like many other African-Americans – he grew up in a middle-class family – he understood the struggle facing every other black American and was more than able to empathize with their hardships. In a time when the heavyweight champion of the world was regarded as perhaps the greatest sportsman on the planet, he used his stature to speak out on issues that sorely required public attention, and would eventually take center stage during one of the most volatile decades of the century.

A key part of Ali's position as a lightning rod for controversy, of course, was his membership of the Nation of Islam. Founded in Detroit, Michigan, by Wallace D. Fard Muhammad in July 1930, the Nation was, in the words of its founder, developed to 'teach the downtrodden and defenseless black people a thorough knowledge of God and of themselves, and put them on the road to self-independence with a superior culture and higher civilization'. Fard disappeared in 1933 with little explanation, and after a brief succession his former assistant, later known as the Honorable Elijah Muhammad, took leadership of the organization from 1935 to 1975.

Though this was little understood by most Americans at the time, the Nation does not adhere to the core tenets of Islamic theology. Moreover, one can argue that its propagated ideology is actually incongruent and abhorrent to true mainstream Islam. The core belief of the organization and its followers was that its founder came in person as God, and at various times the Nation has also argued that 85 percent of the population are easily manipulated 'deaf, dumb and blind' sheep, or that African-Americans are superior to other races. These beliefs became more contentious when one of its most distinguished members, the late Malcolm X, who became a member while in prison, departed in 1964 after friction between him and Elijah Muhammad. Malcolm X became a Sunni Muslim after making a pilgrimage to the holy city of Mecca and began to speak out against the leadership – until in early 1965 Malcolm X was assassinated whilst giving a speech in New York.

Malcolm X has been widely acknowledged as the person who introduced Ali to the group. Ali joined the Nation of Islam in 1964, and was seen at Muslim rallies a few years before he publicly proclaimed his allegiance. Despite Malcolm X playing a pivotal role in the recruitment of Ali, the latter claimed that no one pressured him to become a Muslim; that he did it on his own initiative. It's easy to argue that the Nation exploited Ali, using him as a platform to publicize their message and extracting huge amounts of money from him – but Ali denied it for much of his life.

The Vietnam War, which occurred from November 1955 to April 1975, was another key turning point in Ali's life. The United States entered the war to prevent a communist takeover of South Vietnam, as part of a wider strategy of containing what was seen as a communist threat. However, the end results would be devastating for America's national psyche, as well as for the country of Vietnam and a generation of soldiers, and the war quickly lost favor. The anti-war movement gained national prominence in 1965, peaking three years later, and remained in effect throughout the duration of the conflict. It attracted the support of college campus students, people from middle-class suburbs and even some government institutions.

Ali refused to be inducted into the armed forces at the height of the conflict, in 1967. He rationalized that since he – and black African-Americans – had been denied civil rights in America, he wasn't prepared to venture out to another country to fight against people who'd never done him any harm. He paid a hefty price for his stance, being suspended from fighting for three years during the prime of his career. But his firm stance against the war would later make him a hero.

Both before and after the war, however, Ali captured attention and imaginations with not just his speed and flair, or his lip, but with his heart. As the man himself famously once said, "Champions aren't made in the gym. Champions are made from something they have deep inside them – a desire, a dream and a vision." These weren't empty words – Ali would go on to back them up in his legendary fights the Rumble in the Jungle and Thrilla in Manila, considered to be some of the greatest fights of the century.

The final part of Ali's life, of course, had its own tragedy, but also its own triumphs. Ali, the most loquacious of athletes, could hardly speak in his final two decades on this earth, diagnosed with Parkinson's disease in 1984 and continuing to suffer from it even as he entertained and encouraged others for the rest of his life. Parkinson's stole much from this once mightiest of men, who captivated everyone's attention at press conferences and on TV. He brought streets and airports to a standstill with his extrovert personality, but he ultimately stood up against it, raising awareness of – and funds to fight – the disease worldwide. And so his legacy lives on. Long after he hung up his gloves, according to the Associated Press, in 1993 Ali was tied with the baseball legend Babe Ruth as the most recognizable athletes, out of 800 dead or alive, in America. Ali has signed more autographs than any other athlete ever, living or dead. Most celebrities reach a point where they start to fade into obscurity, particularly once they are no longer in the public eye, but Ali continues to endure. Athletes may be remembered in their sports, but very few are remembered for changing the world. Muhammad Ali's story, without doubt, is an epic one encapsulating all the facets – one of bravery, courage, abundance, castigation and overcoming obstacles with an indomitable will. He touched millions of lives on the way, thousands in person, dozens as a supporter, father or friend.

ONE

FAMILY

Ali's family – the support they gave him, the lessons they taught him and even the ways they couldn't help him – had a huge impact on his career. Despite being married four times (to Sonji Roi, Belinda Boyd, Veronica Porche and Yolanda Williams – commonly known as Lonnie) and having his fair share of domestic problems, Ali was a staunch family man. He had nine children: Maryum; Rasheda; Jamillah; Hana; Laila; Khaliah; Miya; and Muhammad Jr. Laila is probably the most prominent of all, after forging a career in boxing with great success. Two of his daughters, Khaliah and Miya, were born out of wedlock, and Assad Amin was an adopted son. Unfortunately, Ali didn't get to spend as much time as many parents do with his children when they were growing up. Nonetheless, he was a good father and loved all his children.

Ali was first married in 1964 to Sonji, a marriage which lasted a mere seventeen months. Belinda and Ali married in 1967. Belinda was still a teenager when Ali first saw her, a junior at the University of Islam. The couple never went out; Ali went to dinner with his bride-to-be's family in attendance, and their marriage was arranged by her Muslim parents after Ali asked for her hand. After many years of a marriage which had its ups and downs they filed for divorce in late 1976. In the summer of 1977, he married Veronica

Porche, who he had first met in 1974. This marriage also lasted nine years. Soon after his divorce from Veronica, he tied the knot with Lonnie in 1986, a marriage which lasted until his death thirty years later. According to his third wife Veronica, Ali preferred a wife who was the domestic type, someone who would be happy staying at home. He was also adamant that his wives adhere to the Islamic principles, something that Sonji in particular had a very hard time embracing and a key cause of the rift between them.

Though Ali's family tree has its tangles, he endeavored to maintain good relationships with all his children, and with their mothers. Like any good parent, Ali cherished the time he did spend with his children, and sought to make up for his hours on the road or in other cities by showering them with affection when he saw them.

From the intimate accounts of family members, who probably know the man behind the public persona better than anyone else, surfaces the true image behind the legend. Ali was known for his boastfulness and outspoken personality, but behind the facade and frolics he showed the opposite personality behind closed doors, a side of him invisible to most outsiders. In private, Ali was a quiet man, far from the image he portrayed to promote his fights in front of flashing cameras and press-men. The contrast between the two sides of his personality was profound.

For most of us, family is an integral part of our lives. We seek comfort, security and a sense of joy from the few people that know us best. Many people pursue life with the ultimate aim of excelling in endeavors, which they, subconsciously or otherwise, feel will give them happiness, but most of us ultimately grow to understand true contentment is derived from having a loving and supporting family. In his later years, Ali grew to appreciate this, becoming a family man who matured as he came to appreciate the true teachings of his religion.

Like any public figure or celebrity, positive and negative stories have been written in the past relating to Ali's personal history. The media, more often than not, has a penchant for the most controversial parts of public figures' lives. Certainly he made mistakes over the course of his four marriages, as we all do – but as Ali became a much more devoted Muslim, his knowledge and practice of Islamic principles in his life strengthened, and his devotion to his family grew.

Over the following pages you'll find first-hand recollections from Ali's children, some of whom have barely spoken about their father in public before. Most people are aware of the fact Ali has daughters, for instance, but many are oblivious of the fact that he has a son. It's very rare to see most of Ali's children in the spotlight. Ali's son, who has hardly been in the media spotlight for much of his life, shares his memories, and his daughters offer a personal glimpse of the man who is loved by so many. Our family know us as we truly are – not by the performance we put on for the world.

MUHAMMAD ALI JUNIOR

Muhammad Ali Jr. was born to Ali's second wife Belinda. With a personality very unlike his famous father's, Ali's only biological son has kept a very low profile, never attempting to capitalize on his fame. As a result, he comes across as a down to earth person living a normal life.

Q: Your father was perceived as a brash and boastful person. How would you define your father's personality?
Muhammad Ali Jr.: He was very open and we talked about anything actually. We had like a brother-to- brother relationship. His personality is unlike anybody else's. I've never met anybody who had a better personality than my father. My father was actually doing that for publicity, whatever he was doing in the ring. But my father was not quiet; he was outspoken. He's just an all-round outgoing person. When it comes to other people, he didn't mind helping. I remember one time when we were living in California, he had actually moved a family in the house with him to get

them off the street and gave them clothes and fed them. He had a remarkable personality.

Q: When you were growing up, did your father visit you in school like all the other kids' parents did?
Muhammad Ali Jr.: He would come visit us all the time at home and at my grandmother's house. He did come to school once during the graduation. I mean, if you think about what it means to me to be Muhammad Ali's son, I was actually happy to see him.

Q: Did your father give you advice as you were growing up?
Muhammad Ali Jr.: Oh, yeah. One thing he said to me, which I remember, was: I don't care what people call you. I don't care what people think of you – everybody is equal under the eyes of God. He said I care about people being as human and not what color they are. He said look at people and respect them as human beings. Actually, let me put it like this way: don't judge them from their actions and how they look, don't judge people – period. He said what you need to look for is the content of their character. If they've got a good character and they're not stuck up, they're not racists, then they're good people. If they are then just leave them alone. Then you'll be alright. He said watch what you say and watch what you do and respect your elders. And he taught me a lot about chivalry – stop calling people by the names of animals. He gave me good advice.

Q: How hard was it for your father to overcome obstacles in the 1960s when blacks endured many hardships?
Muhammad Ali Jr.: Number one, he was black. Number two, for not having any liable rights at all. Number three, for becoming a Muslim and be slandered for it. Number four, his boxing, decision to not go to war, his title was taken off him. Everybody's entitled to freedom of religion. And another thing he taught me, he said, "I don't care if it's a Jew, Christian or a Muslim in the same room, as long as they believe in God."

Q: Your father went to hajj in Mecca and later became zealously committed to his religion. Did he relate any stories to you how he felt about the experience?

Muhammad Ali Jr.: Oh, yeah. He actually felt sorry for a lot of things that he had said, such as, "White man's a devil." He really felt sorry because the fact that when he went to hajj, he saw black Muslims, purple Muslims, white Muslims, yellow Muslims – all different types of race of Muslims. So, he was really sorry for saying what he had said a long time ago – white man's a devil and this is a white man's world. He was sorry for saying it. Because he realized that there are other Muslims as well as blacks.

Q: He enjoyed joking around a lot.

Muhammad Ali Jr.: He could've been a comedian.

Q: Did you have social family reunions?

Muhammad Ali Jr.: We used to go for ice cream, pies, cakes, etc. We just had a good time. We didn't have too many barbeques. We always had family gatherings such as Thanksgiving dinners. For Christmas we had another Thanksgiving dinner, so it was like twice a year of Thanksgiving.

Q: In your opinion what was your father's biggest and most monumental achievement?

Muhammad Ali Jr.: Regardless no matter what the situation maybe, no matter what the cost, no matter what the circumstances. I mean, my father believed wholeheartedly in Islam. He was ready to die for it. He said, "I'm not going to denounce my religion Islam. If I have to face gunfire, I will."

Q: In the boxing world what was his greatest achievement?

Muhammad Ali Jr.: Well, I'm going to put it like this because my father always told me, he said, "Boxing was just a stage for something greater." That's the way he put it to me. That wasn't his actual thing; it was something greater than boxing. He was trying to liberate his people, even himself. I was at the park in New York and one historian came up to me. And she told me that Martin Luther King was in this park at one time with his wife. And she [historian] said that Martin Luther King got stoned in this park. They were throwing stones at him. It was the non-violent rally which he had. It was unfair. It was just a non-violent get-together for the Muslims. I said, "Man, this is a disaster." So, it wasn't really about boxing, it was just about liberation of black people to be free and to have rights like everybody else.

Q: How do you feel things have changed now, was it not for the 1960s civil rights movement do you think America would not have evolved profoundly?
Muhammad Ali Jr.: Things have changed in the means of: you don't have to go to war if you don't want to. Because of your beliefs, your background, your religion, your upbringing, you don't have to go to war. I mean, really the thing about war is to kill, kill, kill. In Islam it's peace. So a lot of Muslims don't have to go to war because it's against our religion to kill.

Q: Your father got on with everybody, from the old to the young kids, is it true that he would often let strangers into his house?
Muhammad Ali Jr.: Like I said before, when we were growing up he took in his home a family, clothed them, fed them and made sure they had a roof over their heads. I mean, he was just an all-round caring person. He had no bad heart at all.

Q: Which people were close to your father during his career? Herbert Muhammad was his manager and Angelo Dundee was his coach.
Muhammad Ali Jr.: There were a lot of people around my father that didn't do my father any good. Herbert Muhammad was one of them. There's a long list of people but I don't want to get into all that.

Q: What path did your father pursue after hanging up the gloves?
Muhammad Ali Jr.: Helping people, doing things for charities, feeding the homeless, feeding the hungry. It was stuff like that he got involved in because it made him feel good. He said I'm doing something good because Allah wants me to. This is what Allah sent me over here for, to help people. So the best way I can help people is by feeding and clothing them, make sure they have homes. It was his way of giving back to God – giving back to Allah.

Q: Your father wasn't motivated by money, he gave a lot away. Fame didn't get to his head, but a lot of celebrities let fame get to their heads.
Muhammad Ali Jr.: He gave all he made away. My father was grounded in Islam and Islam humbled him. He wasn't a big-headed person in the first place.

Q: Did you go to any events?
Muhammad Ali Jr.: The last one I went to was to collect an award for my father who couldn't make it. So that's all I've done.

Q: Your favorite boxing fight?
Muhammad Ali Jr.: I have one favorite fight and it didn't happen in the ring – it happened in the courtroom. He stood up for his beliefs in Islam by not going to war and Allah blessed him with his title match.

Q: When your father became a Sunni Muslim it opened his eyes, he prayed five times a day.
Muhammad Ali Jr.: Oh, yes. He couldn't really move around too much in his later years and do his prayers, but he was still devoted to Islam. He didn't stop devoting to Islam until the day he passed away.

Q: Is there anything that the people don't know about your father or are unaware of?
Muhammad Ali Jr.: Well, a lot of fans don't know he has a son.

They know he has daughters. A lot of fans think Tatyana Ali is my sister, but she's not.

Q: Did your father let you choose your own path in life?

Muhammad Ali Jr.: My father let me be my own man. But I was actually sheltered my whole life because of whom my father was, who I am to my father, because we had family threats on our lives. So they sheltered me. Actually, it was my mother's parents. I was raised by my mother's parents. I was raised by my grandparents. They actually sheltered me and it really hindered me instead of helping me because I wasn't able to go out there. I wasn't able to get my own, this and the other. It really put a dent on my whole life. But everything's OK and it's not a total loss.

Q: What goes through your mind when you look back watching your father on TV?

Muhammad Ali Jr.: I mean, it seems like a dream to me, to be honest with you. But I just look at him as daddy. He's my daddy. I love him and he's my father. That's how I see him. I don't see him as the Greatest of All Time. I don't see him as the great humanitarian. I see him as daddy.

Q: When you were growing up did you get to spend much time with your father?

Muhammad Ali Jr.: When I was little I spent more time with my father than I did when I was older because he used to come and visit us. But since he was sick, he wanted to come visit me but his wife didn't bring him around. Actually, when he came to visit us he'd give us money and we wouldn't have to ask for it. We'd take summer vacations to California, Deer Lake, Pennsylvania; just go to a lot of places. He used to travel a lot. We'd go to Kentucky to visit his parents – my grandparents. I mean, there were a lot of things we used to do. And I found out – it took me thirty-eight years to find out – I had certain cousins that I never knew I had.

Q: How did you take it when you found out your father had Parkinson's?

Muhammad Ali Jr.: Like anyone else takes it. I mean, I look at it like this: if it's going to happen then it will. That's how life is. Whatever happens is because of Allah's will. It really doesn't bother me too much. Everybody's going to pass away some time, you can't live forever.

Q: Your father wasn't a big spender but he liked cars. What other things did he have a passion for?

Muhammad Ali Jr.: He used to like music a lot. He used to like the old-school music. He was around all those (music) people back then. Everybody knew everybody. I've got to tell you another thing. My mother used to babysit Michael Jackson and her karate instructor was Jim Kelly [*Enter the Dragon* co-star].

Q: Interesting. Your father never met Bruce Lee, who died in 1973. A lot of people compare your father to Bruce Lee. What's your opinion on Bruce Lee?

Muhammad Ali Jr.: He's like the Muhammad Ali of karate [martial arts]. I'm going to put it like this: I think it would've been a good fight between my father and Bruce Lee. Now, my father and Mike Tyson, my father would've kicked his butt. Everybody says Mike Tyson would've kicked your father's butt. I said no. Mike Tyson can't go the distance. He couldn't go fifteen rounds. He's not a boxer; he's a street fighter. He's a knockout artist. He can never hold up to my father! Sonny Liston was like a Mike Tyson, an older version of Mike Tyson. He would never be able to beat him. Bruce Lee, on the other hand, that would have been a good fight. They were both young, they were both agile and both took it to the limit with their training. They both were the best at what they did.

Q: Your father is idolized around the globe, just how much of an impact has he had on the world?

Muhammad Ali Jr.: Let me put it this way: if my father was a bomb, he'd be like the Hiroshima bomb. That's how much impact he had on a lot of people.

Q: He seems to have influenced people from a diverse background.
Muhammad Ali Jr.: He influenced Michael Jackson and he influenced a lot of people. He would meet anybody, he didn't care who it was. People gave him energy. The love from the people gave him the love from his heart. He loved being around people and he's a people person. He would never say no to anybody.

Q: What's the most fascinating or compelling moment you witnessed of your father on TV?
Muhammad Ali Jr.: The most interesting thing I've seen was when he lit the torch at the Olympics. I heard there was going to be a guest, a pious person, who would be lighting the torch. And when they said this, the first thing that came to my mind was my father. And sure enough it was my father doing it. I didn't know who was going to do it, but I looked at it and I thought it's got to be my father. He's a living legend, why wouldn't he light the torch?

Q: Did you have any icons when you were growing up or do you idolize anyone?
Muhammad Ali Jr.: I didn't really have any idols because I don't believe in idols; I was born a Muslim. I'm going to put it like this: the only one that caught my eye, as far as my father's like, the only one I really like who held up to my father is Hulk Hogan. I don't know why I geared towards wrestling, but I've just grown to love wrestling. I've been watching wrestling since the WWF. Hulk Hogan, Iron Sheikh, Bret Hart. I still watch WWE. I think it was a good thing [Ali-Inoki fight]. After I saw my father go to the WWF [special guest referee appearance] I always wanted to go. I used to wrestle in my high school.

RASHEDA ALI

Rasheda Ali and her twin sister Jamillah were born to Ali's second wife Belinda, two years after their elder sister Maryum and two years before Muhammad Ali Jr. She is a speaker who has worked tirelessly to raise global awareness of Parkinson's disease and its treatments, a published author and a former talk show host. Here, she reflects on how her relationship with her father changed over the course of their lives together.

Q: Would you say that your father was born to box, was it in his blood?
Rasheda Ali: Yes. I feel that he definitely was a natural in his boxing ability. He started at age twelve. And he immediately took on the challenges that adult males would take on. He boxed for nearly thirty years, which is very unusual nowadays. So I do think he was a natural talent and born to box.

Q: It's no secret your father had an extrovert personality. How would you describe his personality from a personal perspective?
Rasheda Ali: Well, I think as a boxer my dad was a different person in the ring than he was outside of the ring. As he boxed, he challenged a lot of his opponents. I think a lot of the times he was very brash. He was very confident and he was very sure of himself, cocky and funny – all those things. But in real life he was still confident and very sure of himself. But he wasn't as cocky in real life, behind closed doors, he's very humble. And he didn't make a big fuss about who he was in his real life. A lot of that was show – he had to sell tickets and he had to get people come and see him box. So, naturally, he was more of an actor portraying the role. It was very interesting for reporters to film him. I think that's why he was very brash and overwhelming in his personality, it was interesting for people to watch. It was part of his makeup and it was a part of his role as a boxer. He was a very interesting character and I think he did a very good job of it.

Q: The media paints a picture of a celebrity in the public eye, but is there anything the media missed as far as Muhammad Ali the real person behind closed doors?

Rasheda Ali: You know, I don't think so. I think my dad, when he was out in the public as a humanitarian, what you see is what you got. People have indicated that when they've met my dad they found him to be very warming, sincere and a sweet person. He was like that all the time, that's part of his personality, that's who he is. So, no. I think when the media showed my dad promoting Parkinson's and helping people through his Muhammad Ali Parkinson's Center, trying to educate children at the center in Louisville, that's his personality, that's who he is.

Q: Rasheda, can you relate to me any intriguing stories pertaining to hanging out with your dad when you were growing up?

Rasheda Ali: Where do I start? He was so fun to be with. My dad was really one of a kind, honestly. I've had the honor of meeting so many wonderful people in my life, and I don't think any of them stand up to my dad. I think he's just definitely one of those few human beings sent on earth who was sincere. Off the top of my head, I do recall an incident with my dad. We were all hanging out one day, because we visited him every summer when we were kids, and I think we were driving around in California. My dad ran across to a family. I think they had lost their home so they didn't have a place to stay. My dad brought them home with him and he fed them and he gave them money. It was just really amazing. We were all frightened, of course, because we were thinking, *Oh, you don't know these people*. But my dad didn't have the fear in the world. This poor family needed a shelter and everything my dad had done for them was just wonderful to see. That's a perfect example of something my dad would do. And really for me it kind of set the stage as one of my heroes for that reason. That's part of his loving and giving self.

Q: Did you have family gatherings where all your sisters got together with your dad?

Rasheda Ali: It's unfortunate because we all live all over the place, and my dad has been married four times. We all live in different states. I have sisters in Philadelphia and California. I grew up in Chicago. We're all over the place so it was very, very rare. Then when we were older and we had our own families, it was even more difficult because our schedules didn't allow us to all be in one place at once. I will say when my dad opened up his museum in Louisville – which was back in 2005 – I remember all of us were together. Even then we were missing a sibling. But even at that event at the opening of my dad's museum we still had somebody missing. So it was very difficult for all of us to get together, so we had to make a great effort to come up visit one another. It was a challenge on all of us because we have our own families and we have our own jobs and lives. But we'd make an effort to try to make time to see my dad in later years because it's important.

Q: As a father, did he ever give you any specific advice?

Rasheda Ali: Sure. My dad did give me a lot of advice and I used to go to him for advice, too. Because he set some really good examples of how he...I think he has something which is really strong about him and his attitude is incredible: how he never complained and he just enjoyed his life. He gave me lots of advice. I'm trying to think of one that stands out. Of course, I was in the television industry, as you know this is very competitive, it's cut-throat, it's tough.

And my dad gave me advice about being in that industry. He told me if you like it then go for it. And I think that's what my dad did his whole life. He did what he really enjoyed doing. He never really settled for a career that he never liked. And I think my dad was blessed in that. He was gifted and he pursued it. But he did tell me if you enjoy it and it makes you happy, go for it. I think that's really advice that we should all take – we should all be happy in what we're doing and everything else will follow. So I thought it was pretty good advice.

Q: Obviously, he joined the Nation of Islam but then became a Sunni Muslim and performed Pilgrimage. Did he touch on this subject with you and your sisters?

Rasheda Ali: I think he lived by example. I think at the time when he first joined the Islamic faith, it was an organization which was not orthodox. Obviously, it was more of a sect. You know, it says in the Quran you're not supposed to break up the sects. I think that was one of the sects of the faith, and I think it was a little distorted. Of course, it wasn't really true Islam and my dad found that out, of course, when he visited Mecca. And he tried to see real Islam, and real Islam is all about being together. There are all different races in the religion; it's not just African-Americans.

So, I think he was able to see real Islam when he went to Mecca and hajj, which I think opened his eyes. I think it was really wonderful how he embraced the religion. And he spoke to people about that because a lot of people have a lot of misconceptions. People really don't realize there are billions of Muslims in the world and they're from different races, different cultures, different nationalities and different skin colors. I think that's very important that he was able to come out at the forefront as a very famous American who happened to be a Muslim and share the true beliefs of Islam. It's about love, harmony and peace and I think my dad was able to do that through example how he lived his life.

Q: When your father retired what path did his life take?

Rasheda Ali: After he retired from boxing, he did dedicate a large percentage of his time to helping fight racism and helping children with obesity issues. He really spent a majority of his time helping other charities and things like that and, of course, Parkinson's came along and he was diagnosed. His main focus was to create a Parkinson's Center to help people who have Parkinson's, and help them get proper diagnoses and programs to help them improve quality of life for families dealing with Parkinson's.

So he really went out and he became more or less a world ambassador of peace. He traveled all over the globe helping certain organizations in their causes. So he became from a boxer to an instant humanitarian. I think that's how he spent most of his time: helping organizations and their causes. I think, like I said, he transformed from this incredible boxer, from his incredible skills into a very warm, really peaceful human being. And my dad really did enjoy his life. He had a lot of fun and he was a giving person and he never stopped. That's part of his makeup and he enjoyed it, he really did.

HANA ALI

Hana Ali is the youngest of Ali's children, born to his third wife, Veronica Porche, just before they married. When her father and mother moved to Los Angeles in 1979 Ali's boxing career was coming to an end, and as a result Ali spent more time with Hana and his other young children, strengthening the bond between them. Later, Hana would move to live with her father in Michigan in 2001 and stayed for just under six years, until the two were almost inseparable.

Q: Hana, when you were living in Los Angeles with your father, can you divulge any stories pertaining to celebrities visiting your home to see your dad?

Hana Ali: My dad didn't sit around talking about celebrities when he was with family. He wasn't the kind of person who would tell us stories about celebrities. I was too young to understand. The only one I did was Michael Jackson. When my dad first met Clint Eastwood they were on the same TV talk show together in 1969. And in the greenroom he said to him, "Clint, Clint, do me a favor. Walk across the room and turn around real fast and draw your gun and say, 'You've got four days to get out of town.'" He did it for him. It was funny. My father didn't consciously try to separate his professional work from family or social life. He didn't sit down and think he needs to keep it separate, it just wasn't important for him in that regard to talk to us about celebrities. He talked about spiritual enlightenment instead.

Travolta would come over to our house a lot and he would also go to my dad's training camp in Deer Lake. At the time, my sister Laila and I didn't really understand who John Travolta was because we were way too young. We hadn't watched his movies such as *Saturday Night Fever*. My dad would say to me, "Hey, Hana, do you know who this is? He's a big movie star. He's a greater dancer!" John would dance at the house. My father would say, "Dance, John!" John would dance and my father would egg him on saying,

"Come on, John, that's right. Come here, Veronica. Go, John, dance!" He got a kick out of that. He would show my father how to dance. John would tease my dad saying, "Man, you have two left feet." Dad would say, "I only dance in the ring." Everybody thought it was strange that my father couldn't dance because he was so graceful and elegant in the ring. He had no rhythm for it outside the ring, though. Instead, he liked others dancing.

Hollywood actor Kris Kristofferson's daughter would come with her father and we would play. And an actor that played in films, he had his daughter – I can't remember the names now – come too. I'd take her shoes off and we would play. She was about five years older than me. I remember she had high heels little girls wear and I would try wearing them and never take them off and go to the mirror to check because I loved those shoes so much. Hollywood directors sometimes had kids they'd bring over.

Q: Your father, of course, became a world figure who seemed to endear himself to the political fraternity?
Hana Ali: My father was such a world figure that they admired and respected him. He was able to open up the doors to communication for America when they couldn't get things done. Anywhere he went he could make it easier for the American government. Jimmy Carter sometimes was relying on my father. OK, not relying but would call my father who would offer help. Jimmy Carter could make decisions from information presented to him. Sometimes things turned out good, while other times things didn't turn out too good. It made him conscious of doing things because being a famous world figure his mere presence could condone something that was going on. So he was careful of where he went and what he did. He didn't want to give the wrong impression of being somewhere by supporting a nation where injustice was happening to people.

Q: What made your father different to all the other famous faces, and continues to do so?
Hana Ali: Everything was looked upon from a spiritual standpoint.

He was so humble considering he was this mammoth figure. He never lost that humility. He would call random strangers on Christmas Day to wish them a happy Christmas. A lot of celebrities want to get famous, have all that money and accolades but they're not people person. But my dad was. My father enjoyed being with normal people; he didn't try to hide. He would walk in alley ways, ghettos and mingle. He gave access. Even regular everyday people don't do that. It was easier for a homeless man to see him than the president. He'd make an appointment with a president but a homeless man could walk right up to our house and my father would tell him to come inside.

Q: What can you tell me about behind the scenes personal family get-togethers with your dad at his home?

Hana Ali: The birthday that comes to mind, the more prominent one, was his last birthday six months before he passed away. It was such a blessing because eight of his nine children were there, and his grandchildren were there. He got to do huge magic tricks. He regaled us with his tricks all through our childhood. Even though all my father's kids stick to the birthdays over the years, we never really got all together because of our responsibilities such as jobs and kids. However, that night we all came together after quite some time in Scottsdale. Lonnie hired a magician so he did a show. We were all sitting around clapping. My father tucked into his favorite candy bars and butter fingers. His eyes were open wide and he looked happy. So the year before I spent it with his kids also.

Q: Lastly, is there anything that is often misunderstood about your dad?

Hana Ali: He didn't have bodyguards. The bodyguards that you read about were not in the form of stopping people from meeting him. He had these naturally in case something happened because some places there were big crowds such as at the fights to protect the wife. He never used them for himself. He never had a bodyguard in the traditional sense. In his later years he never kept them around.

MARYUM ALI

Born and raised in Chicago, Maryum Ali – better known as 'May May' – is the eldest of Muhammad Ali's children. She has appeared in several documentaries produced charting the life and career of her famous father, and in 2016 went undercover as an inmate in an Indiana jail for A&E documentary *60 Days In*. Currently, she lives in Los Angeles and is a public speaker as well as working in youth development.

Q: Can you share some memories when you and your siblings used to visit your dad at his Los Angeles mansion in the early 1980s?

Maryum Ali: My father was a practical joker. He lived in a big house so it had long dark hallways. He loved scaring us. He got a kick out of that. He would wait in the dark hallways and we would walk down and he'd scare us. He'd just laugh. He loved playing practical jokes and he was a very fun-loving person. He liked to play with his kids a lot. A lot of parents don't do that. So, that's some fun stuff he'd do. He would laugh so hard then we'd all start laughing with him. You see, my father was a regular person. People make him like he's so different. What does any family do? You go eat out together, go events together. If he had events he'd take us with him. We hung out and watched TV at the house. We went swimming in the back yard swimming pool. We did all the regular common day stuff that a family would do. People are so much idol worshipers, celebrity worshipers and they always think he's something different, but he was just a regular person. He'd do whatever anybody would do from going to get ice cream to praying together.

Q: What is one of the most thought-provoking conversations you ever had with your dad?

Maryum Ali: Thought-provoking conversation would be how we talked about God a lot. You don't realize how serious he was about that. He wanted his kids to be God-conscious. He wanted us to know that our real purpose is to be in eternal heaven, paradise – all Muslims believe in. He would always talk to us about how this life was a testing ground. That would be the most thought-provoking thing. Materialistic things, all the fame, money, that's just nothing, he told us. Are you going to help people with it? So, everything you're doing in this world should be to please God. And it was those lessons of him reiterating the importance of our true purpose on earth that leads to a peaceful happy person. That's the stuff you should be grounded in. He taught us those kinds of lessons and he said, "Always value your religion, your faith and never believe that you're better because you're Ali's daughter." He said to us, "Your name Ali doesn't mean anything. How you treat people means something. Not your last name, not my boxing career." So, that's the most important thing he tried to teach his kids.

Q: In terms of guiding you and your siblings as far as career or education is concerned, did he gravitate toward anything particular?

Maryum Ali: No, he didn't gravitate toward anything like that. He wanted us to do what we wanted to do. He felt whatever we thought was our career purpose then we should follow it. He didn't say you should be a doctor, or you should be this. He didn't believe in doing that. No one had told him what to do. Everybody has a skill or talent. So it's up to you to find that. He didn't try to guide us to anything, or press us. He did want us to get an education and finish college. So that was important. He wanted us to do that. He did want us to be educated and take care of ourselves, but he never tried to force us into any career. That was for us to decide on our own.

Q: Can you talk about any celebrities visiting your dad when you were present?

Maryum Ali: Lots of celebrities would come to his house in LA. He was such a practical joker we sometimes didn't believe what he said to us. Once he walked up the stairs at the LA home and he said to me Clint Eastwood is downstairs. I didn't believe him, I said, "Oh, you're lying. You're not telling the truth. There's no Clint Eastwood downstairs." I said, "Whatever." He said, "You better come downstairs with your clothes on." I had pajamas on. I said, "Yeah, right. It's one of your jokes." Anyway, I go downstairs with my pajamas and my hair all messy and Clint Eastwood is sitting there. I'm like, "Ahhh!" and I ran back upstairs. My father started laughing. While I was running upstairs to get dressed, I overheard him say, "I told her you were down here, but she wouldn't believe me. I joke with them all the time. She came down with her pajamas with her hair messed up, now she's running back upstairs." It was so funny. I was like, Oh, my God! He would tease us all the time. He would say, "Michael Jackson is downstairs." And Michael Jackson would not be downstairs and we'd all come running downstairs but there's no Michael Jackson. This time he said, "Clint Eastwood is down." I told him, "You're trying to fool us again." I was so embarrassed. I have a picture of me with Clint that was taken after I came down again. I was like, "Oh, my, God, he's really here." People would always come over visit him.

Q: Did you pursue a rap career in the 80s and what type of music did your father discuss with you?

Maryum Ali: My father loved Doo Wop, which was in the 1950s and 60s. He loved the music that he grew up on. He also liked the Supremes with Diana Ross and he liked Sam Cooke. I think probably his favorite music acts – which I personally think – were Little Richard, Chubby Checker and James Brown. But when he would see Little Richard, he'd get excited. Every time when we saw Little Richard in person or an event, my father would say, "Little Richard! That's Little Richard!" He acted like a fan. I'm looking at my dad and thinking, "Oh, my God. I've never seen you act like that. People treat you like this." He loved Little Richard, he grew up listening to him. Chubby Checker too. "Oh, there's Chubby Checker! There's Chubby Checker!" he'd say excitedly. He liked the old school music he listened to.

Q: Your father visited Iraq to free hostages, what can you remember?

Maryum Ali: He always wanted to use his fame and notoriety to help people. He understood the importance of that. He wanted to use it for something. I think when he went over there Saddam Hussein wasn't responding to him at all. But my dad was so kind to the people there and he ran out of his Parkinson's medication and couldn't talk much. Saddam respected him. He respected how kind he was with the people. My father was being patient waiting for Saddam's response. And I do believe that the way my father carried himself, his humility with the people there made Saddam release those hostages. Because initially it didn't seem like it was going well, but my father was a very pious person who wanted to do things in a soft way, it wasn't pushy. He didn't go in there pushy. Of course the United States government didn't want him over there, but he's his own man. That's not the first time he went up against the United States government. He was his own man and he felt, "If I can help if American lives are important, then I will. Bush is telling me that I'm playing in the hands of Saddam." My father was right. He didn't play in the hands Saddam. He was connecting with real people. These people, the freed hostages, thanked him but he said you don't need to thank me, God works through me. So he didn't want to take the credit for it. So, it wasn't like he was paid to do it. He was dealing with Parkinson's and it was hard. He just wanted to help save lives. There are not a lot of people like that nowadays, that's why a lot of people are fascinated by my father. My father would say, "Don't be fascinated by me. Turn to your creator and be what your creator wants you to be like. When you do that, you'll be like me. You don't have to be obsessed with me as a person. Try to be a great person in your own right. It doesn't mean you have to be famous. Just do right in your own circle, in your own family and your own community and help people. You don't need a lot of money, millions of dollars or be a big celebrity to do what you're supposed to be doing in your own community." That's what he used to say.

Q: You got to meet President Obama, a man who admired your father?

Maryum Ali: We met him after my dad passed away. It was at the White House where they had an Islamic event. Me and some of my siblings and my stepmom went. He said to us that he admired our father. Our sister Rasheda gave Obama some Ali cufflinks, but the official present said, "You can't give the President any gifts. It's against the rules." Valerie Jarrett, his advisor, said, "No, no, no!" But Obama accepted them from my sister Rasheda. He was very nice and he said how much he loved my father. He had met him when he was a Senator and later again at the Inauguration, and at the Ali Center. I went to the second Inauguration but as a regular person, not as a guest. It's a blessing that people like these admire my dad.

Q: You spoke on the podium at your father's funeral. What can you share with me in terms of your personal feelings and thoughts at the time?

Maryum Ali: I write poetry like my father. I love poetry. I write when I'm inspired. So I wanted to write a poem about what he was like as a father and what he taught us, mostly girls, he has two boys. I wanted to share some of the messages he wanted for his daughters – having self-respect, and not allowing anyone to demean you or disrespect you as a woman. That was very important to him. I wrote about that in the poem. I thought about putting some of the highlights and strong messages I got from him. It was easier to do this in poetry form. I actually wrote that poem on the way to the funeral as I was so busy with all the family members and cousins in Louisville. I wanted to make sure they were all taken care of. It was a big stable of people, so I wanted to make sure all our family members were waiting outside in a line. So I was so busy working on that list I didn't have time to write the poem till I got on the plane. I write poetry pretty fast when I'm inspired. It was a tribute to him.

Q: Any last words on Muhammad Ali, your father who has endeared himself to people from all walks of life beyond the confines of the sporting fraternity?

Maryum Ali: I think anyone who loves Muhammad Ali a lot wants to be like him. I just say he was the way he was because he was always trying to seek what God wanted him to do. He wasn't a perfect person of course. I think whatever religion you are, tap into your spiritual self as much as possible, especially if it's prayer time. And tap into that and exercise that muscle. That's what Muhammad Ali was. And if you admire him, that's what you should learn from him the most.

TWO

THE JOURNALISTS

Two days after his first fight with Liston in 1964, Ali revealed at a press conference that he had joined the Nation of Islam, which was arguably the most feared and reviled organization in America at the time. The press vilified him, even though by that point he'd been selling their papers for years – first as the brash young Olympic champion, then as the cocky loudmouth who had no hope of beating the taciturn champion, and even, for a day or so, as the new champ who told them all to eat their words. It was another remarkable moment for a man whose relationship to the world was, in a large part, defined by his press.

Given the fact Ali became the most famous face in the country, it's perhaps surprising that he was also one of the most accessible athletes for anyone asking for his time. He would talk to reporters for hours, spending far longer than scheduled at press conferences, but also granting access to the gym or inviting them to his home. According to Bobby Goodman, who worked with Ali as a PR man for many years, Ali would do more than anyone – fighter, promoter or otherwise – to promote and publicize his fights. And while high-profile stars can often, understandably, be reserved and distant Ali's relationship with the media was, by and large, excellent.

This open-door policy approach continued even after the champ retired. Moreover, he treated everyone the same regardless of how big and well known their media outlet was. Ali's worldwide fame can be attributed to many things: his in-ring exploits, his unique personality and the controversy that followed his political pronouncements, but sportswriters and journalists played a pivotal role in shaping the myth of his life. Some of the most insightful came from the strangest places.

Ali was also unafraid to use the press for his own ends. In his official statement refusing induction into the armed forces in 1967, he proclaimed: "I strongly object to the fact that so many newspapers have given the American public and the whole world the impression that I have only two alternatives in taking this stand: either I go to jail or go to the army. There is another alternative and that alternative is justice. If justice prevails, if my constitutional rights are upheld, I will be forced to go neither to the army nor jail. In the end, I am confident that justice will come my way for the truth must eventually prevail." At the time, few were predicting that the anti-war movement would gain the momentum it did, which would ultimately change the public's views on the war. Ali was one of the pioneers of the movement: after he became eligible for the draft, Ali made his feelings clear to a reporter, saying, "Boxing is nothing, just satisfying to some bloodthirsty people. I am no longer Cassius Clay, a Negro from Kentucky. I belong to the world, the black world. I will always have a home in Pakistan, in Algeria, in Ethiopia. This is more than money." It was one of many occasions when history would prove him right.

At other times, Ali's exploits outside the ring were just as enthralling as they were inside: his understanding of how to hype a fight by trash-talking and taunting his adversaries in front of the media and the public was ahead of its time. His idioms and quips captivated people's attention. It drew the media in giving them something riveting to write about even when the outcome of his fights was in little doubt, making memorable figures from also-ran opponents. He showed an early flair for pre-fight poetry, which he would recite to the assembled press-men's delight – a skill he developed over the years. In press conferences, he exuded confidence and he was charming.

The media's interest in Ali, of course, went far beyond his fighting prowess. In the 1970s, when one interviewer asked Ali in front of a TV audience what attracted him to the Muslim faith, Ali offered a philosophical answer:

> *"The truth – I can't say how good I am, and no true Muslim will brag or even will take a chance on saying he's good, he's halfway good. It's up to Allah, God, to be the judge. So I'm not going to say one thing about how good I am because I don't know. You never get good enough. I'm always trying to be right. And you asked me another question: why did I change? Because I was raised a Baptist, and after touring the world I found out (there are) over 600 million Muslims on the planet, and all religions are good. I wrote something once, it said: Rivers, lakes and streams, they all have different names but they all contain water. So does religion have different names and they all pertain to guidance and truths, only expressed in different ways . . . what Jesus taught was good; what Moses taught was right... what Isaiah, Luke, Noah. God always sent Prophets to different people at different times with messages for those people, and people have decided to choose those Prophets as their leader."*

It's no secret that Ali felt strongly about his heritage – he was proud to be black. On another occasion when a TV reporter asked him what attracted him to Islam, he exclaimed, "The teachings of Honorable Elijah Muhammad. On how black people have been brainwashed, how they had been taught to love white and hate black. How we've been robbed of our names. We were robbed of our culture. We were robbed of our true history. So it left us as a walking dead man. So when you've got black people in an all-white country – and they don't know nothing about themselves, they don't speak their language – they're just mentally dead." Journalists often tried to challenge him on his staunch views. Another time when Ali was interviewed on Michael Parkinson's chat show in the United Kingdom, Ali launched into an extraordinary tirade when the host mildly challenged him on the nature of his religious beliefs. Despite his outspokenness, though, by and large, Ali had a good relationship with the reporters and interviewers.

Probably the most famous broadcaster to follow Ali's career was Howard Cosell, who died in 1995, but dozens of other journalists spent enough time with The Greatest to cultivate a relationship with him and get an insight into the man himself. In the following conversations with the journalists and photographers who were closely associated with Ali, they share their memories.

ROBERT LIPSYTE

Robert Lipsyte was born in New York and worked for *The New York Times*, becoming an award-winning sportswriter who followed Ali's career from its early stages, becoming one of the first to accept the champ's controversial political stances. He is the author of many books, including the 1978 *Free to Be Muhammad Ali*. Lipsyte's in-depth insights are the result of his close working relationship with Ali, whom he interviewed countless times during his career.

Q: When Muhammad Ali, back then known as Cassius Clay, won a gold medal at the Rome Olympics in 1960, did you cover this story?
Robert Lipsyte: I was just starting off my career as a young reporter at the time. I must say, he was a great story for us, but we did not take him seriously. He won the light-heavyweight championship, as you know. And I think the understanding was that at the time the Cold War was going on and the thing that excited most people about Cassius Clay was when a Russian reporter had asked him about conditions in America, in particular the oppression of black

people, Clay snapped back. He said something clever along the lines of: at least in our country they don't live in dirt shacks the way they do in your country – something to that effect. I forget the exact words now. He immediately became, and this is very ironic for later on, a minor political hero. But when he came back to America, he turned professional and he was still not taken seriously. He really did not beat anybody of note convincingly until he beat Liston.

Q: What was it like for him to grow up in the United States, a country where segregation was rife, before he went to the Olympics?

Robert Lipsyte: He grew up in Louisville, Kentucky, which is a place of great white wealth. It's kind of the heart of horse country, known for horseracing in that area. The most celebrated horserace, the Kentucky Derby, is raced in Louisville. At the same time, it was totally segregated so he came out of a totally separated environment. He went to a totally separated grammar and high school. After the Olympics, as the story goes, he still could not be served in restaurants. He was known as the 'Olympic Nigger'. His first contract was owned by a group called the Louisville Sponsoring Group, which was a group of some of the richest white men in the area. I think there was a general feeling that he was very lucky to have that kind of sponsorship, rather than organized crime and whoever was sponsoring boxers in those days. But I think in many ways they looked at him and treated him as if he was a prize racehorse.

Q: He was refused to be served in a restaurant after winning the Olympics. Can you elaborate on the restaurant incident?

Robert Lipsyte: That I think is half true. The half part of it that's probably true is he went into a restaurant in downtown Louisville, possibly wearing his Olympic gold medal around his neck, but they still refused to serve him. The second part of the story is that he went out to a local bridge, took the medal off and threw it into the water. This part most people who know him do not believe in. They generally feel that much later the medal was stolen and pawned by one of the people from his entourage.

Q: You were present at The Beatles meeting at the 5th Street Gym. Can you shed light on this, please?
Robert Lipsyte: I was not the regular boxing writer [at the time], *The New York Times* felt that Cassius would be knocked out in the first round. Most people felt that way. The odds, as you know, were seven to one. So, my paper decided to send a kid whose time wasn't very valuable – that was me. As I went down there, my instructions when I was there were to hire a rental car immediately as soon as I got to Miami. And drive back and forth between the arena and the nearest hospital, so I wouldn't waste any time following Cassius into intensive care after Liston beat him into submission. I did that as soon as I got there. After I did that I drove to the 5th Street Gym where he trained. It was the first time I'd been there. As I walked up these old stairs up to the gym, behind me I saw these little guys, four little white guys. They were wearing matching jackets and pants.

As we went up the stairs somebody mentioned Cassius had not arrived yet. He was late for his training session. And the four little guys started cursing and they turned around and they tried to leave the building. But there were these two big security guards, and they kind of pushed The Beatles right up behind me and the five of us were pushed up into the gym. Then the security guards pushed The Beatles into the dressing room. I allowed myself to get pushed along with them because by this time I kind of figured who they were. They weren't that big yet, certainly the consciousness of my age group. They were kind of a teenage bopper deal. So, five of us were pushed in this dressing room and he walked in.

And as I found out later, their publicist had set up a shoot with Sonny Liston, the champion, for their publicity – not his. Liston took one look at them, and he said, "I'm not posing with those Sissies." The publicist was desperate so he packed The Beatles back into a limousine – obviously, if he [Liston] could treat them like that then they were not that big yet – and ship them off to Cassius Clay's training place hoping to get a publicity shot with him as a second choice.

So now the five of us have walked in this dressing room. They're cursing and pushing. I kind of introduced myself. I was very pompous. I said, "Hello, I'm Robert Lipsyte from *The New York Times*." John Lennon said, "Hi, I'm Ringo." And Ringo said, "Hi, I'm George." We talked about the fight. And they were all convinced that Clay, 'that little wanker', was going to get knocked out in the first round. We were locked in there for about ten minutes. Then suddenly the door burst open and there he was. I think we all kind of gasped at the same time. He really was the most beautiful thing we'd ever seen. He was much bigger than he appeared to be because he was so perfectly formed. He was huge, glowing and he was laughing. And he said, "Let's go, Beatles. Let's go make some money." And he kind of leads them out to the ring.

If I hadn't known, I guess I would have thought they had prepared all this and had it all choreographed. But they all got in the ring. And it's still on YouTube or wherever, you can see these pictures. It's classy. All four Beatles line up, he taps the first one on the chin and they all go down like dominos. They jump up and kid around. They spent about ten or fifteen minutes. They were very playful, very funny and then they left. I don't know if they ever met again, but they go their separate ways into history. It was really quite amazing. What was particularly amazing for me was afterwards when Cassius was having his rubdown in his dressing room. He and I didn't know each other yet at that moment. He had beckoned me to come over. He had noticed that I had come out of the dressing room, so he said "So, who were those little Sissies?"

It was a really quite wonderful and startling initiation into Cassius Clay. And then during that week leading to the fight, I remember thinking, *God, wouldn't it be fabulous if this guy could win. What a shame he's going to be hurt.* I think I felt that way right up till the moment he and Liston stepped into the ring and came together in the middle of the ring for the referee's instructions. And I certainly realized, and I think the crowd realized at that moment, too, how much bigger Clay was than Liston. I mean, we had been thinking of this like the David and Goliath story. It wasn't really that simple – David was bigger than Goliath, taller, he was broad, and that certainly was a moment that we thought this could possibly happen.

Q: You were at his house in February 1966, when he was told his draft status had been changed. Can you tell me about his reaction when he heard the news?

Robert Lipsyte: It's kind of painful, it's a story I blew. I really didn't see the significance of that story. I'd been with him all day. I was going to do a feature story. It was a very 'hot' moment in American history that day. There were hearings on the war on Vietnam. Senators who were against the war were being called traitors by generals. The country had really begun to polarize over the war in kinds of ways that we're seeing now. I was just kind of sitting on the wall. I had watched the hearings in the morning and then went to his rental apartment in Miami. We did not talk about the hearings on the war. It was obviously something he thought about, or was on his mind. We're sitting there talking [on the balcony] and he's trying to pick up [jokingly] high school girls as they're coming home from school. Telephone rings in his cottage.

He's called out and he answers. Then he comes back and he's angry, he's flamed. He's just found out from the Associated Press that he had been reclassified in 1-A, which meant that suddenly he was qualified to be drafted. Up till that time, he had a classification which made him exempt from the draft. And the general feeling was, since those draft classifications are done on a local level, those powerful guys in Louisville that we talked about, they had fixed it so that he wouldn't be drafted. But he had left them because the contract was over. He had left them and he was going to another group, a group which was dominated by the Nation of Islam, who would hold his contract.

So the Louisville guys were no longer interested. So suddenly now he is 1-A. Within a few minutes of him getting that information, the lawn was crowded with press, with television trucks who were reporters. Members of Nation of Islam showed up, they started telling him if you go to Vietnam they're going to kill you. If they don't kill you, in training some white American sergeant is going to put a grenade down your pants. Meanwhile, reporters would ask, "How do you feel about being drafted? How do you feel you're going to Vietnam next week?" It was crazy. I mean, obviously that wouldn't have happened. He was heavyweight champion of the world. Even if he had been drafted, he would have given exhibitions. He would have been paraded around like a trophy. They'd never send the heavyweight champion on the frontline. This went on for several hours. He was getting battered by all these interviews. "So how do you feel about Vietnam? Do you even know where Vietnam is?" He said, "Sure." He didn't know where Vietnam was! I barely knew where Vietnam was. So it went on and on. "How do you feel about Vietcongs? How do you feel about killing the Vietcongs? How do you feel about being drafted?"

Then sometime after hours and hours of this, without thinking he said, "I got no quarrels with them Vietcongs." He meant he had nothing against the Vietcongs, but the way he used the word 'quarrel'. After having heard this so many times during the course of the day, and realizing he was just kind of responding in a moment of exasperation, that was not the lead to my story. But I think everyone else had just come in for that moment. And AP just flashed it all around the world as if he was making a statement, as if he was holding a worldwide press conference, as if he had nothing against the Vietcongs. The point was that his very first response was: why would they want to draft me? I'm the heavyweight champion of the world who spends so much money on taxes. I buy them so many guns, planes and tanks. Why would they want to draft me when they can draft some poor boy who doesn't pay any taxes at all? That was what was in his head. But the whole thing just turned into this convoluted diatribe against the war, but it wasn't. It was years before he caught up to what was going on in Vietnam.

Q: Can we talk about his relationship with Malcolm X, which later turned sour?

Robert Lipsyte: I think Malcolm was very important early on in his education as a Muslim. I spent a lot of time with Malcolm at the time. Malcolm was funny, brilliant and charismatic. I think the relationship was more of an older brother and a teacher. I think the adult figure that had real power in his life was the Honorable Elijah Muhammad, who was the revered leader of the Nation of Islam. And in my psychological theory, which may or may not be true, I think he replaced Muhammad Ali's own father who was kind of a volatile, abusive man who drank a lot. I think with Honorable Elijah Muhammad, once Elijah and Malcolm became adversaries or, at least, kind of rivals to control the group, Muhammad Ali had to make a choice. The choice he made was Elijah. I think also the fact he stepped away from Malcolm, sometime along the lines there were comments made to the effect: anybody who is against Elijah should not be living. This kind of opened the way to Malcolm's assassination. I've always been upset about that. I think Malcolm was a great man.

Q: Malcolm, of course, underwent further transformation after he performed the holy pilgrimage. Why do you think the Nation of Islam and Elijah Muhammad started to dislike Malcolm?

Robert Lipsyte: I think that Malcolm was a highly intelligent man, still in the process of educating himself. I think he was moving away from the tenets of the Nation of Islam, which were very cultish. He was moving towards more traditional Islam, the larger aspects of the religion. Number two, he was beginning to see himself more as a world figure interested in peace and reconciliation and, ultimately, possibly years later had they both lived, they would have found some sort of ground with the Reverend Martin Luther King. But at that time, he was moving away from the cultish and the mumbo jumbo aspects of the Nation of Islam. I think he was also aware of the fact that Elijah was impregnating the teenage secretaries – some of the hypocrisies of the organization. So Malcolm was moving away, but Muhammad Ali was still loyal to Elijah and did not move away with Malcolm.

Q: What did Muhammad Ali mean to black people in the 1960s? Do you think the Nation of Islam used him to propagate their message?

Robert Lipsyte: Absolutely. They certainly did. But I don't believe that Muhammad Ali had won moralistic impact. I think a lot earlier on before he became a member of Nation of Islam, a lot of African-American black people thought he was just a loud, noisy kind of a guy. Certainly, the middle-class black people didn't look at him in particular favor. I think once he became a Muslim, I think the Nation of Islam wasn't that widely popular in the black inner cities. So a lot of black people thought it was some crazy cult religion. I don't think that he became a widely popular symbol for black people that we remember now until white people started coming down on him.

If you recall it was within minutes of him refusing to step forward in 1967 to be drafted that every boxing commission in the country, which are basically political appointees or politicians, immediately withdrew sanction for him to fight in the region or to recognize his title. I mean, it was such a put-up job. The government had moved on him right away because they didn't really understand, or the lack of, the importance of the Nation of Islam. And they believed if the black heavyweight champion of the world refused to be drafted, no African-American will serve in the armed forces, which is absurd!

So it wasn't until he was stripped of his title and was not allowed to fight, lost his livelihood, being oppressed by the government, that black people began to realize this was another form of oppression they had suffered in America through the history. During the years of his exile in boxing, three-and-a-half years, his key prime years, the entire country's attitude towards the war was changing. The civil rights movement in America was taking incredible force and more power in the country. So he became very important and symbolic to young white people of the 1960s, particularly college young white people. And he became a very important symbol of black resistance of standing up to the man for black people. But that all came as a result of his persecution and prosecution.

Q: Do you feel black people and black boxers gained respect and opened the doors for acceptance through boxing in the 1960s when racism was rife?
Robert Lipsyte: Yes and no. That's a question I asked Malcolm and his answer was good. He said white people will always let black people get as big as they could as long as they're entertaining them, they're dancing for them, singing for them, they're bleeding for them. On one hand, yes. Joe Louis, Muhammad Ali and later Mike Tyson, they all became objects of certain kind of respect. But I think to compare that with Obama as president shows the tremendous gap that sport offers and what real power does. Compare that now. I mean, people are comparing in terms of popularity and power. Tiger Woods with Michael Jordan and then with Ali. We can see Tiger Woods is a figure only to make money for other people.

Q: In 1975, you were with Muhammad Ali in Miami when he was giving a speech at a junior high school, can you recall this?
Robert Lipsyte: He was doing a series of boxing exhibitions in the area and I was traveling with him. I remember that it was not so much a speech that he gave to the kids. What he did was it was their annual awards ceremony so he gave out the medals and awards. And he did it in a kind of a comical fashion, kind of making funny jokes as the kids came up to get the awards. It was not a kind of inspirational address.

Q: What was the most fascinating conversation you had?
Robert Lipsyte: I have to tell you that I don't know that I had a real...I started talking to him in 1964, so what's that? So many decades ago. Wow! So I started talking to him before you were born. I think in all that time I'm not sure we had the same kind of conversation that you and I could. Either I was asking him questions or he was

talking at me. I mean, it's not like we were buddies. The closest thing that I can remember to a real conversation was in 1968. We were both waiting for our first child to be born. I remember that we were talking about how nine months was such a long period to wait for a kid.

But other than that I think what I found fascinating was the process in which his mind worked, and the fact that over the years he developed. I think that when he won the championship through his twenties, he was still very young. He matured very specifically to box and he was inside a bubble of this religion. I don't think he was a worldly person by any means. I don't really think that he really began to use his mind to think until he was not allowed to fight.

So he went to college campuses to talk to college kids. Then over the years he began to have the rounded attitudes that most people get much earlier. The irony, of course, is by the time he really was a formed human being, he could no longer speak. It's like Beethoven going deaf. He relatively became mute, but I think that in terms of pure fascination, I keep coming back to the day after he won the championship from Liston. We entered the arena and he was asked whether he was a card-carrying Muslim. In 1964, the phrase 'card carrying' had a certain kind of historical resonance. Because that's how people referred to Communists at a period America was scared of Communists.

They called them 'card-carrying Communists'. So they said, "Are you a card Muslim?" He kind of looked at him [the reporter] and basically said, to paraphrase it: why are you giving me such a hard time? Here is a group who don't drink. They don't fornicate. They eat right. They tried to have jobs and take care of themselves. And you're telling me there's something wrong with that? Maybe there's something wrong with you. Then they asked if he was a segregationist. He said, "Well, blue birds stay with blue birds and red birds with red birds." You've heard that? After that it was all done and he could see that. And this is mostly the younger reporters now, who stayed with him through the end of the press conference and were kind of disappointed that he seemed like this nationalist, segregationist.

The one thing that I always thought was fascinating was when he said, "I don't have to be what you want me to be. I'm free to be who I want." I thought as an individual declaration of independence, those were the most powerful words I ever heard. I remember being struck at the time and fascinated with them at the time. But as the years have gone on, I have been more and more fascinated and struck by them because no other really important athlete has ever achieved that kind of independence. I mean, the Michael Jordans, the Tiger Woods, all the great athletes, the American athletes of our time, have all rolled over to the material side one way or another. They have done what their sponsors wanted them to do. Ali has always kind of [been his own man] in a sense: I don't want to be what you want me to be. That was the most powerful and fascinating thing I ever heard him say.

Q: When Muhammad Ali fought Sonny Liston for the title, did he or anyone have suspicions that Angelo Dundee may be involved with gangsters?

Robert Lipsyte: I became a boxing writer after Ali won. No boxer ever loses a fight. He was over-trained. He was under-trained. He was sold out by his trainer who was with the Mafia. There's always that kind of reason and those kinds of suspicions have always followed. But not seriously. The point is: we knew Liston was mobbed up, but I don't think anybody felt that way about Angelo, whose brother Chris was a big-time promoter who certainly would have had more connections with organized crime than Angelo. Even then these are the people you do business with, but I don't think that there was any serious concern Angelo was operating...not seriously. Of course, people talked about it. There was some thought Liston threw the fight either because he was threatened by the Muslims or because he knew if there was a rematch it would be a very big payday, which there was. But as time went on, it's possible he laid down his job, but I doubt very much it was a clear fix.

Q: According to Milt Bailey and his team, they thought Muhammad Ali was crazy. And they also had the notion that he expressed fear at the weigh-ins. What's your opinion?

Robert Lipsyte: At the time, I was such an inexperienced reporter that I personally thought that it was an act to get Liston scared. You remember Liston came out of jail. Liston was a very powerful thug. The only way he could scare Liston would be to do something crazy, to make him think he was up against a crazy person who would have no fear of him and could do something totally unpredictable. So, I thought that was part of the strategy. But I wasn't 100 percent sure because of my inexperience. But a few weeks later, I had an exclusive interview with Cassius in his hotel room in New York. And he went through step by step the entire crazy act. He said it had been planned out beforehand and he showed me step by step everything they did.

Q: When Floyd Patterson first fought Muhammad Ali, he refused to call him Muhammad Ali, instead he called him Cassius Clay. How did this fight come about and what was the highlight?

Robert Lipsyte: All those fights which came about were totally about making money. I think Floyd was a decent human being in most instances, who really saw himself as the protector of America and champion of Christianity. He refused to call him Muhammad Ali. He refused to be respectful to Ali's religion. During the course of the fight, Ali totally dominated the fight, but he dominated it in a very cool fashion. My metaphors of the fight when I wrote it, it was like a little boy picking off the wings of a butterfly. He kind of poked him and tortured him. He could have knocked him out at any time in the early rounds. Patterson was much smaller, much weaker. He had a bad back. He was not returning blows. But Ali would hit him a few times and dance away, make fun of him and mock him. It was truly gross and an ugly fight. It was really a terrible low point in Ali's career.

Q: You have said that Muhammad Ali never got the support from the media, but he got the attention back in the 1960s. Do you feel he was worthy of veneration from the media?

Robert Lipsyte: Well, in the beginning they treated him as this kind of a charming clown, this admiration. Everybody knew he was going to get knocked out in the first round of the Liston fight – we assumed that. They believed that he had no right to be challenging for the title at that stage of his career. But he was good copy. He was fun to cover. There was a real split between the older reporters and the younger ones. The older reporters remembered having covered Joe Louis, who was your idea of a boxer, who was respectful and did his talking in the ring and he wasn't a boastful braggart. Remember: I am the greatest. I think nowadays we have been so inured by wrestling, also by other athletes as well, about boastfulness. It seems part of the promotion. But in those days it was obviously new. He would say, "I am the greatest. I am the prettiest. If he gives me any jive I'll knock him out in five." This was kind of new, the wild boastfulness, basically very common street corner talk in black ghettos. Certainly to the white media it was new. It wasn't new to me because I had written a book with a well-known black civil rights activist. I mean, I'd seen all this, but to most reporters it was really wild and new. Certainly, totally new in sports.

So he was great copy. But he was treated particularly... the older reporters called him 'The Louisville Lip'. They made fun of him constantly. The younger reporters, we loved him because the older reporters hated him. There was a generational gap. So he was our age and he was fun. And he kind of reflected the new times. He was not treated respectfully by the powerful older reporters and columnists. But he still did get a lot of space. They did write about him. In a sense, he was the first celebrity athlete. And in many ways he was kind of a model, the kind we see now of people who get covered for no reason at all. Of course, Cassius Clay delivered all of his boasts. But at the time he was being covered, he seemed to be as empty as Paris Hilton, or whoever.

Q: Were you in his presence when he was with any movie or music star?

Robert Lipsyte: Some of the fights were star-studded. At one fight I remember Frank Sinatra – you didn't get bigger than him in those days – taking photographs for *Life* magazine. And Burt Lancaster, the movie actor, was doing play-by-play commentary. These were very big people in their time. Then later on, his fights would bring in Diana Ross of The Supremes. Everybody you can think of, Bill Cosby, Belafonte. He was constantly being surrounded. He was bigger than they were.

Q: Elvis?

Robert Lipsyte: I don't think they interacted that much, you know. I mean, the way celebrities shake each other's hand, hug each other and stand for pictures and then move out. If there were private moments, I was not there.

Q: When Muhammad Ali retired, did you keep in touch or see him in the 1980s and 1990s, and did you cover any stories?

Robert Lipsyte: Yeah, sure. There were some pathetic stories. I remember he was doing some promotion for a Don King fight. I think it was the Tubbs and Witherspoon fight. And he seemed kind of sad. I remember the terrible picture of him sitting in a hotel room with his feet in a pan of water. Somebody was putting electrical wires in the water to give his feet little shocks to stimulate the muscles. I guess it was the beginning of the Parkinson's at the time. I remember thinking how pathetic that was. But he came out of that.

And I think I traveled with him later when he started the Muhammad Ali Center – the big museum he has. I remember white men who were college students in the 1960s coming up to him with tears in their eyes. He's doing little magic tricks. Until he stopped talking freely, which was in the last fifteen years of his life, he was always telling these terrible jokes. He knew I was Jewish. So whenever he saw me he would say to me, "What's the difference between a Jew and a canoe?" And I would always say, "What!?" He would say, "A canoe tips." Does that come through to you? A canoe tips over, but a Jew is too cheap to tip. Something else, he would say, "There's three guys sitting together in the back of a car, a black guy, a Mexican and an Arab. Who is driving?" I would say, "Who?" He would say, "The police." What was interesting to people was he could say these very politically incorrect jokes. But if you or I said it we would be running out of the room.

But he would tell these jokes and people would say this shows how much he loves all people. I said earlier that he matured as he grew older, but I think there was also a kind of innocence to him, kind of innocence of some sort of a holy man in a way. I mean, I think he has been beatified now. He still had kind of a sweet glow. I had not been in his presence for two or three years. I hadn't seen him in the last two or three years. He barely talked. When you do talk to him he'd mumble something. His wife would answer as if she could understand it. She may very well could. I don't know. There was this kind of sweetness emanating from him.

Q: He met a couple of presidents, were you ever in his presence?
Robert Lipsyte: Yeah, actually I was there when he met Clinton. I was there for the public part of it. They shake hands, they hug and they greet each other. They say some nice things. If there was anything more in private, I wasn't there for that. You'd have to ask Clinton. I think Bush gave him a medal. I was kind of pissed off that he took a medal from that guy, but...

Q: Did you ever travel with him abroad, when he went to Iraq or Afghanistan?
Robert Lipsyte: I remember a couple of occasions when he went on peace missions, or trying to release hostages. But I don't think he was particularly effective. He also refused to condemn Osama Bin Laden after 9/11, which was kind of a big deal here. He said he wouldn't talk ill about them, about Al-Qaeda, because he had business interests in that part of the world. So, I mean, there's

always kind of a paradox about Muhammad Ali. This goes back to: I don't have to be who you want me to be. He was a man who was always talking about family values, how important it was to be loving to your wife and children, but he was a man who was fooling around all the time. This was a man who was representing a segregationist cult at a time when the country was struggling in bloody fashion for fairness for old people and integration. I think it's a complicated subject.

Q: Do you think he set a benchmark and transcended the sport of boxing?

Robert Lipsyte: I think he elevated everything. I think I am not in sympathy with everything he said over the years or everything he stood for. However, I do love him because I think that he gave people a standard in and outside of sport – standard of courage, bravery of standing up for what you believe in and for being brave. I think he was brave. I think people can use that aspect of him. The principle stand of being brave and standing up for what you believe in. He certainly elevated boxing. I don't have to tell you that it doesn't take too much to elevate boxing. But he also elevated sport, all sport, and he elevated America. He certainly was one of the most important sportsmen of all time. Also, let me say something: compared to people like Michael Jordan and Tiger Woods, there's no comparison. I don't think those guys stand for anything except their own financial advancement. In both cases they are owned by corporations and they act as really very expensive clothing models. That's what I think they are. But Ali really stood for something far greater.

Q: Did you ever witness Muhammad Ali becoming impudent and lose his temper and become angry?

Robert Lipsyte: Sure! Absolutely. He was angry that day he became 1-A when he became subject for draft. I think over the years he became angry when he felt he was misunderstood or attacked unfairly. He once got angry with me. The only time we had bad words between the two of us was in the mid-1980s when I was interviewing him. I think he felt vulnerable, weak and depressed. It was one of those situations when Don King was giving him some money to promote a fight.

I asked him some serious questions. I was working for television at the time. Ali started screaming at me, he said, "You're a tricky man. You've come to ask me questions to make me look bad. You're a white man and you get the biggest boxer nigger you can find!" I was very embarrassed and angry. My producer said to me black guys are allowed to call black guys nigger, don't worry about it. I think that it was his moment of vulnerability. He's a human being. There were moments of vulnerability when he became threatened. He became angry, he got serious and responded that way. But for the most part, I would say over those last five decades, this was a man who was kindly, really! That incident was a very small moment.

I remember we were both racing to catch an airplane. We really had to catch it because it was the last flight that night and we were late. We were running through the airport and this little old lady took a picture of him. And he stopped. I said, "Come on, let's go." He said, "No, no, no." She had the lens cap on. So he reached over delicately, took her lens cap off so that she can take another picture again. He didn't want her to be disappointed. I think his life has been marked by many acts of kindness. I think he's basically a really good person. Your question about did I see him angry? Sure! But in over forty-six years I can only think of a couple of times when he was angry, serious or mean, but I can think of many times when he was kindly.

Q: Any final thoughts on the greatest sports personality of modern times, you've known him since the early 1960s?
Robert Lipsyte: I think the country has been richer for having had him. Even though in many ways he is kind of a 'holy child', I think he's not Mahatma Gandhi. He's not Malcolm X. He's not Bishop Tutu. He's not any of these real holy people who have tried to elevate a country to leadership and by the force of their thinking. But I think he has kind of enabled a lot of people to think in ways they personally can be brave and can stand up for what they believe in.

BERT SUGAR

Recognizable from a distance by his trademark fedora and unlit cigar, Bert Randolph Sugar worked in the advertising industry before buying *Boxing Illustrated* magazine and working as its editor from 1969 to 1973. He went on to be the editor and publisher of *Ring* magazine and has written over eighty books, mostly pertaining to boxing. He is one of boxing's foremost historians, earning himself the title of The Greatest Boxing Writer of the 20th Century from the International Veterans Boxing Association. Sugar even took the unusual step of sparring with Ali, over a career that saw the pair meet many times.

Q: Can we start off by you telling me how Muhammad Ali pursued boxing, and was one of his influences Jack Johnson?
Bert Sugar: Somebody stole Ali's bicycle and he went to complain to the police. They directed him to a boxing gym, at which point he took up the sport. I don't think he ever got back his bicycle. I don't know who his influences were. I think he was naturally gifted. If he had an influence it was Sugar Ray Robinson, who was in his training camp at given times including the time he fought Liston the first time to win the title. But I don't think his influence was Jack Johnson. When he was out for three-and-a-half years, he saw the play *The Great White Hope* and said the only difference between Johnson and him – because they both were persecuted – was Johnson the women and he the draft. But, no, I don't think Johnson was an influence.

Q: Let's talk about Sugar Ray Robinson, who was one of the legendary great boxers, when he snubbed Muhammad Ali by refusing him an autograph.
Bert Sugar: I've heard about it, but I don't know the story to be honest. I only heard it. It was rumors. I don't know. But I do know Cassius Clay, then not Muhammad Ali, followed boxing and watched it on television. After he took up boxing, if anyone

influenced him it was Willie Pastrano for his moves. Willie Pastrano was a great defensive fighter. He took from Pastrano's moves to stay out of the punches, which became his great defense – the quickness.

Q: How did the friendship between Muhammad Ali and Sugar Ray Robinson ensue?

Bert Sugar: Well, he sought out the greatest fighter ever. And Robinson identified his skills and they became a mutual admiration society. I don't know exactly the time, but Robinson happened in his training camp. Now, Ali, this is when he won the light-heavyweight championship medal at the Olympics in 1960, had met Angelo Dundee because Dundee was bringing fighters to Louisville. And he had taken great nourishment and great inspiration from Pastrano who fought in Louisville. He [Ali] was always there carrying bags, doing anything he could just to associate with professional boxers.

Q: Can you shed light on Sugar Ray Robinson's background?

Bert Sugar: Sugar Ray Robinson was the greatest fighter ever – period, end of paragraph. He could do everything. Everyone saw something different in Ray. He was fast. He had explosive power. He could move and he gave angles. I even saw him throw a knockout punch flying backwards, which is a hell of a lot of leverage. Sugar Ray Robinson would get upset if you messed his hair. He was the greatest at everything he did and he was without a flaw.

Q: What was Joe Louis' relationship like with Muhammad Ali?

Bert Sugar: Muhammad Ali was from a different generation. He even called Joe Louis an 'Uncle Tom' at one time, which was unfair. Joe Louis, in the 1940s, quietly worked his own version of gaining civil rights for the African-Americans. He would not fight in training camps during World War II if the crowds were not integrated. And he basically was for America, one of our heroes of World War II. He's the one who coined the phrase 'we will win because we're on God's side' and that became, if not the slogan, one of the famous sayings for the Americans during World War II. But Joe Louis was a quiet man and he spoke economically and efficiently. He would say things like, before the second Billy Conn fight in 1946, "He can run but he can't hide." Once during a telecast when he was a commentator, the co-commentator was trying to bring him into the discussion. He said that the fighter, whoever he was, doesn't like punches to the body. Joe Louis responded with, "Who does?" But he spoke with his gloves. He had fast hands. Once he had a man on the hook, he was through. Ask Billy Conn how that worked. When Joe Louis hit Eddie Simms with the first punch of a fight before he became champion, Eddie Simms, eighteen seconds into the fight, was knocked down. He gets up and says, "I'd like to take a walk on the roof." At which point the referee called the fight off.

Joe Louis was probably the hardest puncher in the history of the heavyweight division. Ali had a totally different style. Ali could move like no other heavyweight ever. Joe Louis was a plodding fighter who didn't have footwork – he had handwork. He was a different type of a fighter completely. He was the orthodox all-time fighter. When writers first saw Clay they didn't know what to make of him. He ran and he moved. Heavyweights didn't move, they were all in the Joe Louis school of left cross with a right. Ali would flick that left out, move and cross with a right and move. No heavyweight had ever done that. And the writers didn't particularly care for him because he was out of a new school. They didn't understand. I don't think he and Joe Louis' style, nor his appreciation of Joe Louis, was such that he could comment on because it wasn't his style.

Q: How did Muhammad Ali get involved with Archie Moore training him?

Bert Sugar: Archie Moore trained fighters. Remember Archie Moore fought till he was forty-nine and one of his last fights was against Clay, which he lost in the fourth round. Now, he sets up shop. He had gotten to what was the Louisville Group who underwrote Cassius Clay's professional debut. They sent him to Archie Moore. And Archie didn't even want him to fight; he wanted him to do all the chores around the house to gain discipline like sweeping the floors. Clay didn't like that. He just walked out of the camp. But Archie Moore would come back as a trainer of George Foreman. One of boxing's great sagas is the man who has more knockouts than any man in history – period, end of paragraph. What he was going to teach Clay was beyond me because his style wasn't Clay's style.

Q: What was the most compelling conversation you ever had with Muhammad Ali?
Bert Sugar: I don't know. I went up to spar with him once and I got the shit kicked out of me. I went up to Deer Lake in the early 1970s when I was the editor of a magazine at the time. I told them that for publicity sakes, for both of us, I would like to get in the ring with him. I'd been a fighter but I was no damn good. I think my nickname as an amateur was 'The Great White Hopeless'. I went in there and got a couple of rounds with him. All he did was hit me. And he finally figured out that I had very little to offer, so he just grabbed me in a clinch and hit me on the backside a couple of times. But we would talk. And he was Muhammad Ali saying wonderful things.

But I must tell you the greatest story I ever heard of Ali, which wasn't me by the way, it was [told by] Bob Lipsyte who was a young reporter just out of school for *The New York Times*. Before the first Liston fight they sent him to Miami to cover it. They didn't want to send one of their regulars. They tell Bob the first thing you do is find out how close the hospital is to the arena in Miami because he'll probably be there by the end of the first round – meaning Clay. So Lipsyte does that and then he goes to the 5th Street Gym, Angelo's gym, to see Clay. He's got time to kill and he starts walking up the stairs of the 5th Street Gym. Four kids with long hair are trying to get out. And there's someone at the door who won't let them out because the publicity man is screaming at them.

So they stick them, along with Lipsyte, in a room till Clay gets there because he's out doing roadwork. Finally, Clay gets there ten or fifteen minutes later. They open the door and all four guys, along with Lipsyte, are piling out. They get in the ring and they all stand there in a line for the camera. Ali hits the first one, Ringo, hits the second one, Paul, hits the third one, John, etc, and they all fall down and go boom! Afterwards they leave and Clay turns to Lipsyte, and he says, "Who were those fags?" not knowing they were The Beatles.

Q: You were the publisher of *Boxing Illustrated*, did Muhammad Ali ever frequent the offices?
Bert Sugar: And *Ring* magazine and *Fight Game*. Of *Ring* magazine, yes. He walked around looking at the exhibits. He was Cassius Clay then. He told me he was going to be the next heavyweight champion. He was a very refreshing boy and person. Then he went outside and stood on the corner to see if anyone recognized him.

Q: Did you attend the press conference of the first Floyd Patterson fight?
Bert Sugar: Yes, I was at the press conference. Ali was calling him a rabbit because he ran. "He's going to run, he's a rabbit." Patterson kept calling him Clay even though he was now Muhammad Ali. And he [Ali] didn't take to it well. He said that's my slave name.

Q: How would you sum up the fight?
Bert Sugar: Well, I think Patterson was way up the hill, and he was. And it was an ugly fight because all Ali did was keep taunting him with, "What's my name!?" And Patterson fell back on the line he used in the press conference. He would say something that sounded like, though I didn't hear it clearly, but I'm sure it was: "You're mama calls you Clay, your name is Clay." It was ugly because it was Ali trying to taunt him repeatedly rather than win the fight, which he did.

Q: Second Patterson fight . . .
Bert Sugar: It was a continuation of the first one. Patterson couldn't catch him. Patterson wouldn't know how to catch him. Ali was too fast and he kept popping his left and Patterson's back went off. And

the referee kept sending them to the corner after every round, but it wasn't much of a fight.

Q: In your opinion, what was Muhammad Ali's defining fight during his long and illustrious career?

Bert Sugar: There's several. There's the Foreman fight, The Rumble in the Jungle, because when he came back after three-and-a-half years, he lost his speed so what he did was go to the rope-a-dope. But he out-psyched Foreman. He had Foreman swinging till he went down like a water hose, which loses its pressure, and he knocked him out. But he hit him end of every round. He hit Foreman so you knew that he could. And then he got Foreman off balance. He caught him and caught him again and he went down, although, I never heard the count of ten by the referee Zack Clayton. But one of his greatest fights was against Cleveland Williams. He knocked Williams down and out, I think, four times that night. That was his most powerful. Cleveland Williams was a powerful fighter. He carried a 357 Magnum bullet in him, it had never been extracted. He'd been shot by the police. And you're not sure if he was injured going in, but he took every shot but he kept going down. One of his best performances and his best peak performances was against Zora Folley. Then he was stripped off his title for not volunteering for the draft.

Q: During the period he wasn't active for three-and-a-half years, how was he spending his time and did he pursue making a living by doing speaking engagements?

Bert Sugar: He did a lot of speaking engagements. I would reach him at some of them – black colleges, small gatherings, anywhere to get change. He was even in a play called *Buck White*. He did everything and he was supported by people. Joe Frazier gave him money. His business manager, Gene Kilroy, got him money. He had stepped away. He had done something nobody else would probably do. He'd given up his livelihood for his beliefs.

Q: At this point of his career some people liked him, whilst other people's animosity towards him was somewhat visible. Later, his mythical status elevated him to the level of hero-worship.

Bert Sugar: Well, it was a divided nation. It was 'divided we stand'. The young kids, because they were against the Vietnamese War, loved him, particularly the blacks. The Hard Hats hated him. Even Joe Louis said that he should have volunteered. Jackie Robinson volunteered to go into the draft. But those three-and-a-half years were his peak years, when he comes back he's past his peak.

Q: Because of your journalist status and position, did you get invited to any celebrity gatherings?

Bert Sugar: I was at some of them. I was at the opening of the Ali Museum in Louisville with President Clinton. And people like BB King and others were there. And we just talked. I went with Angelo Dundee. Its purpose is to honor its most exalted native son in Louisville. It's a very beautiful museum. This was the opening and there was a massive concert held.

Q: Do you think Muhammad Ali may have been overrated as a fighter, or do you feel he had his own distinctive style, which stood above all others, elevated him in a league of its own?

Bert Sugar: Probably both. Probably both. By those who adored him, grew up with him, young kids who embraced him, yes, he was overrated. But he also was great! He might not have been the greatest as he called himself. Ray Robinson was, and a couple of others who were, including Joe Louis. But he was great. So we're not talking specie, we're only talking degree. And to that end I must tell you every day he gains more, if you will, a myth to be associated with, like movies made of him. So his legend grows after the fact . . . but during the fact . . . he was a great fighter. So the answer to that question is: both! Was great but he wasn't the greatest, but he called himself the greatest. He often did that by tapping himself on the shoulder with his own gloves and people bought it.

Q: Do you think his unique personality and persona played an integral role that elevated his status?

Bert Sugar: Oh, yes. He was the first. Up to then African-Americans had been quiet. Like Joe Louis they were just humble. The 1960s was a new age and that new age was basically personified by Muhammad Ali, who spoke out on everything and at any time. Like, "I ain't got no quarrel with the Vietcongs." Here was a unique fighter, with the help of Angelo Dundee, which we'd never seen before on anybody and in any field. So he was refreshing and new and his personality was part of him.

Q: Do you feel he should have exited the ring before he actually did? The final couple of fights he fought in, he seemed to be over the hill.

Bert Sugar: Yes. You see, boxing is different than any other sport. In any other sport you must make the team. and if you don't make the team, you just can't go out there playing soccer, football, baseball or basketball, or whatever the team sport is, and say, "I'm here because they'll say good, go there." But in boxing you're an individual and that's one of its basic attributes, I think. And when you say I want to fight, there's going to be some promoter who's going to put you on or a State Athletic Commission is going to endorse you because they see money. And Ali, like a lot of fighters, stayed on for too long. And I think in particularly his last two fights, against Larry Holmes and Trevor Berbick, were much too long.

Q: His condition was deteriorating, Ferdie Pacheco who was his physician had left him by then . . .

Bert Sugar: That physician was just a member of his entourage, but, yes, he fought too long. I don't know if his condition could be attributed directly to boxing. I know there's two million people who have Parkinson's disease syndrome, which is what he had. But getting hit in the head ain't going to improve him growing toenails. It didn't but it probably worsened it.

Q: How much money was Muhammad Ali making in the early 1960s when he turned professional, and to what extent did the financial situation change in the mid-1970s when he fought the likes of Joe Frazier?

Bert Sugar: The fight with Joe Frazier, the first one, March of 1971, was the first time ever any athlete in any field made what he and Joe Frazier made – which was $2.5 million apiece. They changed the economic face of the sport. He had been fighting for the Louisville syndicate in the beginning and he was getting a stipend. They underwrote him and just paid him money and took the purse in order to pay themselves back. But he changed everything with that fight in 1971, everything for everybody who ever played a sport.

Q: What about people who were around Muhammad Ali? Obviously, some took advantage of him. He had a large group around him. Was he a much more laid back type of a person?

Bert Sugar: They joined the entourage and he underwrote them. Yes, I don't know if they took advantage. He might have taken advantage of them. He likes people and the more people the happier he is. And he would adopt people like Drew Bundini Brown, he just brought him into the camp. He had previously been with Sugar Ray Robinson as a hanger-on and he starts hanging around with Ali. He becomes the camp clown and Ali loved it! So he might have used them as much as they he.

Q: How would you define Angelo Dundee's relationship with Muhammad Ali?

Bert Sugar: Oh, it was excellent. Dundee did a wonderful thing and he'd let him be him. He'd let Ali be Ali. He didn't try to change him. He just maximized his efforts and minimized his deficits. But Ali was Ali, and he was always going to be Ali. And Angelo would phrase everything so that Ali thought it was his idea even though it was Angelo's. Angelo was a psychiatrist and a psychologist and a wonderful person to be around him. In fact, when they asked Angelo, after Ali changed his name from Clay to Ali, "What do you think of it, Angelo?" He says, "I don't care. My name isn't Dundee originally." That's how he operated. He would tell Ali that was a good uppercut you threw in there, wow. He hadn't thrown an uppercut, but he thought it was his idea. Dundee was the perfect match. He was the Ying to Yang. He would finish his poems and rhymes. They were a pair, a twosome.

Q: How much of a part did Chris Dundee play in the making of Muhammad Ali, and can you tell me about the 5th Street Gym?
Bert Sugar: He promoted a couple of his fights but it was really Angelo. I mean, Chris put up the money for the 5th Street Gym, but it was Angelo. Chris promoted his fight. They are resurrecting it. They're going to start it again by the way. At the 5th Street Gym there were a lot of Cuban fighters. And because he had Pastrano, he was the first selection they made after Clay left Archie Moore, the Louisville syndicate, and Clay fit right in. Angelo had done so much work with the 5th Street Gym down in Miami. Basically, it became famous for all the great products he turned out – many of them Cubans. But now with Clay there it becomes even more famous.

Q: How often did you cover Muhammad Ali in your magazines and what was the biggest story you ever printed? Do you think his fan base was beyond the confines of the boxing fraternity?
Bert Sugar: Well, every time we put him on the cover we sold. So we covered him a lot. Because he had so many fans and followers that to put him on the cover even if we didn't say anything inside sold. So he was on the cover a lot. Everybody loved him on that side. The people who didn't love him weren't going to buy boxing magazines anyway.

Q: How popular was boxing compared to other sports like baseball in those days?
Bert Sugar: Outside of the time of Jack Dempsey and Joe Louis, baseball was always the most popular American sport. But it [boxing] was an individual sport and there was still the belief, at

least in America, that the heavyweight champion was the strongest man in the world. So there was that individual cliché that Ali had, that he was the strongest man in the world and his constant search for publicity. I mean, he never met a camera, reporter, photographer and writer he didn't like, because he knew they could write about him. So we had articles and articles on him covering his fights and the build-up to the fights.

The biggest seller ever for any other magazines I ever edited, this was *Boxing Illustrated* before I took over *Ring*, was the first fight with Frazier. We sold hundreds of thousands of copies! I always think my relationship with him was wonderful, not only as a writer but I'm social, he's social. So he searched me out. We had a good social time. I always identified with him. And I loved his constant, if you will, his life the way he exuded it and his persona. He made great copy and he was a great friend.

JERRY IZENBERG

Jerry Izenberg has written about some of the most significant sports events in history, and is one of only three writers to have covered every Superbowl. He had a long and distinguished career as a columnist for the *Star-Ledger*, ultimately earning him a place in the National Sportscasters and Writers Hall Of Fame, as well as the Boxing Hall Of Fame. Izenberg first met Ali in Rome in 1960 at the Olympics, after which both men became firm friends and traveled around the world. He was nominated for the Pulitzer fifteen times and is the author of nine books. He received the Red Smith Award in 2000.

Q: Can you please shed light on the first time you met Muhammad Ali at the Olympics in 1960?
Jerry Izenberg: He was just another guy at the time. I used to cover a lot of boxing and I was in the Olympic village. He was sitting on the steps with his medal on. And he's yelling at everyone, "I'm the greatest! I'm going to be the heavyweight champion of the world!" Most of the people didn't know what the hell he was saying. But I noticed all the girls stopped to take a second look – that never changed all through the years.

Q: How would you evaluate Muhammad Ali's performance at the Olympics?
Jerry Izenberg: Well, you know, we had other guys win who were there. He was not a heavyweight. Honestly, I'll tell you what I feel: most Olympic boxers that I've seen over the years are . . . I think compared to other kids he was OK. We thought to ourselves, *He's young and we'll see what he does.* It wasn't like I was looking at the future heavyweight champion of the world. He wasn't even a heavyweight; he was a light-heavyweight. Well, it wasn't anything spectacular. You didn't really look until he [later] started to become Muhammad Ali. But what happened was it was his performance away from the ring at the Olympics, sitting on the steps waving to

people. They didn't know what the hell he was talking about. Half of them didn't speak English. But they all laughed when he waved at them saying, "I'm going to be the greatest fighter that ever lived." And I noticed at that time, all the girls came back for a second look. So that told me that he had some kind of charisma.

Q: Did you interview him or have any conversations when you were in Rome, and how would you sum up the atmosphere at the Olympics?

Jerry Izenberg: Nah. I just said hello. He was holding up the medal and shouting. Like I said before, he was very outgoing. Guys didn't know what he was doing, but the girls took a second look, and that stayed with him the rest of his life. Well, there wasn't really much atmosphere. We're talking 1960. It was very, very hot. It was really hot. In fact, they might have moved the marathon to later in the evening. It was like all the Olympics. It didn't really have great heroes that I can think of. I think it might have been a sense of atmosphere when the Ethiopian Abebe Bikila won the marathon. He ran barefooted. Everybody was excited about that. It was just another Olympics, really. Everything that grew out of it came later. Ali was just another guy who won the Olympic medal. We had a lot of them and very few of them have gone on to fight as pros significantly at that time. Boxing wasn't producing. We had Floyd Patterson who was not a heavyweight at the time. He didn't think he'd be a champion till after he turned pro. I think the Olympics were very undistinguished.

Q: When did you start to regularly communicate with him when you got back to the United States?

Jerry Izenberg: I knew a guy named Bill King – not Don King – at the time who was a promoter. And he told me about how it must have been like for Ali to fight with his first opponent. He started getting a lot of attention. Years later I remember the first guy Ali fought who I went up to see. The guy said he hurt his leg playing football. He was a white guy who fought Ali. I really began to get to Ali when he fought Charlie Powell. Angelo Dundee called me at my office, and he said, "You've got to come over. It's going to be a great fight." I said, "I'm not coming. Charlie Powell's just an ex-football player trying to make a couple of bucks fighting. I'm not coming to Pittsburgh. I don't like to stop for gas in Pittsburgh! I'm not coming to Pittsburgh to see a fight." Ali recited a poem. I don't know what it was, but it was the first time I ever heard him read poetry. And I laughed. And that was the end of it. Then he said he was going to knock him out, in whatever round it was. But he did knock him out in that round.

Then we began to stay in contact. He came to New York for a few days and I went to see him fight. I never felt he could beat the world champion. It was a big story. He was easy to write about. He was easy to interview. So, that's really how the relationship began. Little by little I got to know him. He had a great way of attracting attention. And he fought a guy named Doug Jones, which was a very important fight. I thought Doug won the fight. It was a very close fight. Doug Jones was a light-heavyweight but had put some weight on, which made him a heavyweight. They said it would be an easy win for him [Ali] and that he could move up, but it wasn't easy at all. It was life and death. I think looking at the scorecards, Jones lost by a point.

So, Ali did not really distinguish himself at all until after that fight. When he fought Henry Cooper he cut him. Cooper was really hurt but he showed a lot of guts. I got confused when Ali said to his corner he could not see. The thing about Angelo Dundee blinding him with the towel, that's bull. He ran the whole round – he boxed a little bit. Cooper was one of the greatest underrated heavyweights of all time. The only reason Cooper never became a world champion is because he was short-changed by God – the way God made his bone structure. I always wanted to see a fight with Cooper and Wepner.

Q: He wasn't going to acquiescently let the government beat him. Were there any peculiar incidents during Muhammad Ali's draft trial?
Jerry Izenberg: The thing with Ali is, when he was coming back

[comeback], well, they did a terrible thing to him. He had no money. I'm going to tell you a story not everyone knows. You know, there's ways you can tell if a person is lying or telling the truth. I'm going to tell you this. The FBI came in his bedroom to check out things [when they were monitoring him]. And they come to a conclusion. The court appoints an examiner and the examiners are almost always right. They picked a guy who was a retired judge from Louisville whose name was Lawrence Grauman. They thought they'll put him in there, thinking he's not going to listen to Ali and everything will be fine. And what happened was he came out after about an hour and he said to the draft board something. What happened was the draft board overruled him, and this had never happened before. They changed the rules. It's the only time – I could find, and I did research – where they overruled the examiner and went by the FBI report. And as it turned out the FBI report was used.

Later on when he won the case, a guy by the name of Chuck Morgan, who was the civil rights lawyer in Atlanta, demanded to see the tapes. But the government said, "We're not going to let you see them. But on the other hand, we don't need them because he's obviously very guilty." And he [Chuck Morgan] said that we've got a mistrial and a tremendous case to appeal here. My opinion – I never proved it but it's my opinion – is that I think that somebody in one of the African embassies called Ali or he called them. Not for any specific purpose, but Ali would talk to all kinds of people. He wasn't going to leave the country. He wasn't going to run away. That certainly was proved to be true later on. But I think the government was tapping an African embassy. In those days everybody tapped everybody. No one's ever confirmed this with me. His name and his words came up on the tape and that's what they were using [as evidence].

But they didn't have to admit to tapping an embassy. The only reason that I could think of why they would . . . the reason I know why he never tried to leave the country is, you may remember when his fight with Ernie Terrell was kicked out of Chicago. He went to Toronto to fight George Chuvalo. Three days before the fight I wandered into his gym and he was at the back. He was alone. He was getting a massage on the table. He said, "What are you doing here?" I said, "There's going to be a fight." He said, "You know there's not going to be a fight, why are you here?" I said, "Muhammad, I came to see when you are going back . . . getting sanctuary or asylum. And I'm not going to go home." He jumped off the table and got in my face. He said, "What's wrong with you? You should certainly know better than that. That's a disgrace. No one's going to chase me out of my home country. They have rules. If the rules say I have to go to jail, I go to jail. But I'm going home after this fight, don't you forget it!" He was visibly annoyed at me. So this was confirmed to me that he was never going to run away.

I went on a television show to push a book I had written. It was *The Dick Cavett Show*. He was a big-time late-night show host like Johnny Carson and Jay Leno. And while we were on the show we got to talk about the Olympics, which was also in the book I had written. I mentioned the story about Judge Grauman and I just knew his name and the whole overrule incident. One of the producers was waving his hands frantically. When it went to a break, he came running at me and told me Grauman's son was on the phone. He said to the producer that I was right and he wanted to talk to me. So we put it on the air. He said not only did they overrule his father, but the society people broke his heart. They wouldn't associate with him after that. What happened to that judge is that he was atomized by all of those in Louisville, Kentucky.

Q: Did you travel with Muhammad Ali extensively and can you tell me about your travels to Asia and the Ali–Inoki fight?

Jerry Izenberg: Yeah. I went to Africa. I went to Zaire and Malaysia and the Philippines. In Africa the people started with the chant "Ali bombayi, Ali bombayi". He had everybody doing this. George had cut his eye during sparring so the fight had to be postponed. Foreman had never been challenged before. He had never had a tough fight. And I liked George. George became a whole different person. George went in for the weigh-ins. I'll tell you the story about Ali. We're in the gym in a military compound where they had set up a gym. So we go into the gym there and Gene Kilroy, who was the guy who handled the check book for Ali and did other things for him, was there. He was like the facilitator. Ali trusted him a lot. Ali says to him, "Who are these people?" He told him who they were. Ali takes the microphone and he says, "I have to tell you something about George Foreman. Do you people want to hear about it?" They said yeah, yeah, yeah. He said, "I was told that in hard times the authorities used dogs to handle people here." Everybody said, yes, yes, yes. "And I was told they put dogs after you to keep you in line." They said, yes, yes, yes. And he said, "Well, did you see George Foreman's dog when he came in, that big dog?" [Ali had the crowd work against Foreman].

Q: What was the most compelling conversation you had?
Jerry Izenberg: I'll tell you what touched me the most. I did not discover until later. I pick up the phone and call Ali to ask him about attending a function. I get his secretary Kim on the phone. I told her why I was calling and that I want to talk to Ali. She said he's at the hospital because he had an accident crash. She was lying to me – because he had signed a confidentiality agreement about not telling anyone about his Olympic appearance. I said alright. Later I found out. I looked up and there he was, lighting the torch at the Olympics. Everybody is looking at him. By the time Ali approached the ring, he usually put his hands in his pockets because they shook, but now there's no pockets in his sweat suit. I'm looking at the screen. He lights the torch. I'm looking at his face and he's sweating, and I noticed that he did it. They had asked one of his people if he could light the torch at the Olympics. That was a touching moment.

At the end of that touching moment – it's a long story – I hear the phone ring and it's him. I said, "Who is this?" He said, "Muhammad." I said, "Muhammad who?" He said, "Muhammad who? Muhammad Ali, the greatest fighter of all time. What do you mean?" I said, "You mean Muhammad Ali that told me Muslims could never tell a lie. Is that the Muhammad Ali you're talking about?" He said, "What are you talking about?" I said, "Kim said you were in hospital and that you can't attend any events presently." He said to me, "That's OK. Kim ain't no Muslim." It's a long story. The next thing he says to me is to come over right away. I said to him I don't know but I went over. So I went up to his room and I sit there talking with him. And finally we find ourselves alone in the room. He opened his closet and there it was – his Olympic torch. Now he takes the torch and he puts it in my hands. That torch meant a lot to him but he gave it to me. And I was very, very moved.

Q: Can you recall the United States embassy siege in Iran? Did the United States government bring in Muhammad Ali to be the middleman for negotiations? Also, can you shed light on when he was sent to Africa and Russia on political missions?

Jerry Izenberg: Jimmy Carter was the president. What happened was when the Olympic boycotts happened in 1980, they sent him to Africa to try to talk to the heads of states about why we were boycotting, trying to drum up support for the boycott. He got a mixed reception, very bad reception in Nigeria. I think in Ghana as well.

Q: Did you go to Japan for the Antonio Inoki fight and was it a fixed fight?

Jerry Izenberg: No. I refused to go. I thought it was very bad and I thought it was dangerous. He had to go to hospital afterwards. I don't know whether it was a fixed fight but I know this: I think the concept was bad, there were no rules. Maybe they had decided what they were going to do. I'm not saying they did, I don't know. But I will say that I had no interest at all.

Q: Did you often bump into him at showbiz parties or social gatherings?

Jerry Izenberg: We spent so much time together I probably did see him, but it didn't mean anything because there were so many other guys around. I've actually known him since the early 1960s and I was very close to him.

Q: What was one of the most compelling moments in the boxing ring?

Jerry Izenberg: I could tell you that. Cleveland Williams had a bullet in his brain, were you aware of that? He [Ali] said he was worried. He said this guy's a great fighter but how far back is he gone? He said I don't want to hurt him if I can help it. And this goes very far back, and I'll tell you a story which might help you. There was a fighter named...I've forgotten his name, but he was a former light-heavyweight champion who was fighting Joe Louis. The guy said, "I need the money, you've got to fight me." So what Louis did was, he said, "OK, I'll fight you." And he told his people he was going to knock him out in the first round and wasn't going to punish him, so he's not going to get hurt. That's what happened to the guy. I think he had the same last name as Louis. But I'm not sure. Anyway, that's what he did. I said [to Ali] if you want to help this guy then don't fight the way you usually fight, just knock him out. And he knocked him out in the third round.

Q: Do you feel Muhammad Ali should have hanged up his gloves much sooner than he actually did?

Jerry Izenberg: I do. I think the signs were obvious. I don't think it's a question of whether he was ill or not; it's a question of what happens to a fighter and his reflexes weren't the same. He liked the gloves. He had to be with people and it was very important to him so he kept coming back. I'll tell you when I think he should've retired. I think he should've retired right after Frazier – the Ali–Frazier III. That was the most ferocious fight that I've ever seen in my entire life, and I've been watching for over seventy years.

NEIL LEIFER

Neil Leifer is widely regarded as the greatest sports photographer in history. He turned professional while still in his teens after taking classes in the Henry Street Settlement House alongside a young Stanley Kubrik, before working for *Sports Illustrated* and *Time* magazines. He often noted that the nicest athletes in sport were boxers and hockey players, and followed Muhammad Ali's professional career from beginning to end. His image of Ali standing over a fallen Liston has become one of the most famous and memorable sports photos of all time. Leifer cultivated a close friendship with Ali that endured for decades after the champ stopped fighting.

Q: How and when did you first come into contact with Muhammad Ali and what was your initial impression of him?
Neil Leifer: The first time I saw Ali, I remember very well. I was assigned by *Sports Illustrated* to shoot the first Floyd Patterson and Sonny Liston fight. I believe it was 1961. The fight was in Chicago. Muhammad was Cassius Clay then. He had won a gold medal at the Rome Olympics and had just turned pro, and he was getting a lot of publicity because he was so different, you know. He had this loud mouth and he was always telling people how great he was, that he was going to be the champion one day. Angelo Dundee was already training him and he had just begun his professional career. He was about a year into his professional career. I went to the weigh-in of the Patterson–Liston fight. We were in a hotel in downtown Chicago and I was riding up the escalator to go to the weigh-in. There was Cassius Clay. He was three or four people in front of me on the escalator, or behind me – I don't remember. But he was screaming for everyone to hear that he's the next heavyweight champion, and that he could beat both these bums – things like that. Which was very funny, but certainly very different than the kind of fighters I had grown up watching.

But when we got off the escalator, it was the first time I ever saw the young Cassius Clay. And I remember you asked me what my first thought was: I realized how big he was! I had no idea this guy was that big. I mean, he was much bigger than Floyd Patterson. I mean, way bigger. And a lot bigger than Sonny Liston, which most people just didn't know. Sonny Liston was known as 'Big Bad Sonny Liston'. Sonny Liston was much shorter, no way near in the shape Ali was in. Liston, probably, could've weighed 195 pounds if you trim him down, certainly 200 was legit. Muhammad, Cassius Clay then, was 6ft 3, about 215–220 pounds with not an ounce of fat on him. I just remember thinking what a big athlete he was. I'd never seen a heavyweight that big before.

Q: Can we talk about the first Liston–Ali fight, you photographed both fights?

Neil Leifer: Yes, I did. The first Liston fight in Miami, I covered for *Sports Illustrated*. I was at the weigh-in, which was a great scene. But, you know, for photographers Muhammad made the weigh-in interesting. Weigh-ins were boring events until Muhammad came along. The two fighters would get on the scale and they would announce the weight and they would pose for a picture, and that was it! With Muhammad, the weigh-in became an event. There were sportswriters who thought Muhammad was so crazy that he was so frightened of Sonny Liston they suggested the fight get called off. When, in fact, the opposite was the truth. What he was doing was creating the fight itself. I mean, I was so excited I can't really tell you much about it. I was on the apron ringside shooting for *Sports Illustrated* and my picture of the fight was used on the cover of the magazine.

Q: When he knocked Sonny Liston down, the famous picture you shot, what was your opinion as far as performance is concerned?

Neil Leifer: I had none. I've been asked that question a hundred times over the years. First, remember in 1965 there was no such thing as autofocus on cameras. There wasn't anything. I was using strobe lights, and you have to wait for the lights to recharge. I had so many things to think about, like focusing the camera. I didn't really . . . you're watching the fight quite differently through the camera. You're trying to evaluate what's happening because you want to obviously be ready to shoot a moment that would make sense in terms of winning and who's losing. But I've been asked: did he really hit him? I have no idea. I mean, I believe he did but I have no idea. I know more from watching the film over the years. I never realized, at the time. For example, the most interesting thing I can tell you of my best-known picture of Muhammad standing over Sonny Liston, in Lewiston, the best thing I can tell you about this thing is that until I saw the film years later, I realized it happened so quickly. If you see the film, he just flashes his arm across his chest for a tenth of a second. I assumed, for five, six years, until I saw the film one day, he stood over Liston for a couple of seconds taunting him with his arm across his chest. That, in fact, is not what happened. I was worried about focusing the camera and getting the frame right, not about anything else.

Q: For this second Liston–Ali fight, what was the atmosphere like for this rematch?

Neil Leifer: Again, I was a young photographer. I was photographing on ringside right up close – all the atmosphere was behind me. You know, it was a strange place to be. The fight was originally scheduled for Boston. Muhammad had an emergency surgery so they had to cancel the fight a week before – about ten days before the fight. So it was rescheduled. Other than the fact that the fight was in this small town, I mean, big events, big boxing matches had always taken place in Madison Square Garden, in New York, in Chicago, Miami or Los Angeles, but this was unusual to be in a small town. But other than that I certainly didn't think anything unusual about it.

Q: Can you shed light on the photographic sessions you did with Muhammad Ali and what was he like to work with?

Neil Leifer: I did thirty-five sessions, maybe more sessions, where he posed for me. I've said this many times: there are subjects that like the camera. You turn on the camera and they light up. I always call it a sort of 'visual charisma'. Muhammad was just a delight. The reason that journalist, if you were interviewing Muhammad today . . . OK . . . I was in my early twenties when I was starting a career. Muhammad made a hero out of me. But he did with everybody! Because when you came back your boss thought you were terrific. *Wow, what great pictures!* But you got great pictures because he was accessible. He gave you a lot of time. But he did this with everybody. He did this with every reporter.

If you would have called him from where you are, like you did, I promise you Muhammad would have got on the phone and talk to you until you ran out of paper. That's the truth! It made you look good, your boss would have said, "Wow, Fiaz, what a great reporter!" The fact he was a great subject, you couldn't miss him. So I had many, many sessions. We would do covers to preview the fight. And Muhammad was a delight because he always made me look good. He always gave you enough time. One of the things photographers fight for all the time is not having enough time to shoot what they need. You get a session with somebody, but they give you ten minutes, twenty minutes. With Muhammad you always got as much time as you needed.

Q: In the early days was it often hard to get to him because of people who were part of his entourage?
Neil Leifer: Remember, he was a member of a Muslim group called the Black Muslims those days led by Elijah Muhammad, who were preaching the hatred of white people. You know, I'm white. So, yes, of course there were people around him that were not very nice. And the truth was, they simply didn't like white people. But you never saw any of that with Muhammad. I mean, he seemed to love everybody. I never had a single problem with Muhammad. He used to wink at people – white people – to let you know everything was going to be OK. One important point I want to make so I'm quoted correctly is that I've known Ali for over fifty years now. I never saw one ounce of prejudice or bigotry from him – ever!! And

I spent a lot of time around him. There were people around him who were not very friendly. But he made it easy because basically you dealt with him.

Q: Can you recall any memorable situations during any of the sessions?

Neil Leifer: My favorite story is the very first time I ever photographed him, which was in 1965, in the studio. I was twenty-two years old then, but I looked like I was about fifteen because I had a baby face. Muhammad was the heavyweight champion of the world for a year. He had posed for all the world-famous photographers from Karsh in Canada, Avedon in New York, Gordon Parks of *Life* magazine. He knew all the famous photographers who are all older men, right? So when he saw me, he thought I was just a kid. He kept on saying, "Where's the photographer?" When I showed a Polaroid of the first picture I took – you have Polaroid before you have the color film – he looked at the Polaroid. He had some people there. He was always entertaining his entourage. He had some people with him who had come with him. And when I showed him the Polaroid he took a long look at it and he smiled at me, and he said, "Wow, this is really good." Then he paused for effect. Then he had a great line, which I will never forget. He looked at me and he said, "How could you miss with a subject like me?" That's my favorite personal story with him.

We were good friends for many years now. I mean, Muhammad and his wife were good friends of mine. When I was photographing, you might find this interesting. When I photographed Ali, he was a subject of mine. I worked with him and when we finished, we finished. We became personal friends in the last twenty years, long after he had finished fighting. His wife Lonnie and Muhammad were very good friends of mine and I got to know them very well. We had dinner whenever we were in the same town. I've certainly had lunch with them many times. I just really enjoyed being around them, which is something that happened after he finished fighting.

Q: Did your work take you to his place of residence when he was still fighting?

Neil Leifer: Many, many times I photographed him at his residence. He had a couple of places. I did a wonderful cover for *Sports Illustrated*, when he fought Ken Norton for the first time when he got his jaw broken. You know, when you wire a jaw you can't talk. Can you imagine Muhammad when he couldn't talk? And we did a cover story. So I went down to his home and photographed him with his wife and his kids. He was then married to Belinda.

Q: How did he spend the time at home and what was the atmosphere and his surroundings like?

Neil Leifer: Oh, he was bored! He liked going to the gym. He liked being around a fight crowd. I think he was bored. He was delightful being around. I had a good time. We really had a fun session, but I don't think that was Muhammad's happiest time when his jaw was broken. One, he must have been a little uncomfortable. Here's a guy who loves to talk, now he couldn't talk. But he was always a gracious host. Muhammad was a wonderful man. He was just a nice guy. Anybody that was around him will tell you that.

Q: He treated everybody the same, including people who weren't famous.

Neil Leifer: Fiaz, I was working for the most important sports magazine in America, and he treated me wonderfully. I watched a kid from a high school newspaper come up to him and photograph him, and he treated him the same way! He treated everyone the same way. He just liked people! He enjoyed giving interviews. He enjoyed posing for pictures. He loved doing television interviews. He liked the writers who covered the fighting. He was very good to everybody. And I'm saying this from working on the top of the game. I was working for a magazine that probably could do more to sell fight tickets. *Sports Illustrated* had three-and-a-half million circulation in those days. Of course, it was good for *Sports*

Illustrated, but he was nice to everybody. He still was after retiring, by the way. I've been with him in a restaurant, and although he has difficulty because of the Parkinson's disease, if he's in the middle of eating dinner and if someone comes over who wants a picture, many celebrities just look at them like this, but Muhammad puts his fork down and poses for the picture. I wouldn't do it! I would say come back when I've finished eating!

Q: What's the most compelling conversation you ever had?

Neil Leifer: You know, I never. No. Not really because I was photographing him more than thirty-five years ago. We didn't really have a deep conversation. I told you that he gave you as much time as you needed, but it wasn't to sit down and talk to him; it was to pose for pictures. So, when Muhammad came into the studio, if I had an hour with Muhammad I spent an hour photographing him. I never really had a compelling conversation with him till many years later. And then I never talked about politics, we never talked about religion. I just never had a conversation like that with him that I can remember. I sat once and watched fight footage with him. It was fascinating to listen to him talk about the fights and how he was as a young fighter. But I can't really tell you that I ever sat down and had a conversation with him. I never talked about politics with him. I never talked about religion with him. I just didn't, you know. Being a sports journalist, you just don't. It was a different kind of world that I worked in.

Q: Did you go to events where Muhammad Ali and countless other athletes were present?

Neil Leifer: Many over the years. At the end of the century *Sports Illustrated* did a huge event for one of the greatest athletes of the century, but I didn't really hang out with Ali at those events. I was just around, Michael Jordan was there, and there were a bunch of people there. Again, I can't really tell you I ever had much attention. To me, Muhammad was a friend after he retired, but when he was fighting he was a subject of mine.

Q: After he retired . . .

Neil Leifer: I would say Muhammad spent a good amount of time doing charity work. He is the first one. As you know he's a Muslim. And he certainly traveled. I think anytime he was invited it's hard because he had Parkinson's disease. But if the King of Saudi Arabia invites Muhammad to an event, he goes. If the president of China invites Muhammad, he goes. He was traveling a lot but he was doing less of it later because his health was not that good.

Q: What was it like shooting pictures at the press conferences?

Neil Leifer: Ali had so many, but maybe the most interesting one ever was when he didn't step forward for the draft to go in the army. But I don't really remember much. Again, it's like you asked me earlier about what I thought about during the fight. As a photographer, I'm not there to write a piece, I'm not paying careful attention to what he's saying. I'm looking at what the light is looking at. Does it make a better picture from side lit or front lit or back lit? I just didn't pay a whole lot of attention. If you were there you'd have to listen to the words he was saying. I'm looking to see how to take the best picture of him.

Q: Can you comment on the 1977 film *The Greatest*?

Neil Leifer: I don't remember it very well to comment. I saw it but I surely don't remember it well enough. The one I know is the one Will Smith played him. And I liked the movie. I think Muhammad liked it from what I remember, and his wife liked it. They were very happy.

Q: You spent a considerable amount of time with Muhammad Ali on a social level. What elements of his personality did you detect, which stood out?

Neil Leifer: I had dinner with him three or four times in restaurants, in cities that are used to seeing celebrities like New York. I had dinner with him one night in New Orleans. The thing about Muhammad is when you walk into a restaurant with him, as soon as you walk in one or two people start clapping. In America we clap hands. By the time Muhammad gets halfway into the restaurant, he's getting a round of applause from the whole restaurant. He's very well-loved. When he gets to an airport he'll sign every autograph. He talks to everyone. He had difficulty speaking, as you know, but he still tried to talk to everybody. The expression I would use is he's a 'people person'. This is a guy who likes people. A lot of celebrities don't; they want to be left alone. Muhammad seems to like people to the point where he doesn't need to be left alone.

I'll tell you a very good story. I went once with Howard Bingham, who was his best friend. Howard and I had an exhibition together on 5th Avenue in New York and Muhammad was a guest of honor. And after this was over we all had dinner in a restaurant down in the East Side in New York. When dinner was over Muhammad wanted everybody to get into one of the limousines. There was a group of us, about eight of us. There were two limousines. Because his daughters were now grown up – the twins. He had twin daughters with one of his wives. He moved on to another wife so he really didn't see them grow up. But now they were grown-ups. Anyway, he directed the limousine driver to go to Times Square. And he parked the car in the middle of Times Square and he got us out. First, two people came. Then six, then ten, then there was a crowd of a hundred people wanting autographs. The police had to move us into a side street because the traffic couldn't go through. What he said when we got back in the car, he wanted to show his daughters that he could still draw a crowd in New York even though he was retired.

The other experience I had is a very good one, really interesting. In this country Muhammad was the best-known opponent of the Vietnam War. He fought the government for three-and-a-half years in court when he didn't want to go in the army. I photographed him when he was sold. We did a cover on *Sports Illustrated* of him with Howard Bingham. Muhammad was getting an award in Washington D.C. and I asked him if he would go to the Vietnam Memorial in Washington. You would think this is the place in America that Muhammad would be hated – that would be the place because those were the people who did go in the army and died.

So we got there and I took a picture. Nobody knew we were coming, of course, we just got there. We got out of the car and I walked him over to the wall and I started photographing him with Howard Bingham. Pretty soon people recognized him. Instead of any hatred, it was the same scene as it was in Times Square. There were two people, then six people, then a group of girl scouts came and they surrounded Muhammad – they were too young to even know who he was. But he was signing autographs and posing for pictures. We were on our way to the airport in Washington and his wife had to get him finally out of the group or else we would've missed the plane. I was very surprised to see the reaction he got at the Vietnam Memorial.

I think that in this country when Muhammad lit the torch in Atlanta, he was shaking at the Olympics, it changed the opinion. Anybody that disliked Muhammad had to change their mind. Here he was with the President of the United States. He's been a very popular American for the last twenty years, certainly ever since 1996 in the Olympics. I think that changed the perception of Americans who didn't like him. I mean, I always loved the guy so that doesn't apply to me, but there were plenty of Americans who thought he was a loudmouth. All the boxing fans weren't used to somebody who bragged. Athletes never supposed to brag; they supposed to be modest. He was quite different.

Q: Did you travel abroad with him?
Neil Leifer: Many times, many times. I did every one of the fights. I photographed him in London fighting. I photographed him in Zaire fighting. I photographed him in Manila fighting. I went to the Frankfurt Book Fair when the big book *GOAT* came out. I flew with him – me and Howard Bingham, and Leon Gast who did the movie *When We Were Kings*. We flew over in Lufthansa. We were in first class. As soon as the plane was in the air Muhammad got up and he starts working his way down the aisle. He had difficulty talking and he has difficulty walking. But he likes to do these magic tricks. He would stop every three or four rows and he would do his tricks.

And you'd hear a round of applause on the plane. The stewardess had to finally ask him to go back to his seat because they couldn't get the serving carts in the aisles because Muhammad was blocking the aisle.

Q: You've photographed many top athletes. Can one make a comparison with Muhammad Ali?

Neil Leifer: I'm not an expert – I never saw Ali play any other sport. But looking at him physically, I mean, he was just a spectacular athlete. I believe if Muhammad had grown up in Europe he would have been a great soccer player. If he played football in America he would have been a great football player. I certainly think he would have been a brilliant decathlete had he gone into decathlon. He's a physical wonder. He's in great shape and he's a great athlete. He didn't do other sports to my knowledge. I don't think he ever played football, or at least, certainly didn't play it seriously – American football. You've got to look at him and think that anything he would've tried to do he'd have been good at.

Q: Did you photograph him at the White House?

Neil Leifer: I was at the White House with him, but not really. I mean, I never got to talk, only on the receiving line. I was there for the event. Muhammad was being honored along with other athletes. So I did see him with Clinton. I was there but I couldn't really give you anything. Howard Bingham was in the Oval Office probably every time Muhammad saw a president, Jimmy Carter, certainly with Clinton. I haven't had that kind of experience other than the one time I was at the White House with him, and I wasn't that close.

DAVE KINDRED

Born in Atlanta, Kindred met Ali as a staff writer and columnist for the *Louisville Courier-Journal*, where he worked from 1965 until before he joined the *Washington Post* in 1977. He has captivated readers by bringing them closer to many of the greatest performers and personalities in the sports world, including many interviews with Ali. Dave Kindred was named the recipient of the 2010 PGA Lifetime Achievement Award in journalism, and the Red Smith Award – sport's journalism's highest honor. He is the author of eleven books including a dual biography of Muhammad Ali and Howard Cosell, *Sound and Fury*.

Q: Can you please reminisce about the first time you met Muhammad Ali?

Dave Kindred: I met Muhammad Ali in 1966. I was a young sports reporter for the Louisville, Kentucky, newspaper the *Courier-Journal*. That was Ali's hometown. He occasionally came back to Louisville to see his parents. And one day when he was in town I was assigned to go follow him around. This was in 1966. He was the world champion. He had beaten Sonny Liston twice by then and he was back in Louisville to see his parents, who were both still alive at the time – Cassius Clay Sr. and his mother, and to see his friends. He was not fighting, there was no exhibition. He was just in town because it was his hometown and he had come down to see his family and friends.

Q: How would you define his personality?

Dave Kindred: He was vibrant; he was fun; he was charming; he was low key; he was not boastful and a braggart but he was clearly having fun. My son went with us that day. My son, at that time, was four years old and Ali carried my son around most of the day because he liked children so much. But he was happy and everywhere he went, he was greeted like a hero by the people who knew him as a child. He was famous in Louisville from the age of twelve onwards because he had been on a television show in Louisville town called *Tomorrow's Champions,* an amateur boxing show that was on television at the time. He first appeared on that show when he was maybe thirteen years old. So everyone in Louisville knew Cassius Clay as a young man and they certainly paid attention to him forever as Muhammad Ali.

Q: How did the day progress?
Dave Kindred: We went to his neighborhood in the West End in Louisville. He was not a poor child. His father was a painter – house painter – his mother was a domestic who cleaned houses. So they had money. I'd say they were like a middle-class family. I remember going to a barbershop and a shoeshine place. And we just drove around and everyone recognized him even in the car. He was always eager to see people and he drew energy from people. He would just stop and get out of the car, it wouldn't take more than ten minutes to see a crowd gather and see him.

Q: In 1966 how did non-blacks treat him in his hometown, or was there ambivalent attitudes among the people?
Dave Kindred: He was not popular, there were many people... Kentucky was what we call a 'border state'. It's not really the South, it's not really the North – it's kind of in between. There was much more of a Southern kind of mentality, so there was a great racial divide. Blacks, of course, almost all blacks, loved him. Almost all whites had great problems with him from refusing the draft to joining the Nation of Islam. I don't think anyone from the white part of Louisville really understood Ali, so there was a great divide. Either you loved Ali or you hated him. And a lot of that divide came down along the racial lines.

Q: What was his father like and how would you succinctly describe their relationship?
Dave Kindred: His father Cassius Clay Sr. was much like Ali himself – he was a showman. He was a little man by the way. Ali

was maybe 6ft 3, 220, at his best, but Cassius Clay Sr. may have been 5ft 10 or 11, 150–160. So he was not a big man at all. He was a very boastful man, full of braggadocio. He saw himself as a great painter. And I don't mean a house painter. I mean a great painter of portraits. I've seen a lot of stuff that he did around churches around Louisville. They were very crude, amateurish, but he thought he was very good. And a whole lot of Ali's kind of showmanship came from his father in a sense of drawing attention to himself.

Q: His mother was a really nice lady . . .
Dave Kindred: She may have been bigger than Cassius Clay Sr. She was very mild mannered, very sweet tempered. She was a member of the Baptist Church near their home. She was very quiet. It's almost too simplistic to say there was this great divide in Ali himself and it was shown in his parents. I mean, the wild, crazy bombastic showmanship came from his father, which could be seen in his father. And the sweet charming – and he could be silent – side of Ali came from his mother. It was an amazing kind of combination of these two people in Ali. And Ali was both those people.

Q: His brother Rahaman would accompany him to his fights, what was their relationship like?
Dave Kindred: Rahaman Ali had been a fighter early on and they did fight on the same card sometimes. In fact, Rahaman fought before the first Liston fight. And Muhammad even came out of his dressing room to watch his brother fight. His brother was a very raw professional. I think he may have fought eight or ten fights. He was not much good. When he quit boxing Rahaman was an integral member of Ali's entourage. He was there all the time. He more or less appointed himself like a bodyguard and security man. He was always there to help Muhammad do anything he wanted done. And he served that role for a long time.

Q: Can you tell me of any press conferences you attended and how did Muhammad Ali conduct himself?

Dave Kindred: He was the greatest promoter of all time. Not only promoting his fights, not only promoting himself but promoting his fighters. He should have got the promoter's share of the money. He made every fight through his press conferences and interviews. He made a drama of every fight and he was always fun. He would tell the same stories time after time, say the same things time after time: I am the greatest. But every time he did it, it was as if it was the first time he had ever done it. He was a great actor. He was a great showman. He was a great performer, and no matter how often you were around him or how often you heard him, it was always fun to hear him again.

Q: When he refused the draft, to what degree did his relationship diminish with the American people and the government?

Dave Kindred: Well, when he refused the draft he was vilified. He was despised by most of America. I believe – most of white America, for sure – there was great resistance to the draft. There was resistance to the draft by the white people who thought the war was unjust and that we had no business [to be there]. I think Ali became a hero to that kind of faction of America, but to the large portion of America he was despised. Because I don't think anybody believed his reasons for refusing the draft. His reason for refusing the draft was he said he was a minister. I don't think very many people bought that.

Q: Do you feel it was political or was there any other peculiar reason behind his refusal?

Dave Kindred: I think so. I mean, I think that Ali is a lightning rod of controversy on all the things we learn to not talk about: race, politics and religion. He was a controversial figure in all three of those areas. And through the 1960s, it was a very tumultuous time in America from fascinations, war, young people protesting in the streets. Ali was at the center of all that. So he caught a lot of heat for that, politically, religiously and racially in every way and he came through it. He managed to survive in the end. Now people have come to admire him for having the strength and the principles. The strength and the principles in his belief that never wavered. He was willing to go to jail. He was willing to accept the fine. He was willing to lose the heavyweight championship to uphold his beliefs and his principles. And I think that people now respect that.

Q: The FBI was monitoring Muhammad Ali and the Nation of Islam.

Dave Kindred: They certainly were. There's documentary evidence of that. The FBI was monitoring everyone. The FBI was monitoring every kind of protest group, every kind of racial group, from Martin Luther King. Ali is heard on audio tapes talking to Martin Luther King, even early in the 1960s. And so, yes, he was on constant surveillance from the FBI.

Q: It's no secret that Howard Cosell supported Muhammad Ali through this time.

Dave Kindred: It was kind of a sophisticated kind of support. Cosell supported Ali's right to his opinions; he did not support necessarily those opinions. Cosell was never on record saying he was against the Vietnam War. He was never on record saying Ali was right. What he said was Ali had the right to have that opinion and Ali should not have been punished for having that right. Cosell was steadfast in that and Cosell continued to appear on television with Ali. Just being on television with a powerful message that here was this white television broadcaster, who was a famous television broadcaster in America, who was willing to stand side by side with Ali and give Ali a podium, gave Ali a chance to express his beliefs. That was Cosell's greatest contribution to Muhammad Ali: continuing to interview him.

Q: Muhammad Ali's relationship with the media in general was excellent. Obviously, he got a lot of coverage . . .

Dave Kindred: Ali was the most accessible of great athletes of all times. I mean, every newspaperman, every author, every magazine writer admired and respected Ali because Ali gave them time. Ali was always accessible. There were people who did not agree with Ali's opinions, and they said so in print and they said so on broadcast. But Ali never took offense to that. I don't believe Ali ever had a cross word. I don't think Ali ever argued with the media. The media was important to Ali because it was a mirror of him. He liked to see himself. He liked to hear himself and the press made that possible. So I don't think anybody in the press ever really had a problem with Ali. They certainly had a problem with some of his beliefs, but not with him personally.

Q: When you interviewed him in the 1960s, do you have any significant memories which surface above all others?

Dave Kindred: It was in the middle of the 1970s. Ali once told me the reason he stayed a member of the Nation of Islam. It was because he was afraid to leave because he had seen what had happened to Malcolm X. Malcolm X had broken with the Nation and had broken with Elijah Muhammad – the leader of the Nation of Islam – and was assassinated. And Ali, while not saying that he expected such a thing to happen, certainly understood it had happened and he stayed with the Nation of Islam until after Elijah Muhammad died. Then the Nation, which is very sophisticated, became a different kind of group. It became much more moderate, much more conservative, much less angry, and Ali reflected that. Ali of the 1970s was a much different person, kinder and gentler than the Ali of the 1960s.

Q: What shape did Muhammad Ali's life take after he lost his license to box?

Dave Kindred: I very seldom saw him during that time. He made speeches on college campuses. He appeared in a Broadway show called *Buck White*. I think he made one or two movies. He was basically at a loose end. He was not allowed to fight in the United States. They took his passport so that he could not leave the country and fight anyone else. So he was scrambling for money. It was a bad time in his life for the three-and-a-half years. It was very hard for him at that time. He had no way to make money and he was alone. Joe Frazier agreed to fight him and that made it possible for him to make a comeback. He lost his three-and-a-half best years in any athlete's professional life. From the age of twenty-seven to thirty-one he lost his time. But he came back and he was a great fighter again. He was a different fighter just as he was a different person.

Q: Why do you think they gave him his license back?

Dave Kindred: Eventually, the people understood that the license should never have been taken away from him. That was an injustice to start with and an injustice that was corrected – one of the injustices Cosell identified – in addition to which he could make money for a lot of people. So that was an incentive for them, New York for instance, to give him back his license. Tempers had calmed down. He had won a reversal and was on his way to winning a reversal in the Supreme Court of his conviction. So it was clear that the tide was turning in his direction so they gave him his license back.

Q: Is it true that the Louisville Group, who initially sponsored him, had something to do with him getting re-enlisted in the draft?

Dave Kindred: I don't know that but they encouraged him to enlist. I don't know if they wanted him to enlist. But they thought that he could serve in some kind of showman role, where he would do boxing exhibitions and satisfy the government's draft without ever going to war, without ever going to Vietnam. But he refused that because he said it was against his religion to serve any country in any war. And that was his stance and he stood by that.

Q: Herbert Muhammad became his manager, what type of a character was he?

Dave Kindred: I didn't know Herbert very well. I was around him sometimes, but he became his manager early on because he was

Elijah Muhammad's son. And when Ali joined the Nation of Islam as Cassius Clay, which was his name then, then Elijah Muhammad put him in charge. He and his son had the responsibility of guiding Cassius Clay's boxing career. So that would have been maybe 1964 because he didn't announce his name change after the first Liston fight. By then Herbert Muhammad was running Ali's business affairs. I didn't really know him at all. He was around me, at least a silent guy, but Ali loved him. Ali worked with him for twenty years probably and together they made a lot of money.

Q: Do you think the Nation of Islam was squeezing money out of Muhammad Ali?
Dave Kindred: I think everyone believes that and Ali never denied it. Ali never seemed to resent it. He felt it was his obligation to help the Nation of Islam. But it is true that Herbert Muhammad, as his manager, was I think given 33 percent of the money and probably diverted other money. I don't know. All I know is Muhammad Ali himself never complained about his treatment by Herbert Muhammad or the Nation.

Q: Do you think Muhammad Ali had a rather soft side to him which consequently allowed people to take advantage?
Dave Kindred: He was the all-time soft touch. Anyone who came to him with a sob story, anyone who came to him asking for help, Ali was eager to help. He never had money himself – he borrowed ten dollars from me multiple times. Money never meant anything to him. As long as he was content, he didn't need big houses and all that. He was not a spender. He would give almost anything to anybody who asked him for it. He was very generous.

Q: Did you cover the George Foreman fight?
Dave Kindred: I covered one George Foreman fight. I did not go to Zaire. I did not see that fight. I covered George Foreman in his comeback fight against Evander Holyfield.

Q: You covered the first fight with his arch-rival Joe Frazier. Just how much hype was there really?

Dave Kindred: The one in Madison Square Garden. How many times have we heard that this is the Fight of the Century? Well, I believe that probably in the ranking Fights of the Century that has to be in the top five. It was crazy. Frank Sinatra was sitting on ringside shooting pictures, it's as big as it gets. It was the biggest sports event I've ever been to and the most hyped sports event. It was two of the greatest fighters of that era who were basically at the top of their game. It was a great event. Both fighters were very good that night. Frazier was obsessed that night, Ali was good. It was one of the great sports events of all time.

Q: Did you interview both of the fighters before or after the fight?

Dave Kindred: Yes, at press conferences before and after. I did not interview them personally. Ali was reprehensible in his treatment of Joe Frazier. Frazier had been his friend in his time when Ali did not have his license. Frazier offered him money, offered to fight him and was trying to help him. But when the time came to fight, Ali turned it into a race war by trying to make Frazier the white guy! It was unbelievable, really. But I think Ali was always his meanest and most cruel when he was most afraid, and I think Joe Frazier scared him. Joe Frazier was a great fighter at that moment, irresistible, unstoppable and Ali knew it. Ali knew he was going to be in for the fight of his life so he said mean things about Frazier. And it only got worse, that relationship. And that's too bad because they were both great fighters who understood and respected what it took to be great fighters. It was too bad they never really came to be friends.

Q: How would you define Joe Frazier's personality, would I be right in saying he was a quiet guy who did his talking with his fists?

Dave Kindred: I think that's probably right. He talked some and that was one of the times Ali called him stupid, saying, "You can't talk." Ali compared himself physically and mentally as superior to Frazier. And Frazier, of course, took offense to that as anyone would. And he never really recovered from those insults. Frazier was a nice guy. Frazier was a common guy who grew up on a farm in South Carolina in a poor part of the state. He came up with nothing to be one of the great fighters ever. Ali never really gave him the respect he should have.

Q: What was your sentiment on the end result of the fight?
Dave Kindred: I was so much a fan. I was Ali's hometown newspaper writer. And I've always had trouble at fights watching both fighters. I see one fighter and I can see what he's doing. I don't see what the other one's doing. That's a flaw in my reporting ability. So I basically see Ali. I thought Ali won the fight. I mean, he beat Frazier's face till he looked like a . . . huge bumps all over his face. I felt that Ali won the fight but it was unanimous decision for Frazier. When I saw the film of the fight, I couldn't argue with that. Frazier was unstoppable. Ali wasted early rounds. I remember Ali leaning against the ropes one time while Frazier was hitting him, and Ali looked down at some of us at ringside and was saying, "No contest! No contest!" Meanwhile, Frazier was beating him up, so it was a contest and Frazier got the best of him. And when Frazier knocked him down in the fifteenth round it sealed it for a lot of people. I don't remember now if Frazier needed to win that round. No. He didn't need to win that round to win the fight. But he did win the round and the fight in a decisive margin.

Q: What were Muhammad Ali's comments to the press after the fight?
Dave Kindred: After the fight he did not do a press conference because he had been hurt so badly they took him to a hospital. So he didn't say anything that night. He did not appear at a press conference. He was gracious in defeat. He did say, at some point, Frazier won the fight. He also said, "I will return." Within the next day, Ali knew that he couldn't stand on that so Ali began saying he had been robbed and that he had won the fight and everyone knew

it. Ali, in one single moment of truth, understood Frazier had won the fight, but then he started promoting for the next fight.

Q: Muhammad Ali had said to Joe Frazier if he loses to him he will crawl in the ring. After the fight Joe Frazier actually told a member of his team to tell Muhammad Ali to come over in the dressing room to crawl.
Dave Kindred: He did say that. I read that in a book Frazier had cooperated with. I didn't hear that myself, but that is one of the stories around that fight. Of course, Ali did not do that.

Q: Muhammad Ali would often predict what round he was going to knock-out his adversary. Do you feel the confidence he exuded was real or merely part of his act?
Dave Kindred: Ali was always very confident and cocky. Early on in his career when he was fighting fighters who were not that good, he could do that. And he did that on several occasions. So it was both confidence and absolute certainty of his ability that he was able to do that against very bad fighters. He couldn't do that against good fighters. And he didn't try that against good fighters. He didn't try that much after his first ten or fifteen fights.

Q: What is the most intriguing incident you remember?
Dave Kindred: In 1973, I actually got in bed with Muhammad Ali. The situation was, in Las Vegas he had a two-bedroom suite. The center room was where everybody gathered. And his room was always full of hangers-on and partygoers and people who wanted to meet Ali. So I walked in to see Ali. I could see him through the door in the bedroom. And he was in bed. So he saw me and waved to me to come on in. I don't think he ever knew my name but he knew I was from Louisville. He always called me 'Louisville'. He said, "Come on in, Louisville." So I went in there and was going to interview him about his entourage. But he couldn't really hear me because there was so much noise. So he raised the corner of the sheet and said get in. So I got in bed with Ali!

We were both under the covers like little boys hiding from their parents and I interviewed Ali while we were in bed. I had on clothes. He didn't. He took my notebook. I wanted the names of the people in his entourage and what they did. He took my notebook and started writing holding it above his head. And he wrote the names in his entourage and how much he was paying them each week. Then I interviewed him for about ten, fifteen minutes and got out of bed. When I left I realized I had forgotten my notebook. So I had to go back and ask Ali for my notebook.

Q: Can you name some of the people in his entourage who were close to him?

Dave Kindred: The one that was always close to him forever was Bundini Brown. He was Ali's alter ego. He was with Ali everywhere at all times. He was as bombastic and as much fun as Ali was and they were like brothers together. Without Bundini I don't think Ali would have been the charismatic character that he was. Bundini Brown – I think he was called an assistant trainer – was basically a kind of good-time guy that Ali loved. He was always fun. Bundini Brown worked with Sugar Ray Robinson before Robinson had suggested to Ali as a young fighter he needed someone like Bundini Brown with him. So Bundini traveled with him forever. And he had couple of others with him. Angelo Dundee was, of course, the trainer with him at every fight. Howard Bingham was the photographer. They were close friends. I think Bingham met him in 1962. He's the person who had been around him the most. He's a great guy. He's done photography with Ali, Bill Cosby and he's a great photographer in addition to being a great friend of Ali's.

Q: Were there any parts of the entourage who were suspicious about the press?

Dave Kindred: Not when I was around. Then again I didn't cover Ali as a heavyweight champion until he came back in 1970. By then there was a different crowd around him. During the 1960s, the Nation of Islam had bodyguards who were called the Fruit of

Islam who were with Ali all the time. I think they were suspicious of the media. But I didn't see that in my time. In my time everyone was welcome around Ali.

Q: Do you think Muhammad Ali should not have taken the Larry Holmes fight because he was no doubt past his best by then? You sat next to Herbert Muhammad, who had his head down throughout the fight as Holmes proceeded to punish his foe.
Dave Kindred: It was a terrible fight to witness. I think I said to someone at some point, "If you cared about Ali it was like watching someone you love in an automobile accident." Ali had nothing that night. He had convinced us, the press, that he was able to fight, but he had nothing. He should have quit. When you're Muhammad Ali and when you've fought against the odds your whole life, you think you still can fight against the odds.

Larry Holmes has never been given the respect that he is due either. Holmes was a great, great fighter. I first saw Holmes when he was twenty or twenty-one years old, when he was a sparring partner with Ali before the Foreman fight. He was a young kid who was as big as Ali and was very good. He patterned himself after Ali in his movements. Not so much his personality but certainly his movements. Holmes was a great fighter. He was a great fighter that night. He was at the height of his powers and Ali was on his way down. Ali was down and should have not taken that fight. Ali should have quit after the fight in Zaire when he won it back. He had everything he wanted, but how do you quit being Muhammad Ali? You don't.

It was terrible. It was horrible. There was nothing. Ali couldn't throw a punch, couldn't avoid a punch. I certainly remember Holmes asking the referee to stop the fight. The referee did not stop the fight and Holmes would come back and attack Ali again. I sat next to Herbert Muhammad who did not look at the fight all night, he kept his head down. Finally, at some point – and I missed this – but someone was asking Herbert Muhammad, and I know Herbert Muhammad finally shook his head in a 'yes' gesture, and that meant stop the fight.

Q: You have said it's the worst sports event you ever covered in your career. Is this true?

Dave Kindred: Well, this was a guy who had been a great fighter. Certainly you had to like him. He had gone through things in life. But under all that he was a sweetheart. And to see someone you cared about, someone who had been a great fighter reduced to that nothingness in a game, that hurt you. That makes it the worst thing I've ever seen. I mean, this was not a basketball team losing a game. This was not a baseball team losing a game. This was a man getting his brains beat out. And I hated to see it.

Q: Before retiring from boxing for good, Muhammad Ali fought another bout against Trevor Berbick. Can you tell me about this fight?

Dave Kindred: The Berbick fight was a farce. Ali again tried to convince himself he still could fight. He came up with an excuse for the Holmes fight that he had taken too much medicine, that he had a froid problem. So he had taken too much medicine, which dried him out and dehydrated him. He felt he could get in better shape. But the only place that would give him the fight was the Bahamas. Trevor Berbick was a journeyman fighter. Not a great fighter, but not a bad fighter. He was in the top ten in the world and Ali, I don't know if he turned forty or was about to turn forty, was better in this fight than he was with Holmes.

But that was small solace because it still was no good because Trevor Berbick was all over him all night, and Ali was not strong enough to keep him off him. Simple of the whole thing was they fought in a makeshift ring on a kids' baseball field in the Bahamas. And they had no ring bell. They had to get a bell off a cow's neck to use it ringside. I think I wrote at the time that Ali's career ended with a cow bell. Ali that night was at a little press conference at a hotel, where we could barley breathe because it was so packed with people. He said, "I couldn't beat father time." And that was the end for him.

Q: Did he announce his retirement there and then?

Dave Kindred: The next morning I think. I'm sure it was the next morning. He said he was not fighting again, although at the press conference he did say, "I shall return to Los Angeles!"

Q: Were you ever present at any celebrity engagements or when he visited presidents?

Dave Kindred: No. Certainly not when he was with presidents. I was around him when he was with celebrities. I remember when he came back to fight Jerry Quarry, the first fight of his comeback. Diana Ross of The Supremes was a huge star at the time and she was in the dressing room and he was flirting with her. But I don't remember that much about this kind of stuff.

Q: Did you keep in touch after his retirement?

Dave Kindred: I'd see him occasionally but not often. He would be at fights. I covered one of Evander Holyfield's fights and Ali was there, but I never spent much time with him.

Q: Any charity events?

Dave Kindred: I think the last time I saw him at one of those he was appearing at a... I'm not sure what it was, but he was going around the world doing charitable events. When I saw him in Bloomington in Indiana, he appeared with the Dali Lama. Dali Lama joked with him and put his fist like he was going to fight Muhammad Ali. And Ali kind of waved his finger around his temple like, Are you crazy! I was never around him that much in those things, but I know he has done a lot of good work over the years.

Q: How would you define Muhammad Ali the supremely gifted boxer?

Dave Kindred: One of the things I've said is maybe two of the best fighters of all time were Cassius Clay and Muhammad Ali because he was a different fighter under both those names. As Cassius Clay, you couldn't hit him. As Muhammad Ali, you could hit him as much as you wanted and you weren't going to hurt him. As Cassius Clay, he was a dancer. As Muhammad Ali, he was a slugger. He was two different fighters. A lot of that came from three-and-a-half years that split up his career before he lost his license. He was so fast you couldn't see him. The ultimate fight at that period was with Cleveland Williams. Cleveland Williams must have thought he was fighting ten guys. Ali was so fast Williams couldn't find him let alone hit him. Afterwards when he came back in 1971, the Frazier period, through the 1970s, then he was a fighter who took a lot of punishment and gave a lot of punishment. He was no longer the guy you couldn't hit, you could find him but you still couldn't beat him.

Q: Any final words on Muhammad Ali, the sports legend who has received profound adoration from millions around the globe?

Dave Kindred: He was the greatest athlete that I ever saw, the greatest athlete I ever will see and the most significant athlete in a social sense that we will ever see. He affected America. He affected the world in ways that we'll remember in a hundred years from now. When people will no longer have any idea who Michael Jordan was, they will still know who Muhammad Ali was.

GEORGE KALINSKY

George Kalinsky has been the official photographer for New York's Madison Square Garden, one of the world's most famous arenas, since the mid-1960s. A world-renowned, award-winning photographer, his work has appeared in major mainstream media such as *Newsweek*, *People*, *The New York Times* and *Sports Illustrated*. Kalinsky is one of the few elite photographers who worked very closely with Ali, attending both the 'Fight of the Century' between Ali and Frazier in 1971, and their rematch in 1974. In November 2010 the national Arts Club awarded him their Medal of Honor for Photography.

Q: What was your first assignment shooting pictures of Muhammad Ali, was it at a press conference or a studio?
George Kalinsky: The first time I met Ali was when he was fighting in 1967. It was a fight he gave a fighter an opportunity to fight for the championship. I can't think of his name, but it was definitely in 1967. I met Ali at a hotel, which wasn't too far from the Garden. So, the first time I really met Ali was when he was the heavyweight champ. Actually, it wasn't the first time I met him come to think of it. The first time I met Ali was in 1966, the year before, at the 5th Street Gym where he was working out. At that time, my career had just started with Ali. But the first assignment I really ever had was in 1967. We started talking and I took some pictures of him. I wanted him to spar and I discussed in relationship to what I wanted to do in the next hour or so.

I took some nude shots of him. Basically shots of him laughing, his hand on his chin, and he was combing his hair in the mirror. I mean, I tried to do things that people normally do rather than [just the boxing]. I wanted people to see what he was really like. I wanted to see what he was really like as this was the first meeting. I want to backtrack a little. A year before when my career started, I didn't know the 5th Street Gym was there. I happened to be walking there. And Muhammad Ali, who was Cassius Clay at the time, said hello to Howard Cosell, who was right in front of me. I was nothing more than a passerby who happened to have a camera. And at that point, I only used my camera to take pictures of my family or some of my designs.

So I followed Cosell and Ali and walked into the gym. Angelo Dundee stopped me, and he said, "You can't come in here unless you pay a dollar." Somehow this came out of my mouth, "I'm a photographer for Madison Square Garden." The words just came out of my mouth. He said, "OK. Come on in." And there were basically a couple of sparring partners in the gym and Angelo Dundee, Howard Cosell and myself. I took some pictures and I really loved it, taking pictures of the heavyweight champion of the world.

To make a long story short, when I left the gym Ali was top of the news because the fight he was training for was going to be canceled. So I brought my film to the *Miami Herald*, which is a newspaper in Miami, and they developed the pictures and they asked if they could use one to send over to the wire service. I said sure. So in a couple of hours, the first time I'd done a picture of anyone famous or anything important news-wise, next day the picture would go all over the world. Then the next week I went back to New York and brought a couple of my pictures to Madison Square Garden to show to them. The next week the head of Madison Square Garden boxing said, "If you have the whole film then come to me with one roll of film. I have to hire you." That's how I became the photographer [for Madison Square Garden]. So the next time I met Ali was in 1967, as I told you.

Q: Can you relate any social moments you both shared throughout the years of your working relationship?
George Kalinsky: I can go back and forth. The time period would be between 1967 and 1977 – in a ten year period. In 1974, Muhammad Ali called me and says he'd like to have a meeting with me. We eventually got very close. When we met I said, "Ali, what's up?" He said, "I've got this fight in a month, but the problem is Foreman is too fast. He's too big. He's too strong. He's too quick.

I don't think I can win the fight." That's when I came up with the idea of the rope-a-dope. I said, "You've been training all your life for this fight. Usually when you train in the gym you always put your back against the ropes and you let your sparring partners hit you. What you've been doing all these years, training for this fight, you act like a dope on the rope." And eventually within minutes the dope on the rope became rope-a-dope.

Anyway, in 1976 towards the end of Ali's career, I remember getting up at four o'clock in the morning to photograph him at his hotel doing roadwork. I was in a station wagon in front of him. He was jogging and I was taking pictures at night with a flash to light him up. When we went back to the hotel, I said, "Are you really sure you want to fight anymore?" I was worried he was going to get hurt. He only spoke in a whisper when you were in private with him, he said, "The more I fight, the more people recognize me because I'm probably the most recognizable person. I probably have the most famous face in the world. So if I stop fighting I'm going to lose my stage. And the stage is the boxing ring. That's my stage. I'm afraid that if I stop fighting nobody will know me anymore." I couldn't believe the honesty behind that and the fear and the emotions behind what he was saying. And it was almost like a low, very whisper-sounding voice.

When Ali did talk to you privately, he was very much opposite to how he was in public. In public he was always like a showman, and he spent many hours planning what he was going to say. But when he was in private he spoke almost in a whisper. So this is the real Ali. When he was telling me this, at this moment in his life he had the most famous face in the world, maybe other than the Pope. He had a fear of people not knowing who he is anymore. I said to him that there's other things in life you have to do when you have to realize that you can't fight anymore, and that there has to be something else. He said he was reading as much as he could about politics, but nothing is going to compare to being in the ring and the feeling of security by being in the ring. He felt more secure being in the ring than anywhere else.

Q: Anything interesting, can you elucidate further?

George Kalinsky: At one time, in the early 1980s, when the first WrestleMania took place, which was at the Madison Square Garden with Hulk Hogan, prior to the build-up for the WrestleMania they had a lot of celebrities who were honorary referees. They had people like Pete Rose, a diverse group of people, and Ali was one of the referees. I was looking at him and it was the first time that I realized – it was a couple of years after his final fight – and feeling sad because you could see he wasn't the Ali that I was used to seeing. I felt really bad. I remember back when Ali said to me the ring is his life and everything and the ring is his opportunity to be famous. Here he is in the ring but not necessarily the star. Hulk Hogan was the star that day and Ali was just one of the supporting athletes.

Q: Being a professional photographer, how would you describe Muhammad Ali's image in his peak in the 1960s, as far as dress sense and other things he had a penchant for – hobbies, cars?

George Kalinsky: Ali was a very conservative dresser. He usually liked to wear flacks – not necessarily dungarees but flacks – and a dark-colored shirt that came over his belt. That's basically what he wore most of the times, except when he had to be in public and making appearances. Appearances meaning showing up anywhere he spoke, where he usually wore a conservative suit. He wasn't into this. Part of his private life is where he wanted to be more conservative. One time I had him on a golf course just to photograph him. He had trouble hitting the golf ball. He said he wasn't really into other sports. Boxing was really the only sport he cared about.

One time Dick Gregory, again, this was also 1967, was into health food and Dick Gregory talked to Ali for a while. I remember Gregory talking to Ali, just the three of us in his hotel room and he spent hours talking. Mainly to Ali about the benefits of health foods and the importance of carrot juice, calories, etc, which may not be a big deal now but at the time it was new. Including vitamin C and vitamin D, vitamin E – all the different vitamins. You put carrots in the blender and make the juice. I said to Ali that it was interesting.

In terms of hobbies, I can't think of any. He was so occupied. For example, I remember when he was fighting Joe Frazier he was learning his lines when we were riding in his white Cadillac. We were riding, I guess from Miami to Fort Lauderdale, which is about half hour or forty minutes' drive. And in the back seat were Ali and me. And Drew Bundini was driving and one other person was on the front seat.

So, I was alone in the back seat with Ali. First of all, the mission was to go see some kids at a school that he wanted to show up for. He felt that by showing up at a school it would be very important for the kids. There was no press or photographers. It was just something he wanted to do for a school he heard of, for kids in one of the poorer areas of Fort Lauderdale. He felt he could be very helpful. There weren't a lot of kids. I think there were thirty kids in total. This is another public side to Ali: he felt he wanted to reach as many people personally that he could, and not necessarily through defeating Joe.

You say hobby, and this was the goodness of Ali. This is the Ali where he cared about people and especially cared about kids. For example, he used to do a lot of drawings at different times when he was signing an autograph. If it's the right person, he might do a drawing of an airplane or whatever and then sign his name after that. As a matter of fact, he gave me drawings two different times. When he did the drawings for you, it meant you were in his inner circle and you were part of his . . . you had his trust. That was very important to me. The drawings were very primitive, but I valued the drawings very much and the meaning behind them. And it came from his heart. On the way to the school in Fort Lauderdale, Drew Bundini was feeding him the lines for, I think 'float like a butterfly, sting like a bee'. And then he needed two more lines. The way he practiced them, when it came out of his head, he practiced his lines maybe for twenty or fifteen minutes each – even if there was only two lines. Then he would go to the next two lines, 'float like a butterfly, sting like a bee', boom, boom, boom, boom, and he studied and studied.

This was his preparation and this is why he was so good. It didn't just come out of his head; everything he did was very well planned and rehearsed. Not that it was dishonest, because if anything Ali is one of the most honest people you'll ever meet in your life! He was totally honest and he was always humble. He knew where he came from and he always reminded me that he was a poor boy, and anything that he had and any success that he accumulated, he always said I cannot ever forget where I came from. I can never forget my roots. I always remember I was very, very poor and I'll never forget that.

And deciding to help people is interesting, where his feelings for being truthful, he was very, very truthful. He was always very prepared. Nothing that he said was necessarily false. I think if anything, he was very honest and humble and he was always trying to be truthful. But when he did say something, he wanted to be well prepared and he always was well prepared in front of the public.

So, I was in the back seat with him. As a matter of fact one time we stopped at a red light, there were four construction people working and fixing the road on the corner. And these guys were really big. As we are waiting for the red light Ali stands up on the back of the convertible, and he says, "I heard Joe Frazier's somewhere around here. Where is Joe Frazier!? You know where Joe Frazier is!" One guy had a shovel, one guy had a pickax. They were trying to break the road so they had heavy equipment, especially the big guy with overalls. Ali wasn't sure. He wasn't secure with these guys coming forward. He said to Bundini, who was driving, "Get the car going!" And then at the next stop he'd say, "Where is Joe Frazier? You guys know where Joe Frazier is! Bundini, get the car going!" He was putting on an act, at the same time protecting himself, as the car would be gone by the time they got to the car.

Q: Muhammad Ali cultivated a close friendship with Howard Bingham, who was his photographer. Did you ever work with them together?

George Kalinsky: Howard Bingham was his best friend. I was around with Ali with Howard on occasions, but very little. I actually saw Howard more without Ali than with him. If I went to Florida, which I did many times photographing Ali working out at the 5th Street Gym, Howard wasn't necessarily there when I was there. And Howard is a very shy person. He usually stayed in the background. Even if he was there he was very quiet. It was a very wonderful relationship that Howard and Ali had. Howard is really a fine person and Ali and Howard were lucky to have each other.

Q: Did you cover the Ken Norton fights – the fight at the Yankee Stadium in New York?

George Kalinsky: Yes, I did. Shooting usually starts beforehand when I do the pre-fight photos to build up the fight. For example, Ken Norton had just come from doing a movie in 1976. He came from the movie to my house on Long Island. The reason he was coming to my house was because it was a very good place to take portraits. Plus the fact that we could go out into the woods and do chopping of the woods shots and whatever else we could think of. All kinds of stuff which simulated what he had been doing and working out for Ali, preparing for Ali. He pulled up in a limo outside my house. Ken Norton was more than a boxer; he was a movie star. And that was a pretty big movie. Anyway, the point I'm making is, I got to know Ken very well very quickly and I honestly thought on the night of the fight Ken Norton had won that fight.

Everybody ran to Ali's dressing room after the fight. I went to Ken Norton's dressing room first. Ken Norton himself was at the door. He looked tremendously dejected and hurt. And he himself was at the door and was only letting one or two people into the dressing room. And there was hardly anybody in the dressing room. He saw me and I hugged him. And I felt bad because this was a fight that really could've gone either way. Many think Ken Norton actually won, but Ali did win the fight and they fought a couple of times. But Ali was a great showman, obviously the greatest showman I've ever photographed. He had great charisma and charisma reserved for people like Ali and the Pope. In recent years, President Clinton had charisma, Frank Sinatra and Elvis Presley had it. These people had charisma and Ali had it as much as anybody.

Q: Do you feel Muhammad Ali was coming to the end of his career at this point?

George Kalinsky: It was 1976 when I told you about the story when he was fighting with Ken Norton. I went to see him at the Concorde Hotel. He was in bed when he talked about the stage, how his life is on the stage and he didn't want to lose the stage. If he quit boxing he wasn't going to have the stage anymore and people would forget him. That was his fear and he had that fear that people would forget him.

Q: What was one of the most exhilarating experiences you encountered during your time with Muhammad Ali?

George Kalinsky: One of the great days of boxing studio photography I ever had was when I got to do [photograph] Ali and Joe Frazier at Joe Frazier's gym in 1971. Maybe two months before the Fight of the Century in Madison Square Garden. It was quite a privilege to have both Ali and Frazier alone in the gym. For example, I took two of them head to head, nose to nose – no one ever did that before. These pre-fight photographs I took of them, the fighters training, no one ever did that before either. Before I came along, the only way a boxer was photographed prior to the fight was he would just pause, a stand-up pause – that's it. Occasionally, you might see somebody chopping wood, but I started taking photographs of boxers doing what they do. So when I got the two men together in the gym, one of the things I wanted to do was go around with each fighter with my camera.

So when I went around with Ali, instead of me having boxing gloves, I had the camera. And he was looking at me, and I said, "Ali, just think I'm Joe Frazier." He kept swinging at me, missing my camera by a quarter of an inch. I immediately realized if Ali hit Frazier with his fist . . . I couldn't believe that he had so much control and he was real fast. If he had hit a nail, that nail would have been hit. He was missing my camera by about quarter of an inch and I felt confident that he was never going to hit my camera. Then I tried to take pictures with Joe Frazier. I had him stop after twenty seconds because Joe had no precision. But more than anything, at that moment I realized if anyone's going to win this fight at that moment, it would be Joe Frazier because, to me, it's about two fighters in that one round in the gym.

Q: Can you tell me about going over to his house for photo shoots?

George Kalinsky: I went to his house. I took a beautiful picture of him lying on his couch after he had done some training. It seems like Ali took every advantage he could to take a nap. He was either working or training. You asked about hobbies [earlier], he did everything he could to stay in good shape. He was an honest person. He ate well. He was into the health foods and he liked to take as many naps as he could. I never really even thought of that before, but as I think back now he would go into a quiet, always thinking mode. Hobbies were almost like planning and thinking than actually playing an instrument. I think he had a lot of feelings about wanting to be an artist. He did those drawings we talked about earlier. He also liked to do magic tricks, making other people happy and making other people laugh. Magic tricks may have been a little crude, but it was important for Ali to make other people smile, especially children.

Q: Can you recall any unusual incidents that happened when working with him?

George Kalinsky: As much as Ali was a talker in front of the public, Ali was not an extrovert. He wasn't loud in private, he wasn't a talker. He was more of a thinker than a talker. He saved his talking and well-practiced lines for using in front of people, which he practiced a lot. As a matter of fact, going back a little bit in relation to one of the stunts, I remember being with him in the mountains prior to a fight. I don't remember which fight it was. One of the gimmicks was they had about forty people from the press and Ali was going to take us on a bus ride. So we get on the bus and Ali's on the front seat. The next thing you know Ali is driving a bus and he drives it into a ditch. And the next day in all the headlines in the local papers in the New York area read: ALI DRIVES A BUS INTO A DITCH. They tried to relate that to training. So it was all planned. He knew ahead of time that he was going to drive the bus into a ditch.

Q: Any last words on your friendship and working relationship with the greatest sportsman of the century?
George Kalinsky: One of the last times I saw Ali was when he was sitting next to Dustin Hoffman at ringside about a year ago. Ali was sitting next to him at the fight. I can't remember which fight it was. I went across to see him, and the way he looked now, it was one of those things love attachment, so to speak. But you sort of feel bad about his Parkinson's disease. Anyway, I wanted to go over and say hi to him.

I didn't know what the reaction would be as I hadn't seen him for a while, and I had photographed Dustin Hoffman. Actually, I know Dustin Hoffman pretty well. The two of them were sitting next to each other and I had my camera around my neck. But my camera wasn't really very important at that moment. I just wanted to go over and shake hands and speak to Ali. He recognizes me and when I walk over his eyes lit up, realizing that he did recognize me. It was a good moment of being able to shake his hand and to be thankful for all those years we had known each other. I've been the official photographer for the Madison Square Garden for a long time since I've known Ali.

So, I've been very fortunate and privileged to photograph the world's greatest entertainers and athletes. You have to put Ali on top of the list. You have to go with Ali, the Pope, Sinatra, Elvis and Michael Jordan. He is the icon of our time. Muhammad Ali was certainly a very important influence in my life. And it's very important that I had the privilege to be able to photograph him. Because when people introduce me to other people and say this is the photographer who photographed Ali, the Pope, Sinatra, Michael Jordan, it's always Ali first. And for me personally, being the photographer of the Garden, the world's most famous names, I had the privilege to photograph them. Not just getting their favorite picture, but a moment that will live forever. Ali certainly has to be top of the list of American icons, not only American but worldwide icons.

GARY SMITH

Gary Smith was a sportswriter for *Sports Illustrated*, where he produced several long-form pieces a year. Before joining *Sports Illustrated*, he worked for various print media outlets: *Wilmington News-Journal*, *New York Daily*, *Philadelphia News* and *Inside Sports*. Smith spent time covering Ali mostly after he had retired from the ring. He is a recipient of the National Magazine Award for Non-Fiction, the closest magazine equivalent to the Pulitzer Prize.

Q: Which was the first Muhammad Ali fight that you covered?
Gary Smith: I only covered a couple of his fights. I watched a number of his closed-circuit TV fights, where they had them on the big screens back in those days. But as far as covering actual fights, I think I remember covering the Leon Spinks fight in New Orleans. I wrote about it. It was more spending time with him after his career. I spent a lot of time with him and interviewing him during his career, but more of my interviews were done with him after his career.

Q: Can we talk about the time you were with him during his career?
Gary Smith: The very first time, when I was twenty-five years old, when I went to see him in the camp there were other reporters who were heading out there. He was going to be fighting Larry Holmes, which was later in his career. I'm thinking, *How am I going to be up there among a big horde of media?* I showed up at Deer Lake in his cabin. He trained up in the mountains. I was the only one there. He was having a deep massage by his masseuse. His eyes were closed, you could tell he had worked out already that day and was tired and was kind of dozing off on the massage table. He showed me a lot about him that day because I was the only one there. I was only a kid. He spent a couple of hours with me. I thought I'd be hiding behind some big-time reporters, just scribbling a few things

out and thought that I might ask a few questions. But nothing like that happened. He gave me a couple of hours of his attention. I was somebody he'd never seen before. I was just a kid. so that showed me there was a special quality there as a human being.

Q: How did Muhammad Ali come across?
Gary Smith: The thing that jumped at you with Ali was his aliveness and sense of humor. He started doing card tricks, magic tricks for me. He wanted to show you a good time and entertain you. He was kind of almost coming out of sleep, waking up basically and turning on the lights, putting on a show and having fun. That always jumped out. And that would jump out throughout the years. When he was older and had retired, I went to visit him at his farmhouse in Michigan. I went to the bathroom, and when I was coming back out to continue with the interview, I couldn't get the door open. So here I am trying everything with the door. I'm locked in Ali's house in the bathroom and yanking. Finally, after five minutes he finally opens the door and I stumble out. He was holding it the whole time. So little tricks and stuff like that he'd do, just being playful.

Q: Larry Holmes was Muhammad Ali's sparring partner for a couple of years, then they fought each other. What is your view on the fight because this fight took place in the twilight of his career?
Gary Smith: It turned out later that he had been on some kind of pills prescribed by a doctor to reduce his weight. He was all shaky, not good for him at all. It was very bad medicine, which he was receiving at the time. Dr. Ferdie Pacheco had left him at the time because he didn't feel he should be part of it. He thought it was over for Ali and dangerous for him to continue to be fighting. He found another doctor who prescribed some pills to help him lose weight, which was really bad stuff. Ali went into the ring and he got his weight down, but it was really bad for him. Holmes just took him apart. It was very painful to watch. I watched that from Madison Square Garden closed-circuit television.

Q: What do you think compelled him to continue fighting? Was it the people around him who were influencing his decisions?

Gary Smith: He was still caught up of having to be something, being in front of everyone and entertaining the crowd and being in the middle of a spectacle and taking care of everyone. There were many reason. Certain point of his career he had to fight for the world in a lot of ways. He was helping so many that in a way he became a figurehead and a symbol and that helped him – that motivation helped him. Against Frazier, when he was in Manila, it was the spirit of realizing. Bundini Brown was relying on him and said to him that if you beat Joe Frazier, you win for the world. That was an incredible motivation for Ali, but it was also the world against him in the end I think. At the end of his career he couldn't give up. He was fighting for the world. He thought he was. And that kept him feeling he needed to continue and he couldn't let it go. Like a lot of people willing to let go is a very difficult thing. He couldn't let go of that status and position, that crusade, that position he'd been placed in by people and others. And he felt like he had to fulfill their needs and that double backed on him in a very painful way.

Q: You've interviewed and interacted with some of the top sportsmen and personalities in the United States. Can you compare them to Muhammad Ali?

Gary Smith: I think he's in a category all by himself. He had a much larger vision of himself in the part he can play in the world and he embraced that. Most athletes find that would get in the way and become an obstacle in achieving their goals within their sport, so they funnel down into their sport. Whereas Ali opened up, it was exactly the opposite. He let the whole world become a tidal wave and push him along. It's a very difficult thing to do, to take on all of that. But he could use all of that energy as well and he was able to handle that sort, which most people can't. So he rode the world's energy and he was drained. That's a very complicated relationship to hold. Eventually, it's part of why he stayed so long and couldn't give it up, as I mentioned earlier. He's the last major athlete who has become a high social figure, changing the world and culture and society as well as being an incredible sportsman. It's very rare people are willing to care to be both. You see many major superstars who really want no part of that role.

Q: Did you travel with him on the road?

Gary Smith: I was with him in 1984. He was obviously retired by then. We were on Santa Monica Freeway traveling back. He'd taken me to see some boxing training for the Olympics in Los Angeles. Parkinson's was already hitting him at that point, so the medication he was taking made him very sleepy. I'm in the passenger seat and he's driving. The car starts to weave back and forth at sixty miles an hour on Santa Monica Freeway. I'm seeing his eyelids closing. I'm getting very nervous, but I didn't want to reach over and grab the steering wheel from the greatest heavyweight champion of all time.

Part of me as a writer wants to let it go and see what happens here, but a certain part of me as a human being side of me clicks in with fear. I'm just not sure what to do. I'm on the edge. His eyes were totally closed and his hands are off the wheel. There's cars honking, at that point I was about to reach out and grab the wheel. All of a sudden a little arm comes out on his shoulder. I think he was nine years old, a little boy, he reached over his dad's shoulder and grabbed the shoulder and steering wheel. He was not driving the car in the back seat. That went on for a moment. Finally, he opened his eyes and took over the wheel again. He's such a jokester and prankster. I don't know whether this was something he'd done before and set up. He liked to play tricks on people. Whether he'd fallen asleep for a moment or not, I don't know. I'm hoping it was a prank. But anyway, it was a very humorous moment but a very unusual moment.

Q: Do you feel the *Ali* movie, starring Will Smith, did justice to Muhammad Ali or could it have been better, as some people feel it didn't hit the mark?

Gary Smith: No, it really didn't quite capture the whole spirit I think. It's a very difficult thing to do when a man's still alive to play his part and do that – make a movie which is really effective.

Q: What do you think was Muhammad Ali's reaction?
Gary Smith: I have no idea how Muhammad would have taken that, to be honest with you.

Q: Did you see him often in the last few decades after his retirement, and do you think he became much more complacent?
Gary Smith: More in the late 1980s and early 1990s. In 1984, he was still living in Los Angeles with Veronica Porche. Then his marriage was coming towards an end. Then he remarried a woman from Louisville who he grew up with in the same street. She was younger than him. He married her and he was living with her in the Michigan farmhouse. She was very quiet. She was much more loving and there was much more spirit of a relationship going on between them. The house was quiet, there was a barn there and all the pictures of his career were in this barn. And he took me up there and showed me. Pigeons had crapped on them who had come through the rooftop which was open and it needed repairing. So the pigeon crap had come through the room and hit the pictures and stained them. So he just went around and started turning the pictures of all his moments of glory, turning them one by one, facing them against the wall so the pigeons can't keep crapping on them.

Q: Having known Muhammad Ali and spending time with him, how would you describe him as a person?
Gary Smith: Very religious. He would take his time five times a day and pray on his prayer mat. That meant everything to him. Anybody he signed an autograph for, or even me coming as a reporter, he'd hand a little thing which had some words about peace in Islam. Very important, it was very clear his relationship with God was what mattered the most to him and he was in a very spiritual mode. He had been the center of the world and now he's in a quiet Michigan farmhouse, where he was still. He was working his way through that and God was a big part of that.

Q: Do you feel he evolved as far as religion goes because in the beginning he was drawn to the Nation of Islam, which was not mainstream Islam?

Gary Smith: I think he softened. He definitely softened as he went on. He softened as a man and his religion.

Q: Any deep conversation you had with him that really touched you?

Gary Smith: We talked about stuff and I tried to take it all deep as I can. So I'm sure there were some very deep conversations. I can't remember the nature of them at this moment, really. It was about life and how things had quietened down and how he was dealing with that. I wasn't at the midst of the glory [years]. I was there at the end of his career and after his career.

Q: Anything that really touched you about Muhammad Ali?

Gary Smith: One thing I remember was the day on the freeway with the car incident. After that happened, he was waving people over to form a line behind him. They were shocked to see Muhammad Ali waving to them and telling them to get their cars behind him and follow him. Finally, we had a big convoy of cars and he led them back to this big house he lived in and did magic tricks for them. All these people who were total strangers. So again, he's still needing an audience. That was a revealing moment as well.

Q: What sets Muhammad Ali apart from Joe Frazier, Joe Louis, Jack Dempsey and Mike Tyson? Do you feel had he just been a boxer without the personality he cultivated then he would have never achieved the iconic status he did?

Gary Smith: There's no doubt about it. He was something much more, as part of the world as a leader, someone who meant much to so many people and embracing that is what makes him different. The others were, it was more of their singular quest, survival quest for some of them. Whereas Ali rode the world's energy he was the whole thing. That's what makes him different than any others.

THREE

THE OPPONENTS

Before Muhammad Ali turned professional, he built an awesome amateur record. He tallied up no less than one hundred and eight amateur bouts, over the course of which he prevailed a hundred times. He also won the National Golden Gloves tournament twice, six Kentucky Golden Gloves championships and captured the National AAU title twice. After winning the Olympic gold medal in the 1960 Rome Olympics, in the light-heavyweight division, Ali turned professional the same year. He won his first professional fight against Tunney Hunsaker, a police chief from Fayetteville, West Virginia. On February 25, 1964, in Miami, Florida, as a mouthy impetuous underdog then known as Cassius Clay, he dethroned Sonny Liston to capture the prestigious world heavyweight crown. He was only twenty-two years old.

Following his victory over Liston, the young brash boxer began to produce a steady stream of headlines. It wasn't long before everyone started to know him for his lyrical charm and braggadocio. His verbal banter was as sharp and quick as his trademark lightning jab. Yet, he was able to back up his boisterous claims of being The Greatest with his performance in the ring. Ali was a fighter of exceptional skill, extraordinary speed and cunning who reshaped the sweet science with his unique style. He would dance around, flicking out swift jabs and blinding combinations, leaning back to defend in a way that made audiences gasp. The Louisville Lip, as he became known, was a flamboyant ring performer. He developed a habit of dropping his hands at his sides, unlike almost every other boxer of the time. Small wonder that Ali's ring exploits became legendary.

In 1967, his title was revoked and he was sentenced to five years in prison for draft evasion. He appealed, and though it took nearly four years before his appeal was successful he never went to jail. However, the authorities banned him from boxing – a decision reversed in 1971 by the United States Supreme Court, but not before Ali's prime years in boxing were stolen from him by the United States government.

After his return to the ring, Ali started to employ a radically different style, moving less and drawing opponents into wars of attrition where both winner and loser would typically take tremendous punishment. He fought and beat every top heavyweight of his era – a golden age of boxing – and his legendary fights with Joe Frazier and George Foreman are widely acknowledged by fans and critics alike to be the greatest fights of the century. The actual Fight of the Century, between Frazier and Ali, gave rise to a trilogy of bouts that are some of the greatest every captured on film and undoubtedly shortened both men's careers. Sadly, Frazier could never forgive the invective Ali directed towards him during the build-up to their fights – later, Ali stated that his attitude towards his foe was merely to hype up the fights. However, Frazier never truly accepted the apology.

By contrast, many of the pugilists who had the privilege of sharing the ring with The Greatest say that it was an honor to fight him. These one-time adversaries confess that Ali changed their lives forever, both by changing the importance of boxing and by giving them a chance to step between the ropes with the most admired boxer of all time.

Inevitably many compare Ali to boxing champions of the past and present. Nothing sparks controversy and interest like having a debate on who is the greatest pugilist in history. Ali, more than any other boxer in history, is constantly used as a measuring stick by fans of the sport and experts alike. Jack Dempsey, Sugar Ray

Robinson and Joe Louis have all been suggested as worthwhile contenders for the pound-for-pound crown, while if you want to throw in a more modern-era fighter, then Mike Tyson is the name that most readily springs to most people's lips. True comparisons are, of course, impossible, but interesting fodder nonetheless. Dempsey's punching power and aggressive style made him one of the most popular boxers to ever enter the ring, while Sugar Ray Robinson's achievements as a technician are impossible to deny. Joe Louis, who is highly respected by the sport's historians, was named the greatest heavyweight boxing champion of all time in 2005 by The International Boxing Research Organization. He had some of the greatest rapid-fire combinations in the game's history. Furthermore, Louis is widely considered as the greatest boxer puncher of all time; his power shots were absolutely devastating.

Something which should also be taken into account is that the history of sports shows a linear improvement among athletes. To this end, making comparison between fighters from completely different eras becomes somewhat difficult. And yet, in boxing, modern-day greats are often happy to pay homage to the champ. When Mike Tyson, considered almost unstoppable at the height of his fame, appeared on a TV show with Sugar Ray Leonard and Ali in the early 1990s, he himself conceded, "I know I'm great, but can I tell you something, in this situation every head must bow, every tongue must profess, this [Ali] is the greatest of all time."

What's safe to say is that athletic greatness comprised of a myriad of qualities and attributes, some technical, some physical and some mental. And what's clear is that, apart from the speed, reflexes and unorthodox style that served him so well early in his career, Ali had a granite jaw and could absorb endless punishment, while also being a scientific and smart fighter with endless heart. Out of sixty-one professional fights he lost only five – including three between 1978 and 1981, when his best fighting days were behind him.

Ali retired in 1981, immediately after losing his comeback bout to Trevor Berbick. His retirement did not diminish his status as an international personality. The legendary ring exploits of Ali inspired sports fans of new generations. In the following section you will discover exclusive interviews with some of the heavyweight champions and prominent fighters who shared the ring with the three-time heavyweight champion. They offer first-hand accounts and opinions, sharing memories of moments in sporting history typically only available to those brave enough to face The Greatest.

GEORGE FOREMAN

George Foreman is unarguably one of the greatest heavyweights to ever enter the boxing ring. He won a gold medal at the 1968 Mexico City Olympics and turned professional the following year. Foreman defeated Joe Frazier on January 23, 1973, to capture the heavyweight title after Frazier won it from Ali. His battle against Ali in Zaire the following year – the Rumble in the Jungle – became one of the biggest boxing bouts of the century. Later, he became the oldest man ever to capture the world heavyweight championship at the age of forty-five. Foreman now lives in Texas and is a successful businessman.

Q: George, how did the Muhammad Ali fight manifest itself into a reality?
George Foreman: Muhammad Ali bout, he was the next available opponent for me. Of course, I was the champion and he was the number-two contender. I'd beaten Ken Norton and Joe Frazier. No one else wanted to fight me.

Q: Can you take me through the events which happened in your press conference?
George Foreman: There were actually several press conferences. They were mostly apart. I would have one in California. Muhammad Ali would have another in New York. And we would meet up in Salt Lake City – but mostly apart. Because we tried to publicize it as

much as we could away from each other, but the press conferences were all around the country.

Q: Leading to the press conferences, what publicity did the fight receive? It was one of the biggest fights in boxing history.
George Foreman: I think it was because there was so much publicity. I had really established myself as a genuine puncher. Of course, Muhammad Ali ensured me, when we signed for the fight, he was going to make it big, that he's going to do as much talking as possible. And he did, by taking the fight to Africa to a bigger stage because the international press was interested in that country, Zaire, as much as we were.

Q: How did you acclimatize to the environment when you got there? Was it a completely different atmosphere to what you were accustomed to?
George Foreman: The thing about me was I had so many boxing matches all over the world. As a matter of fact, I had won the title in Mexico. I'd fought in the Caribbean, Venezuela and also in Japan. And my amateur career had taken me to Europe. So the climate had nothing to do with it. I had been pretty much acclimated to box anywhere, so it didn't bother me. It would just be a different time of day, but it didn't really bother me.

Q: What training did you do to prepare for this bout and was there anything your team wanted you to look out for?
George Foreman: I didn't train any different than I always did for any other fight. I always do a lot of running and roadwork. I hit the speed bag and the punching bag. I did wood chopping and a lot of sparring. This time, of course, I met a better man who was slicker and had had more tricks up his sleeves. When I fought Muhammad Ali, my trainers and my corner people were like, *Let George out of the cage. The animal will destroy Muhammad Ali.* I didn't have any other strategy but just to go get him.

Q: Would I be right in saying before the fight you thought you'd be able to easily outbox him, but you've also said Muhammad Ali amazed you?

George Foreman: What amazed me most about Muhammad Ali was he would take my most hardest shots. The punches that I'd usually knock people out with, he was able to absorb the punches. And with a couple of punches I would rock him, but he would recover more than anyone I had ever fought [before]. I was certain that I would knock him out in one or two rounds. That's why I didn't conserve any of my energy. I was sure he would be out in two or three rounds. When I looked up at the fourth and the fifth round and saw he was still there, that's when I became amazed.

Q: Would I be right in saying that you hit him with the hardest body shot you ever hit anyone with?

George Foreman: I hit him in the body so hard one time I thought he was just gonna drop. He looked as though he wanted to fight toe to toe with me, but then he changed his mind and he covered up. When he covered up and survived, he couldn't believe it, nor could I believe it. That's when I really tried to finish him off and he was still standing. That's when I thought Ali was on the whole ring. He took it and he stayed on his feet. But I'm shocked he was able to take that body punch.

Q: How would you define his fighting style? He was a speed fighter; you were by far the hardest hitter in the heavyweight division. What was the difference between your styles?

George Foreman: The funny thing is when I fought him he didn't demonstrate much speed at all because I cornered him, and I could hit him pretty good. But when he did the one-two combination, the punch that knocked me down, I had never been hit by a right hand that quick, and as fast as he delivered that night. I saw it coming but I just couldn't get out of the way. When I turned, it just hit like, pap, pap, and it was lightning quick. He was probably the fastest heavyweight that I've ever been in the ring with.

Q: What was your strategy going into the fight and did your cornermen give you any advice?

George Foreman: I think my corner people had been spoilt. They put on my robe and just waited for me to knock-out everybody. They weren't prepared for the adversary because when the fight started to move up on to the fifth and sixth round, my corner panicked. They were not equipped to give me instructions. They just didn't know what to do because they were surprised as much as I was.

Q: Talk to me about the famous rope-a-dope strategy implemented by Muhammad Ali. You threw so many punches and expended energy in the process, which seemed to work against you in the end?

George Foreman: Well, I was a boxer and I always looked for openings. And in that fight when you get a guy against the ropes in the ring, that's an opening to finish him off. So every time I hit him, I tried to finish him off. First round, I'll get him in the second. Each round meant that I was going to finish him off. I didn't know he was going to be standing there round after round. I was shocked and amazed. The rope-a-dope only occurred because of some... I don't think it was a strategy, it was more of survival for Muhammad Ali and he did well because of it.

Q: The crowd supporting Muhammad Ali was in a gleeful mood, and after the fight they were shouting, "Ali bombayi!" What can you remember after he won?

George Foreman: I can't remember. When I always get into the ring I'm totally focused. I was trying to win. There were a lot of people pulling for me and there were a great amount of people pulling for Muhammad Ali. He wanted people to love him. He wanted people to pull for him. That's not what I wanted. That's not what I was looking for. So I didn't even try to cater with that. I only wanted to get a knockout and get my money and go home.

Q: Muhammad Ali taunted his opponents in and out of the ring. In your case, what did he say and did he pursue the psychological game?

George Foreman: He spoke to me, but he wasn't the first opponent to talk to me when I've been in the ring. So that didn't bother me at all. Of course, he kept talking and I figured he was talking because he was scared I was hitting him hard. But it had no psychological advantage over me. He hit me with his fist.

Q: Muhammad Ali was one of the most defensive fighters, and that's the strategy he often used instead of going in for the kill.

George Foreman: I think Muhammad Ali was a great fighter. He'd get you off guard and he'd hit you with a great shot. He was a real great fighter. He was the best of all times.

Q: Can you express your thoughts when he knocked you down?

George Foreman: When I got hit with the one-two combination, I tried to break the fall. I hit the floor and I could have gotten up, but my corner told me to wait till the eighth count. And I waited for the eighth count then I jumped up but the fight was over. All that was going through my mind when I landed on the canvas was, *He'd been covering up all night, but now he's going to try to go for a finish and I'm going to knock him out.* That's all I was thinking about. But when I got up the fight was over.

Q: When the fight was over were you bitter? What was going through your mind?

George Foreman: After the fight is over, of course, you're bitter, sad and you're hurt. Because I lost the most precious crown in athletics you can receive – the heavyweight championship of the world. I was hurt for a long time, devastated really. When I got my thoughts together, what I wanted more than anything was a rematch. I never could get a rematch. For some reason he never wanted to fight me again. I left the ring in 1977, of course, and he continued his career. By the time I came back in boxing he was long gone.

Q: Outside of the ring and away from the press he was a very friendly guy!

George Foreman: The few times I met him beyond the boxing ring, he was always a fun-loving guy. He joked a lot, we were pretty good friends after the boxing match.

Q: When you both retired did you meet up at charity events?

George Foreman: Muhammad and me, after he retired, of course, I became great friends with him. He would come to Houston to present awards for me and, of course, I traveled with him to promote the *Champions Forever* video. We became great friends.

Q: Mike Tyson versus Muhammad Ali in their prime, what's your opinion?

George Foreman: Muhammad Ali told me himself. I said to him, "Do you think Tyson could beat anybody?" He said, "Man, Tyson hits so hard." He felt Tyson hit harder than anyone he'd faced. He told me once that he didn't have the confidence he could have beaten Mike Tyson.

Q: Do you feel Muhammad Ali elevated boxing and took it beyond?

George Foreman: I think he went beyond in elevating boxing because he pretty much elevated manhood if you ask me. I think this earth is better because Muhammad Ali taught a lot of men how to become better at being men – and women. Muhammad Ali was the greatest motivator of human beings I've ever met. I've lived a good life. I've had a great boxing career and I've also become a salesperson. The George Foreman Grill has been really popular. I love to meet and talk to people and tell them about my career, most importantly my ministry. I'm a preacher at the Church of Lord Jesus Christ, that's what I do now. I spread the word about the good news of God and how Jesus died. It leaves me happy and I think everybody finds it makes them a better person as well.

LARRY HOLMES

Larry Holmes, who grew up in Easton, Pennsylvania, was one of the greatest heavyweight fighters of his era, with a career that included victories over Muhammad Ali, Ken Norton and Tim Witherspoon. From 1978 to 1983, he was the WBC heavyweight champion, before claiming the IBF heavyweight championship from 1983 to 1985. From 1980 to 1987 he was *The Ring* heavyweight champion. Holmes made twenty successful title defenses, second only to the Brown Bomber Joe Louis' twenty-five. Holmes was also Ali's sparring partner for a number of years.

Q: You were Muhammad Ali's sparring partner, how did you get involved with him?
Larry Holmes: My trainer took me up to his camp. My trainer knew Angelo Dundee and Angelo Dundee put me in there.

Q: What was it like to spar with him?
Larry Holmes: It was alright. It was OK. I don't know what he worked on, but I worked on getting in shape. I didn't care what he was doing. I was there getting in shape for myself and do a good job with him.

Q: What was Muhammad Ali like as a person?
Larry Holmes: Ali was OK. He was always a good guy.

Q: How did you end up fighting him in 1981?
Larry Holmes: He wanted to fight somebody after he came out of retirement and I was the champion then. I was traveling the world. He said he wanted to win my title.

Q: Before the fight at the press conference, were there any major incidents that you would like to share?
Larry Holmes: Press conference was just like another press

conference. You go in there, you say what he was going to do and what I was going to do. And that was the end of the press conference.

Q: What attributes of his were you going to look out for?
Larry Holmes: I was going to look out for everything. I didn't have to worry about just one thing, but I was looking out for everything he did. I wasn't concentrating on one particular thing. My thing was I went out there to do what I had to do and not worry about what he was going to do.

Q: Any special training you did for this specific fight?
Larry Holmes: No. I kept on what I usually did.

Q: Can we talk about the training you implemented when preparing for the Muhammad Ali fight?
Larry Holmes: I did what I had to do, each and every day, to put myself in top condition so I could win. I work really hard, that's what I do. There was nothing special that I did to train for the Ali fight. I just trained like I usually did.

Q: Some people said that Muhammad Ali was old and was no longer at the pinnacle of his career. What is your opinion on this matter?
Larry Holmes: People can say anything they want to say, but I know what I had to do and I went in there and did it. If they want to say he was out of shape, old, fat or whatever, then that's OK with me. I went in there and did what I had to do and I won.

Q: Before you ever met Muhammad Ali how did you perceive him as a boxer?
Larry Holmes: Ali was a good fighter. He as one of the great guys, but he wasn't the greatest guy in the world. I think Joe Louis and everybody else came in there, too. But he was a good guy. I didn't really think too much of anything. I just wanted to go out there

and do what I had to do and get ready for the fight, and to win the fight – that's it.

Q: What did you think of his personality?
Larry Holmes: A great personality! Ali had a great personality.

Q: Going into the fight, he used to call his opponents names, did he taunt you or use this psychological strategy?
Larry Holmes: He talked to me a little bit here and there, but we didn't care about it. We were concentrating on what we had to do.

Q: What was the highlight of the fight?
Larry Holmes: After they raised my hands, that was my highlight. Ali is a good man. I can't knock Ali. He wasn't ready for me. I was better than he was at that time. So that's all that matters.

Q: Would I be right in saying you have said you were beating him in the gym in your sparring days?
Larry Holmes: I didn't say I was beating him in the gym. I was training. We would go back and forth. I didn't try to beat Ali up. We just did what we had to do, that's all.

Q: Were you confident going into the fight?
Larry Holmes: Yes, I was always confident. I didn't worry about nothing.

Q: After the fight did the reporters talk to you and what did Muhammad Ali say?
Larry Holmes: They come up to you and say what you did, what you think and everything. I did what I had to do, and that was to win the fight.

Q: What was the hardest fight of your career?
Larry Holmes: When I won the heavyweight championship from Kenny Norton.

Q: You fought Mike Tyson and Muhammad Ali. How would you compare the two?

Larry Holmes: I don't know why you guys bring up his [Tyson's] name. He couldn't fight. He's just proved he couldn't hold the title. You're going to measure him as a great fighter? He couldn't fight!

Q: Did you become friends with Muhammad Ali?

Larry Holmes: We were friends. We were friends before I fought him. We were friends back in 1971 when I first met him. We've always been friends.

Q: What was the most interesting thing he ever said to you?

Larry Holmes: I don't know of any interesting thing. What am I going to do, turn the clock back thirty-plus years? I can't remember thirty years ago. How can I tell you that? All I know is I fought him and I beat him. I got in shape to beat him and I worked out with him as a sparring partner. The guy was a great guy. I have no hard feelings. He had no hard feelings. I went out and beat him. He was not giving me advice and I wasn't taking advice from him. I didn't do that. I didn't let him give me advice because I did what I wanted to do because he tried to beat me up every day in the gym. That's what he tried to do – win every day.

Q: Do you think he left a benchmark after he retired?

Larry Holmes: I don't know. It depends on all you guys, you guys doing the writing. If you guys want to say he's the greatest, then he's the greatest. You want to say he's the worst, then he's the worst. Whatever, you guys say! I'm saying he was a great fighter. But I was greater than he was. I'm the greatest fighter that ever walked this earth and I'm still here. I'm still alive. I'm still talking to you.

Q: After you fought Muhammad Ali what path did your career take?

Larry Holmes: I did nothing. I just kept going in the way I was going. I kept winning. That's all I wanted to do.

Q: Do you feel Muhammad Ali should have retired earlier?

Larry Holmes: I can't tell you that. He did what he wanted to do. I can't say Ali should have retired. I fought till I was fifty-two years old. He was thirty-eight when he fought me. So how are you going to tell me he should have retired? I can't tell you. I was fifty-two years old when I quit. He was thirty-eight. So he did what he had to do. So what's the difference?

Q: Anything you would like to add about your friendship with Muhammad Ali?

Larry Holmes: The only thing I wanted everybody to know is I fought him and I beat him fair and square. I have no regrets or remorse. I did what I had to do. If there's Larry Holmes fans out there that like Larry Holmes and respect what Larry Holmes did, then that's great.

JOE BUGNER

Born in Hungary in 1950, Joe Bugner moved to the United Kingdom in the late 1950s. After training as a youth at the Bedford Boys Club, he fought sixteen times as an amateur before turning professional in 1967. He went the distance with Ali twice, after which both Ali and Angelo Dundee proclaimed him capable of becoming world champion. He also held the British, Commonwealth and European titles. Ranked one of the top ten heavyweights in the 1970s, he moved to Australia in the early 1980s, became friends with Ali and continued to see him long after their pair of historic bouts.

Q: Well before you fought Muhammad Ali, you actually went over to the United States in 1969 to train with him. Can you please tell me about the experience?

Joe Bugner: Absolutely. By then, Ali was trying to make his boxing comeback. As you know, he was a conscientious objector. He refused to fight in Vietnam so the courts had stopped him from fighting. By the time I got to America in 1969, he was aching to get back in the ring. He hadn't had a fight yet, but I was one of the first international boxers he confronted in front of the British press and the American press. So it was quite an exciting moment.

Q: Where did your first meeting take place?

Joe Bugner: It was actually at Gil Clancy's gym. Gil Clancy was famous for training some very famous fighters and world champions. He was famous like Angelo Dundee at that time. The actual first meeting with Muhammad Ali took place at a hotel in New York. This was one of the most exciting times in my life because here I am at nineteen meeting the legend. By that time, he had made himself to be a legend because of his refusal to fight for America. He was one of the greatest champions of the world and, to me, it was just brilliant.

I'll give you an example. My trainer and I were having breakfast on the day of his arrival. We thought he'd arrive very quietly, check into his suite and see us at the gymnasium. But no! He made a grand entrance into the restaurant of the hotel, and I've got to tell you something: it was fascinating. He walked into the place, looked around and saw me sitting with a group of people from Britain. And within three or four minutes hundreds of people had piled into the restaurant. The owners were absolutely bloody baffled. I'm sure they were thinking, *Good God! What are we going to do?*

Anyway, Muhammad looked across the room and he saw me. I stood up, and he looked across and he shouted, "You're the white boy who wants to make a name for himself at my expense. Let me tell you something, white boy, by the time I'm finished with you your mother ain't going to recognize you." And whilst he's talking, he's actually coming closer and closer and he's throwing punches. He was throwing combinations – starting with those fast lead jabs of his. By the time he's reached me, he was missing my nose by quarter of an inch. "Do you see how fast I am?" he said. "I'm so fast I scare myself. I'm so fast I could put the light out and be in bed before the light goes out!" I was thinking to myself, *Good God, I'm nineteen years old and I'm listening to this great fighter, speaker.* He was brilliant, absolutely magnificent.

Q: Did you ever get to spar with him in the gym?
Joe Bugner: Well, when we got to Gil Clancy's gymnasium, he'd already given me the talk – the typical Muhammad Ali showdown. The verbal hazing just never stops. When we got into the gymnasium, on that day he was just mesmerizing. He spoke to the press and gave them all the verbal stuff that he was so good at. We did six good rounds with him and everybody wanted to know how good I was so they asked him. "How good is the kid, Muhammad? How good is he? Do you think he'll make it?" It was just the same old typical boxing questions. Muhammad Ali turned around and said, "Let me tell you right now. Nobody, nobody has ever given me a white eye." By that he meant instead of a black eye, a white eye – he called it a white eye.

He and I became not friends but we became sort of 'talking

people' in the boxing world. Within four years of that meeting, I was fighting him for the world title eliminator in Las Vegas at Caesars Palace. So after meeting him and sparring him for six rounds in the gymnasium, four years later I was fighting him for the world title eliminator, which was fantastic.

Q: So how did the first fight materialize and what did you think of Ali's ability first-hand?

Joe Bugner: What happened was obviously my career was doing really well in England. I mean, there I was, I fought a number of British fighters – I think I had thirty-five fights and I fought Henry Cooper on my twenty-first birthday. Anyway, I beat Henry Cooper. Then, of course, I won the British, European and Commonwealth heavyweight championships. Then I go up to fight and defend my European title. And in 1973, after I retained my European and Commonwealth championships, they said I was worthy of a world heavyweight title challenge. That was the world title elimination between Ali and I. I think it was very, very close. It was very exciting for me because here I am now and it's not sparring, but it's the real thing. Muhammad Ali was methodical in the way he said, "I'm going to whoop this white boy. I'm going to fix him up so bad he will retire from boxing." And all this nonsense that was coming out of his mouth.

And fortunately in those days I had a very brilliant cut man called Danny Holland, who used to look after Henry Cooper. Anyway, in the first round of the bout, you won't believe this, I got a right hand clip on the top of the lip and it caused an immediate cut that was pretty serious. Well, when I got back in the corner Danny looks at this, and he says, "Joe, don't worry about it son, everything's OK. I will make sure it will not reopen." He actually fixed it and the fight went the distance. In between rounds, between one and twelve – because it was a world title eliminator – Muhammad Ali talked to me in between the punches. He'd talk to me during the fight. "How do you feel, white boy?" he was asking me sarcastically. "You think you good enough to beat me?"

The nice thing about it was in the eighth round I clipped him with the most beautiful right hand. And I could see him shudder. I could see Muhammad Ali shudder. He looks at me and says, "Do it again, white boy!" And like a moron – I was still twenty-three – I tried again and he absolutely unloaded on me. I thought, *Oh, my God. I'll never ever do that again: listen to an opponent just because he said I hit him with a good shot.* Anyway, the fight went on to twelve rounds. I think he won it by two rounds, it was very exciting. I mean, people like Frank Sinatra, Elvis Presley, Sammy Davis Jr., those people actually were watching it and being there was just amazing. These were legends in music and everything you could think of in those days. I did not let myself down. I thought I had put up a good performance and was very happy.

Q: Can you express what your thoughts in the dressing room were before facing this legend? What was going through your head?

Joe Bugner: The major thing about going into the boxing ring is you should be ready mentally. It doesn't matter who the opponent is. The fact of the matter is that this was the greatest fighter on earth at that time. At that stage Muhammad Ali was only around thirty and he had already been a great champion and had defended his title many times. To answer your question, there I was at twenty-three years old and still wet behind the ears. I'm meeting my hero, in my opinion, who was the greatest athlete that had walked on this planet. So I was absolutely petrified! But I had something that a lot of fighters did not have, and that is I was able to switch off this fear, the tremendous anxiety where your adrenaline is pumping a hundred miles an hour and sucks your strength. I was able to switch this off.

I spoke to my manager, Andy Smith, at the time. I said, "Look, I need to be left alone at least five or ten minutes before going into the ring, so I can just go into myself and concentrate on the job ahead." I used to love to just virtually stand still and go into myself and knock away this adrenaline. Because I've seen fighters actually shit themselves or piss themselves. I've seen them go to toilet seven or eight times before they go into the ring because of this adrenaline, the nervous energy that's trying to make them do all sorts of things. I was able to switch this off about ten minutes before entering the ring. What was fantastic was, when I entered the ring it was almost like a daze. I was watching Muhammad Ali the great athlete, but to me he was just another person by then.

Q: At one point, Muhammad Ali declared you were capable of being a world champion.
Joe Bugner: This particular time when I fought him, he was absolutely determined to put on a great performance. This was the second stage of his career after the American government took away his license. He wanted to show the world that he had smashed everybody before me, and that he was ready to come back and regain and retain his world title. I don't think he was very happy with his performance because he had realized the guy who was standing in front of him had potential. One thing I credit myself to is: I was never a moron when I went into that ring. I never went in there with my head down and just threw punches. When I went in there, I typically worked on instinct. Now, what that means is I could go in there and practice certain combinations, practice the left jab and practice the right cross and I'd work it out. With Ali, you couldn't do that because Ali was one of the greatest pre-thinkers of fighters I'd ever been in the ring with. He would work you out so quickly, it's not even funny.

But then I thought to myself, *I'm not going to let him dominate me or let him do his own thing. If I do then I'm going to end up like Henry Cooper, getting smashed.* You know, it's amazing that Cooper fought Ali twice, and he got smashed twice. And people say, "Yeah, only because he got cut." And I say to these morons, "The only bloody reason Cooper got cut is because the idiot got hit." If you don't get hit, you don't get cut. And they say, "Well, yeah, well..." I say, "What are you talking about? What did he have that was brutal?" Everybody today has the same problem in that if they take a punch to the head they're going to get cut, especially if it's more than one or two times. I say Cooper never had a good defense; he just took punches to the head and that's why they call him the 'Bleeder'.

He was very similar to Chuck Wepner, the guy who fought Liston and Ali. I mean, I smashed Chuck Wepner because he allowed me to hit him. Ali hit Cooper so many times it wasn't even funny. And they say, "Well, Henry could've done better because he cut, didn't he!" I say, "Yeah, it's because he got bloody hit." I'm not exactly a great fan of some of the journalists who wrote stories about that era.

Q: You challenged Muhammad Ali for the world championship in July 1975. The fight took place in Kuala Lumpur, Malaysia. Can you shed some light on the atmosphere when you arrived in Kuala Lumpur?

Joe Bugner: It's amazing – after fighting Muhammad for the world title eliminator, I continued on retaining and winning all the fights that they put to me, eventually having a clash with Muhammad Ali. I retained my European and Commonwealth heavyweight title. Anyway, what a fantastic showdown this was, between Bugner and Ali in a neutral place. I was only twenty-five then and Muhammad was thirty-two. I was in my prime and Muhammad Ali was absolutely in his prime. So when the fight was negotiated and everything was sorted out, I flew across to Malaysia not knowing what to face and not knowing what to expect. It's a neutral country, it's one of these Muslim countries and Muslims run it, with a lot of Chinese people living there.

So, there I was in a country that was run by Muslims and Muhammad Ali was almost a god to them. So when I arrived in Malaysia, I did have a lot of press because I arrived three weeks before Ali did. Because I wanted to acclimatize to the weather, which was continuously over the 100 percent humidity – it was horrible. I went through the period where I was very ill for the first ten to fourteen days. I had diarrhea. I had all the problems that 90 percent of the people coming from other countries of the world would suffer. So, anyway, I got myself in a position that in the third week I was absolutely ready because I'd gone through that period of getting used to the water, the food and the climate and the heat. I took with me two sparring partners, which was fantastic because, I mean, without them I would have been absolutely lost. I had a young fellow from Manchester, he came along and I had this other kid from Norway – I can't remember his name. So these two boys came along and they sparred with me continuously, and we were averaging about eight to ten rounds a day.

What had happened was people in Malaysia were very, very nice, but then you had the radical side, who obviously didn't want Muhammad Ali to lose. So they tried to give me a hard time. And eventually a week before the fight, there was a phone call made to the police by someone expressing that this is a disgrace because there's a Christian fighting a Muslim and it's wrong. Saying, "We are in a position now that we have to take action against this fight because this fight should not take place." There was really a lot of nonsense, but it had to be taken seriously. Then the police chief came to the hotel where we were staying, and said we're going to shut this hotel down and we're going to put soldiers on each floor. I think it was a twelve-floor hotel.

Every floor had police with machine guns. I'm thinking, "This is absolutely absurd. Here I am, I'm challenging Muhammad Ali for the greatest title in the world and these bloody people are trying to threaten me and are getting the word out." You won't believe this, but three days before that the Green Berets were brought in and they took over the hotel. They overtook everything. I actually went down to the fight in the back of a bulletproof vehicle. I couldn't believe it. Anyway, the press conference is done, everything is done and we get these bloody radical guys, whoever they were, talking to people saying, "If Joe Bugner wins this fight he will not leave the ring alive." The Malaysian people themselves are absolutely fabulous – they really are. But the fanatics, on the other hand, are absolute morons. I mean, what on earth am I going to do whether I beat or don't beat Muhammad Ali to upset their rights?

I mean, I don't want to be upsetting them. This is a sporting event.

It's nothing to do with Muslims or Christians. And the Chinese, you won't believe, who were actually there were all fantastic as well because they were all on my side. I had no idea why because I didn't even know what religion the Chinese people had. So here I was protected in some ways by the Chinese fraternity, who I imagine were Christians, or whatever they call themselves. I was ignorant to all this, I was twenty-five. I was a young kid with ambitions and dreams.

Anyway, the fight goes on at ten a.m. in the morning so we can pick up the satellite circuit to feed back to America and the United Kingdom. So the whole of America and Britain can watch it in theaters. I think in England there were about 1,500 cinemas who actually put the fight on, it was chock-a-block. I was told this afterwards. And in America it was a huge hit. So, the fight takes place at ten in the morning. There's two or three hundred Green Beret Marines inside the stadium, it was an open stadium. I thought, *Jesus, this is an open stadium and there's people with machine guns. If somebody dropped a cracker which goes bang, it would be an absolute slaughter.*

I honestly think the fight was much, much closer than what they all made it out to be. And the fact of the matter is, when the fight ended after the fifteenth round, I was told that I didn't try hard enough. I didn't do this and I didn't do that. But you know what, I think to myself, *Hang on a minute, if I didn't try hard enough, I went fifteen rounds with the greatest fighter on the planet. How bad is he? Why didn't Muhammad Ali knock me out? Why didn't he stop me? Why didn't he cut me up? Because I was just too bloody good!* And you know what, it's amazing the reality is the British press slaughtered me because I was able to outsmart Ali at Ali's game. His game was to make sure you don't get hit, when you don't have to get hit.

The fact the fight went the full distance, they said, "Well, Joe Bugner never tried." Well, hang on, if I tried and made the mistakes I'd have been knocked stupid. One thing about Muhammad Ali was he was able to smash people up who were thick, thick from the neck up. And one thing I never allowed him to do is to outsmart me. So he may have beaten me in speed. He may have outsmarted me in some moves, but I'd take credit for being not smashed by a bloke who was brilliant at smashing morons. And there are a lot of morons that Ali smashed. I don't have to go into that.

Q: The fight was a defensive fight, were you both being cautious?
Joe Bugner: What's incredible is Muhammad Ali was one of the most intelligent people on the planet. When he came into boxing, he was so clever he worked his jabs and he tried to suck you in. He tried to pull you into his right cross. One thing I give myself a lot of credit for is not falling for this. I remembered him fighting people like Liston. I remembered him fighting Cooper, Jerry Quarry, all these great fighters. He knocked them out, 90 percent of the time using the big right hand, although his left jab was the tamer. In other words, it looks like a lion tamer. A lion tamer doesn't beat his lions; he just sticks them. You stick a chair in front of the lion, the lion backs up. Muhammad Ali was the same with the lead jab. He just constantly went bang, bang, bang, bang, and out of nowhere he would come out with this incredible sharp right cross that would stop them in their tracks.

And I have studied him and every time he threw that beautiful left jab, I would back off, so his right hand couldn't work. None of the idiots who write about it could see that because they were so mesmerized by Ali. They said, "Why isn't Bugner going in there and getting smashed up? Why isn't he going in there and getting knocked out?" Because I was cautious! I will never be forgiven for this by the media because these bastards destroyed me. I had to leave England in 1975 and move to America because I couldn't stand the morons who write for the press. They are the most horrible people – I'm talking about the writers. I'm talking about the newspapers. On the other hand, *The Boxing News*, as I know it and I remember it, was pretty fair 90 percent of the time.

One thing I will never ever forgive the press for is when I won the world title way back in 1998, when I was forty-eight years old, I got smashed for that because I TKO'd James Bonecrusher Smith in the first round. I hit him so hard I missed his chin by a quarter of an inch. I hit him in the shoulder and his shoulder just flew out of its socket. Immediately he was screaming with pain. I was looking at this bloke thinking, *What on earth has happened here?* The bloke's shoulder had literally fallen out of the body. The referee looked at it, pulled him to the corner, called the doctor in and they tried to put the shoulder back in. But there was as much chance as me flying to the moon. I mean, this guy, James Bonecrusher Smith, I beat him for the title, but I never got one ounce of credit for that, not one ounce of credit from the press in England!

Q: After the Muhammad Ali fight ended, were you in fear of the fanatics?

Joe Bugner: Yes. After my fight in Kuala Lumpur I was literally put back in this armored vehicle and went back to the hotel. Until we actually left the country, I had these armed soldiers who actually took us to the airport and out on the airplane, and everything was fine. I think the worst part about it is that unfortunately when it went public, this was a possibility it could happen, it triggers off all sorts of interest with all sorts of lunatics that are in the world. So they were very worried that this problem may appear in some other areas, some other athletic fields and so on. So when I actually got on the plane with my manager and my sparring partners, it was a relief for me now. I mean, as far as Malaysia was concerned, beautiful country, love the people, but sadly the fanatics are everywhere.

And I just happened to be in Ireland fighting when I was fighting under the Muhammad Ali–Alvin Lewis card for the world contention back in 1972. Just before I fought Ali in '73, I was fighting some young fellow from America, some Irish-American. And the IRA threatened to shoot me there as well. I mean, this was bloody pathetic. A bloke actually got through to my suite on the phone, and he said, "Joe Bugner, you better leave the country because if you don't you're going to pay the consequences." I said, "What's the matter with you lot? I'm fighting. I'm European champion." He said, "No! You are recognized in Britain as one of the most famous athletes." I said, "What's that got to do with me?" I was trying to sort of get out of it. I said to him I'm not even English – I'm Hungarian. He said stop this, as far as we're concerned you are the most famous person in Britain as a fighter. I said this world has become stupid.

Anyway, the threats were real. Again, I had to go on British Airways. This was way back in 1972. After the fight was done in Dublin I had to get in this wagon, slip down into the airport and get straight onto the plane with my boxing clothes on. I had to leave my boxing gear on and I actually got changed on the airplane when we took off. I mean, this incident didn't happen in Malaysia because I had a couple of hundred bloody Green Berets with machine guns looking after me. But it's still concerning because some people say that's why Joe never won. That's not the reason because I smashed the bloke in Dublin. I knocked him out in the sixth round. So it wasn't that, it's just a matter that there could be that one loose cannon out there who could maybe get to you and actually do the harm. So, yes, in simple English: I was very concerned. You just never know.

When you're in the public eye like Ali, I'm not sure but Muhammad may have had plenty of idiots who wanted to shoot him or kill him or whatever. He would either cover it, or won't talk about it or just walk away from it. But in those days the IRA were very active in Ireland. And I think the fanatics in Malaysia, who were Muhammad Ali fans, were just as active because they didn't want their idol to lose to any white bloke who's not a Muslim.

Q: It has been said that it was hard to sell the fight because everyone thought you had no chance of beating Muhammad Ali. He was considered by far the more technical out of the two of you. Is it true Muhammad Ali's people came up with an idea for him to make an announcement that this was going to be his last fight and he agreed to play along with it?
Joe Bugner: This is news to me. It was one of the biggest money spinners Britain had ever seen. Let me tell you something: 1,500 theaters around England bought the fight. Let's say 700 to 1,000

people in each cinema, over a million people [paying fans] watched me fight Ali in Britain alone. If that wasn't a seller, I don't know what is. This is a fact. Morons who say such a thing were people who obviously had money on the wrong person. They would've put money on Ali to say Ali was going to stop Bugner. But they tried it with the first fight in 1973. They said Bugner has no chance.

Do you know how many bloody airplanes flew to Las Vegas? It was incredible. A large percentage of the people were bloody Brits. And when I was able to stick with the best in the world they all got bloody disappointed – I'm talking about the press. And like I said, then I came back in '75, which is two years later, and I fight for the world heavyweight title. As I said to you, 150,000 people watched the fight in cinemas throughout the United Kingdom. If that isn't a seller then I must be a moron because I've never seen a fight anywhere in the world – in one country only – that have 150,000 viewers for one fight in 1975.

I can go to America and I'm very well recognized. And the major thing about it is any restaurant I go into people stop me and ask, "How you doing, Champ?" This is a recognition thing throughout America because they love their sporting heroes. And you know what, Frank Sinatra was one of my biggest heroes. I went to see him in 1981 just before the Larry Holmes fight in Las Vegas. Frank Sinatra turned to his own people in the audience, and he said, "Ladies and gentlemen, I want to introduce you to one of the greatest fighters from England. He's a dear friend of mine. His name is Joe Bugner. I'm going to dedicate this whole evening to him and his beautiful wife Marlene." Now, if I wasn't well known, what great superstar like Sinatra would stop his show and introduce me to his fans in Caesars Palace? I mean, it blows me away. There's petty jealousy and all this nonsense that goes on in England.

Q: What's the deepest and most edifying conversation you ever had with Muhammad Ali?
Joe Bugner: Muhammad Ali and I were flying from Los Angeles to Miami. We were doing a press conference and he wanted to

announce something. I was sat right next to him and he was talking away. I just turned to him and I said, "Muhammad, I'm still besotted with you because I think you have such incredible attitude and incredible thinking power when it comes to boxing." He said, "Listen to me, Joe Bugner, I am so frightened before I go into that ring. The only way I can release my fear is by calling these fighters names. Back then I used to call you 'white boy' this and 'white boy' that. I have to do this because that way I can hide my fear. I know what it's like to go into the boxing ring to fight someone who's on my fitness and my strength and my power level. If I destroy them before I go into that ring, I'm three quarters of the way there." He continued, "I go into the ring with fear that I won't be able to produce what I promised I could."

And I listened to this man who was so intelligent in his thinking. He never said he was fearless. Not once did he turn to the media and said I'm fearless, that he can go out there and do this and that. No, he didn't. The courageous thing I noticed about Muhammad Ali was when I was in his company on many, many occasions, that in private he was absolutely down to earth. He was just another human being who lived life to the full. As soon as a media bloke arrived or turned up out of the blue, he would turn to me and start shouting, "Why did you call me a nigger, white boy?" I'm saying, "Muhammad, we're having lunch."

That's what he would do: he'd put on a front. If you can understand, Muhammad Ali was not shy about being a bloody racist. And he certainly wasn't shy about opening his mouth and accusing you of saying things you never even dreamt of. But Ali was that way because he wanted to make sure he was the man in control. As I said, in private he was an absolute bloody gentleman. I had a beautiful house in Beverly Hills which I bought in 1976, and then he bought a beautiful house in Hancock Park, which is the next little suburb. We're talking about a hundred meters apart.

He would come to my place and I would go to his. I said to Muhammad on many occasions, "Muhammad, why do you allow any Tom, Dick and Harry to come into your house?" He said, "If they need money, I give it to them. If I don't have money, I can't give it to them. I don't need money. I don't need anything. I am what I am. I don't like this business about I'm better than the next man." He said, "In the ring, yes because that's how I make my living. If people come to my door and they need a hundred dollars I give it to them." And that to me just answered one question: he never ever was the arrogant person that the media saw because behind the scenes he as a genuine, fantastic and beautiful bloke. Absolutely.

Q: It's interesting you lived near him at one time!
Joe Bugner: I lived in America in Beverly Hills for ten years, that's where I met my beautiful wife Marlene. She was working for the magnate Rupert Murdoch. I met her in America. My kids went to school there – Beverly Hills High, which is one of the upper schools in Beverly Hills because all the celebs send their kids there. My son went to school with Laila. This is back in the '70s. Occasionally, I would go to Ali's house, but not regularly because I never was a good mixer. I don't like going to other people's places. I'm very private in that way. My wife and I have lived our own life. We don't have to depend on anybody.

Q: Did you attend any celebrity parties?
Joe Bugner: No. Oh, God, no. That's for wankers. I turned professional at seventeen. I was in the *Guinness Book of Records* at the age of fourteen. I threw a discuss 64.5 meters, that's something which is burnt into my memory so I will never forget it. I became a professional fighter at the age of seventeen, the youngest ever. I was the oldest ever to retire at forty-nine. Undefeated in Australia.

My career has been very successful and more up than down. The beauty about it is although I have been in the company of Muhammad Ali since 1969, that's when we first met physically, one of the last times I saw Muhammad personally was in 2000 at the Olympic Games. I flew to Sydney because I was working for Channel Seven for the Olympic Games. Muhammad and I spent three days together. I saw him in his hotel suite because I was actually staying at the same hotel because I was doing the commentary for Channel Seven, which is one of Australia's television companies.

So one of my last physical visual things with Muhammad was at the Olympic Games 2000 in Sydney. The lights pop out in the stadium, everything is pitch black and everybody is thinking, *Oh, my God, what's happening? Is it a power break?* And suddenly this beam of light comes on and they focus the beam on Muhammad Ali coming into the stadium. As he comes in the whole place just roared with applause. I mean, it just kept on and on and he's waving to people very, very slowly because he's got Parkinson's. I'm sitting on ringside with my earpiece and he looks across to the ring and he sees me. I could see that beautiful cheeky smile of his. The two young ladies that are leading him in lead him up to the boxing ring. As he came up to me, I put my arms around him and gave him a big hug and a kiss on the cheek. You know what he says to me? This was no more than thirty seconds. He says, "Joe Bugner, how many children do you have?" I thought that's a strange question. I said, "Five. How many do you have, Muhammad?" He said, "Well, I have nine. Beat you again."

Here is a dear man who has got a serious physical problem, but he is able to still have a joke with one of his friends without any worry of upsetting me. You know what was incredible? He looked in my eye, there were no tears or anything, he says to me, "Joe Bugner, if you ever utter the words 'I feel sorry for Ali' or you tell me 'I feel sorry how you turned out', I will never be your friend again." I looked up to him and said, "Muhammad, how can I feel sorry for you, you beat me twice!" He pulled on a beautiful smile on his face, and he said, "Look, OK. We'll leave it at that." He and I stayed in touch. He wrote me a fabulous letter once. I think Lonnie, his beautiful wife, wrote me a letter with Ali's signature just thanking me for all the friendship.

Anyway, for me, remembering Ali as the great athlete is beyond explaining because you can't. People often say what a magical moment! This was magical for me because as I said, I met him in

'69. To me, I remember him as the dancing King of the Ring. I mean, he was able to dance for fifteen rounds. At the end of the day, after the fight when it was over, if you took annoyance or were upset because he beat you then you're the fool. Because he would be your friend forever. When we first met I said to Muhammad, "I have the greatest respect for you, you know why? Very few people can beat me." He said, "I know. I know. I've told these people you're going to be champion one day." The only problem was when he made that comment, thirty years down the road it happened.

Q: In Sydney did you get time to socialize?
Joe Bugner: I was with Ali for three days because he was staying at a hotel in Sydney and I was staying in a hotel. He and I would catch up on a daily basis. He did come to the fights, I think, on one occasion only. But I kept going back to his hotel because his manager or coach, or whoever he was, rang me asking if I wanted to come up. I said absolutely. So I would have dinner with him and we would talk. I have some very, very precious photographs of him and I together in his suite with his arms around me and my arms around him. These are the moments you can't ever replace because sadly the man was not what he used to be.

But my memories of him are going to be forever printed in my mind because, again, what's incredible is that he comes from an extended family of many kids, but he's the only one who ever achieved great success. His children never did. Laila tried boxing but you can't walk in your father's shadow. Laila is a beautiful girl and thank God she's happily married now with beautiful kids. But what I'm just saying is that Ali will go down, eventually, in my opinion in history as Hercules. That was one of the imaginary heroes but this [Ali] one's a real one. He was just awesome. All you have to do is just look at some of the great fights on film.

RON LYLE

The late Ron Lyle, born in Ohio, learned to box in prison after being convicted of second-degree murder and sentenced to fifteen to twenty-five years. After being stabbed by another inmate and embarking on a calisthenics regime in solitary confinement, he fought twenty-five unrecorded bouts while still behind bars before coming out of prison to become one of heavyweight boxing's most feared punchers in the early 1970s. Lyle turned professional at the age of thirty and faced Ali in 1975, in Ali's second title defense in his second reign as champion.

Q: You fought Muhammad Ali on May 16, 1975, which was Muhammad Ali's second title defense in his second reign as champion. How did this fight come about?
Ron Lyle: Well, I worked my way up the ladder and when I got there I fought Jerry Quarry, Larry Middleton and I fought Vicente Rondon. I fought them all. So I was in line for a title shot and Ali gave me the shot.

Q: Were you aware of his strengths and weaknesses?
Ron Lyle: Ali was pretty much an all-around good fighter. He was a good boxer, very scientific. He had all the skills and the knowledge of the game. When he came back from the Olympics, a guy named Sugar Ray Robinson took him to the side and raised his full skills and a lot of knowledge of the game. And he executed them very well.

Q: Was there any verbal banter at the press conference, and what was the state of your mind before entering the ring?
Ron Lyle: Me and Ali, we never really went through that thing. We pretty much respected each other. Ali was a good athlete; I wasn't a bad athlete. I played all sports so I had a good sense and concept. So boxing came pretty easy. At that time, it was the most important

fight in my life. It was the biggest fight of my life, biggest fight in my career at that point. So my trainers told me to do good, stay in control of him and keep things at my reach. And I pretty much did that throughout the fight. So, I was pretty much pleased at the way I fought. I wasn't pleased with the outcome, but that's the way it goes. That's the way life goes, so you have to move on.

Q: Did your corner give you any specific instructions and was your strategy to be cautious?

Ron Lyle: No, not to be cautious. A fighter can't be cautious, a fighter has to either put it on the line or know his craft. He has to accept . . . I understood Ali was a great boxer, counter-puncher and had all the tools in the game. So I already knew to just go ahead. My thing was to see if I could get in control of him and keep him at bay and keep him at my distance as opposed to his distance. He was in my distance but I was out of his range. They [my corner] told me to keep him in my range and stay out of his, and keep him in front and don't let him get on the side of me. And when you get on the ropes be prepared to defend yourself and come off, don't hit the ropes later. I was never a rope fighter anyway, but I could fight off the ropes. But I kind of like to stay in the center of the ring, which is not on the ropes but not off the ropes.

Q: Please can you talk me through your training and your camp when preparing for this fight?

Ron Lyle: Typically, they brought in a lot of people who they thought could help me with my offense and my defense, as well as my conditioning. So I had a lot of good sparring partners and we worked on things, which we thought Ali would be doing, and my sparring partners would imitate him. Some did a good job. So they prepared me very well.

Q: How big was boxing and Muhammad Ali at the time, and did the fight receive good coverage?

Ron Lyle: No matter who he's fighting or where he goes, they follow him. So it's like Ali don't have to go to the mountain but the mountain came to Ali. So the press followed him, wherever he went the press followed him. They did a good a job.

Q: What was the culmination of the fight?
Ron Lyle: Again, it was a good fight but I thought I had control pretty much the whole way until I got caught with a right hand. I went to the corner and the referee stopped it. But up till that point, I think I was pretty much in control of everything.

Q: After Muhammad Ali threw a right hand he followed up with a flurry of punches and the referee stopped the fight. You were not happy with the stoppage. What were your feelings?
Ron Lyle: I couldn't believe it. I couldn't believe it. There again, that's life, that's the way life goes. It don't always end the way you want it, but it ends and you just have to accept it – accept what it is and move on.

Q: Did you protest to the referee? He wasn't going to change his decision, was he?
Ron Lyle: No. I mean, that's the way it is because once they make the decision that's it. No matter what I say or how I say it, it is what it is and that's the way it is. You either accept it, you've got to move on, you can't live on the past.

Q: After the fight Muhammad Ali said to a commentator you are a scientific and a good fighter. You said to the commentator that the fight should not have been stopped. What was the public's reaction?
Ron Lyle: We didn't talk too much after the fight. I think we acknowledged each other's skills. We respected each other as people. I think he acknowledged me as a good person. I think the most important thing today is that he got to know me and I got to know him. I respect him for what he's done for the game. I'm a fighter, too, and there's a sense of respect with both of us. Those are

the words which can't be expressed – it's between the two people. I think the public respected what I did and I think he appreciated my efforts. I think they saw my ability and what I was capable of doing. I think it's all necessary because the decision to win, a win or a loss, a lot of times people who are around the ring, the boxers are involved, so it's a matter of opinion and we all have it. Sometimes we see it our way, sometimes we see it their way. For me, to have the opportunity to fight one of the greatest fighters in the history of the game, so in order to compete in that class of those fighters, I feel pretty good right now.

Q: Your coach or cornerman wasn't too happy, did they believe there was something more to it?
Ron Lyle: I don't know. I had a very professional corner, we didn't like the decision but we accepted the decision. Because the people that made the decision control the game. So it's really not much you can do anything about that, but we conducted ourselves very well. Quite soon my corner felt we weren't happy about the decision, but that's the way it goes and we have to move on.

Q: Muhammad Ali was a defensive and gifted fighter and was extremely fast, did he surprise you?
Ron Lyle: Ali had very fast hands and I was very fast. I actually played all sports from football, baseball and basketball, so I was a good athlete as well. It was down to skills, really. That's what it falls down to.

Q: Did you meet or talk to him after the fight?
Ron Lyle: I used to see him all the time. Sometimes when I go to the Hall of Fame or go to Vegas they have a party. One time, it was on I think his fiftieth birthday party in Vegas at the MGM Grand. I went to that. Boxers got together and talked about how they fought and say some comical things, typical gathering of all ex-fighters – all in fun.

Q: Did it make you a better person after coming out of prison?
Ron Lyle: I would say it did. Before I was young and, you know, young people make mistakes. Young people are usually influenced and I was no different. I made mistakes then. Again, recovering back after the mistakes is harder than the mistake itself because you're constantly battling against the odds up the hill. And if you make it, it's because out of the presence of God you do make it. You understand?

Q: If you had won the fight with Muhammad Ali would that have been the highlight of your career?
Ron Lyle: When you are a fighter, win, lose or draw, that's the battle right there because even to get in there, it takes levels. You have to pick yourself up so it takes a lot of energy just to get in there, not to win but just get in there. And to win or lose, that says a lot about the fighters. If you win you're courageous. If you don't, and lose, that means you've missed the mark and it's tough. I gave it my all. I didn't hold back. I put it all on the line. Win, lose or draw, I am satisfied with how my career turned out. I have no qualms at all on how my career turned out. I'm very pleased and happy and I met a lot of people. I'm living a good life.

CHUCK WEPNER

When Chuck Wepner fought Muhammad Ali, no one knew the bout would go on to influence a then unknown Sylvester Stallone, who would create Rocky, the story of an underdog who goes the distance against a brash, big-mouthed champion. Wepner turned professional in 1964 and went on to have a total of fifty-one fights. After going fifteen hard rounds with the greatest boxer of all time, Wepner was catapulted to fame, and was the subject of the 2019 film *The Brawler*.

Q: Chuck, when did you started to pursue boxing?
Chuck Wepner: I really started when I was about eight or nine years old. We used to have little amateur bouts as little kids, which used to be three one-minute rounds. I did a little bit of that when I was a kid because P.A.L's [Police Athletic League] owner was on 23rd Street and I was on 28th Street. So, my mother raised my brother and me. We didn't have a lot of money, so what they did was they gave you membership to waive the P.A.L from the city. So I went three times as a nine-year-old, then I stopped. And I really didn't start boxing again until I was in the Marine Corps. I was eighteen years old and I was playing basketball for the Marines team. I was a pretty good basketball player. I was scoring a lot of points and they asked me to play with the base team – the big team. I was good enough to be a local player, a local star, but I wasn't good enough to play with these guys in the Marine Corps. I mean, they had All-Americans in that team. So I didn't make that team.

But I met a guy there at the athletic program and he asked me if I had ever done any boxing, because I had a fight at Fort Bragg. He said, "Have you ever considered boxing?" And I said, "I used to do a little bit of boxing when I was a kid." Anyway, I went out for the team and I won the heavyweight championship at North Carolina. I had three bouts. I won two by knockouts and one by decision. They were just 'smokers' – they called them 'smokers'. They were inter-platoon bouts, like one platoon against the other. Then I stopped boxing. I had only three bouts and that was all within two months. I got discharged in 1959. I came home and I started working in a couple of clubs as a bouncer. The coach at the P.A.L was a guy named Joe who saw me one day and came into the club. It was actually a Go-Go club, the only Go-Go club the town had. He said, "I heard you had a fight with Tommy Mullin," who was one of the top guys. Anyway, I beat him up pretty good. He said, "I heard your hands are pretty good. We've got a boxing team and we have no heavyweight. We have the smaller guys but no heavyweights. Would you like to come down and try out for the Golden Gloves team? We're going into the New York Golden Gloves."

Right now they have Jersey Golden Gloves, which is nothing like... the New York Golden Gloves is the whole East Coast's big one. And to be honest with you, I'm a fairly tough guy, and I'd never done any real serious boxing, but he said, "I want you to come down and we'll see what you've got." I went down and trained for about two-and-a-half months. There was another assistant coach named Ralph, who really didn't think too much about my style. I wasn't really known as a classic boxer. I was more like a brawler. Joe wanted to put me in the Golden Gloves in New York, but Ralph said I don't think he's ready. Anyway, I said to them, "Look, I'm twenty-five years old now. Let me go in." So they changed their minds and they put me in there in 1965. I won five straight fights, two by knockouts, three by decision. I wanted them to put me in the New York Heavyweight Golden Gloves championships. And I wanted to fight another guy who won the Youth championships that year. I beat him, a guy named Burt Whitehurst.

Anyway, I won a couple of championships in the amateurs and then they turned me pro. They asked, "What do you want to do?" I said I wanted to turn pro and see if I could make some money, never dreaming that someday I'd be fighting for the heavyweight championship of the world. So I turned pro in 1965. And I was undefeated until I fought Sonny Liston in the armory. Sonny Liston was a former heavyweight champion of the world. He had just come out of two loses to Muhammad Ali. He lost the title to him in the first fight and he was knocked out in the first round in the other one in Lewiston in Maine. Anyway, we thought it would be a shortcut to the big time to the rankings because Liston was ranked two or three in the world, and him being a former champion. We fought in the armory in New Jersey City. I don't know, I guess I just wasn't ready for him.

In the first five or six rounds, I was in the fight and he started to cut me up, closed both of my eyes and broke my nose. I had to have seventy-two stitches, but I went ten rounds with him. They stopped it with a minute and twenty-one seconds to go in the tenth round on cuts. But that's where I got the name 'The Bayonne Bleeder'. A guy named Rosie Rosenberg, who was the editor of the *Bayonne Times*, a local paper here in Bayonne, was sitting ringside. Every time Liston hit me, I was pretty bloodied. So I was spraying blood all over the place and it got all over Rosie. He said, "Jesus, they ought to call this guy 'The Bayonne Bleeder'. The headline the next day was: THE BAYONNE BLEEDER GETS STOPPED BY LISTON IN THE TENTH ROUND.

Q: OK, how did the memorable fight with Muhammad Ali come to fruition?
Chuck Wepner: At that time, I was ranked seventh in the world. I was in the top ten in the world. I was in an eight-bout winning streak, and my manager Al Braverman, who had known Don King many years before in Las Vegas, had been around a long time. King was an up and coming guy then. Ali had just come off that tough fight with Foreman where he knocked him out in the eighth round. They were toying with the idea trying to get me a shot against Foreman, who was the champion of the world at that time before he lost to Ali. Don King, who was a promoter, started to promote me. He said, "I'm going to send you out to Salt Lake City, Utah, to fight a guy called Terry Hinke," who was a big, big puncher who nobody wanted to fight.

Anyway, he sent me out to Salt Lake City. A couple of years earlier I had won the North American championship by winning Ernie Terrell in Atlantic City, who was a former WBC heavyweight champion of the world. For that fight Rosie Rosenberg was the promoter. That fight was going to be for a new title called the National American Heavyweight Championship of the world. It was going to be for two titles – Ernie for the North American Championship, and my new title, which they were going to introduce. Now they've got all these titles, but back then there were only two or three. I beat Terrell in a twelve-round decision but they protested the decision. The commissioner at the time, Althea Gibson, who was a tennis pro, if you could believe it, knew nothing at all about boxing holds up the recognition of the world title. They were going to present it to me in the ring after the fight if I won it. I won it. Anyway, she held it up and never recognized the world title, but she did recognize the North American title because Terrell had it and I beat him.

So to make a long story short, I was in the top ten in the world at the time. And a couple of years later, Ali fights Foreman and everybody figures that Foreman's going to knock Ali out because Foreman was unbeatable of sort because he was knocking everybody out. Don King said to me if you take that fight with Hinke in Salt Lake City and you win it, I'll try to get you a shot at Foreman for the title. I went out to Salt Lake City and I stopped him in the eleventh round. I retained the North American championship and I was supposed to get a shot at Foreman. Three weeks later, Foreman fights Ali in Zaire and Ali upsets Foreman and knocks him out.

To make a long story short, Don King says to me, "I promised you a shot. You're going to be fighting Ali someday." I was like, *Yeah, sure*. I didn't believe it. Three months and a day later, I was sitting at home and watching television, a program called *Kojak* starring Telly Savalas. I had met Telly a couple of years earlier and we became friends. The phone rang. It's my mother. I said to her, "I thought I told you never to call me during *Kojak*." I love *Kojak*! I said, "Look, Mom, I don't even answer the phone when Telly is on. What is it? What is it?" She said, "Oh, my God, you've got to get the paper. The whole back page in the news tonight says: Ali is defending against Wepner March 24 in Richfield, Ohio."

I couldn't believe it. Don King had been out in Cleveland with Ali at the Hall of Fame and brought up the proposed fight between us. He said to Ali, "Look, you had a tough fight with Foreman. This guy Wepner is a pretty tough guy but he cuts easy, you'll probably cut him up and it will be an easy fight." Ali said, "OK. I'll take the fight." So Don King, as smart as he is – and he's very smart – broke it right away with AP and UPI all over the world and it made the paper that night. I ran up where there was a place where they sold newspapers. I ran up there and I got to the guy who was just closing up. He had four copies of the *Daily News* left. The whole back page had a picture of me and Ali with the headline. The rest is history. I got the shot and I got to go away to the camp. That's the only fight I ever trained for full-time in my life because I was just a part-time fighter, really. I used to run in the morning and work during the day and train at night. I went fifteen rounds, had him down, and Stallone saw the fight and made the movie *Rocky*. And the rest is history.

Q: Into the fight, what was going through your mind in the dressing room before facing the legend?

Chuck Wepner: First of all, like I said, Don King sent me up to the camp. A lot of people say things about Don King, but I'll tell you what, he never took anything off me. He paid everything up front and never tried to rip me off. We had a contract. He kept to that 100 percent. He even helped some of my sparring partners, one who had to leave early because his wife was very sick. He sent me up to the Granite Hotel in upstate New York and I trained seven weeks there. I got in the best shape of my life because all I had to do was train and not worry about work or anything else. I was ready for the fight. I was sitting in the dressing room and I couldn't wait. I was a little nervous, but I was never nervous in a fight about getting beat. I knew I wasn't a great fighter; I just knew I was always in great shape and a tough guy. I was more nervous about maybe not looking good. I mean, let's face it, this was Muhammad Ali. It was against the greatest fighter and heavyweight that ever lived. I knew I would be on national television and all over the world, and

I didn't want to look bad. I wanted to go out there and give 100 percent, which I intended to do. I wanted to be proud of what I did there. And if I went for fifteen rounds I definitely would.

One quick story, actually a couple of quick stories. The night before the championship fight, I bought my wife Phyllis a powder-blue negligee. I was confident. I was on a nine-bout winning streak. And I bought the negligee and I gave it to her in Cleveland the night before the fight. I said, "Tomorrow night I want you to wear this in bed because tomorrow night you're going to be sleeping with the heavyweight champion of the world." She said, "OK, no problem." After the fight I came back to the hotel – I lost the fight – and walked into the hotel room. And there she is sitting on the end of the bed with the powder-blue negligee, and she says to me, "Am I going to Ali's room or is he coming to mine?" She had a real good sense of humor.

Back to the fight. When I dropped Ali, believe it or not, I was just warming up. I couldn't believe the tremendous shape I was in from doing the training. It was a great punch. Ali pulled away from the jab. I hit a right hand and hit him under the heart and he went down. I went back to my corner and said to my manager Al Braverman, "Stop the car we're going to the bank." He said, "Chuck, you better turn around, Ali's getting up and he looks pissed off." I thought, *Oh*. He really turned it up after that. Bundini Brown started to scream at him at the end of the round, "What the hell is wrong with you!? This guy's kicking your ass! You're lazy, get out there!" For the next six rounds he did turn it and it became a much harder fight than the first nine rounds. For the first nine rounds he was doing a lot of rope-a-dope, dancing, punching and tapping. With Ali, I knew that I would have to knock him out or beat him so decisively in order to get the win. So I kept the pressure on. Because I was in great shape, it paid off.

The only time I was tired was going into the fifteenth round. At the end of the fourteenth round I came back to the corner, and I said to my corner, "Feel my legs." I started to quiver. My legs started to bother me from an hour of chasing in the ring. The punch he hit me with, he actually hit me on the shoulder, and it hit my side of the head and I went down. I remember going down, everything was clear. The referee came over and I started getting up. I got up by eight. The referee looked and waited, nineteen seconds to go, he said my eyes looked bad and he didn't want me to get hurt. I mean, I was standing looking at him in the eye. That was the only time I was ever down and stopped that way in my whole career.

Q: Before the fight a reporter had asked you if you could survive in the ring with the champion, what did you tell him?
Chuck Wepner: I said, "If I could survive the Marine Corps, I could survive Muhammad Ali." I mean, thirteen weeks in boot camp was the toughest thing I ever had to do in my life. It still is. Thirteen weeks of psychological and physical abuse. That was in 1956 when I joined the Corps. That's how it toughens you up to go to war and to be a Marine and be ready. When you go through it, everything's hard and it seems unfair. But after it's over you are proud of what you did for the thirteen weeks. And you're ready for just about anything.

Q: In the final round of the fight Muhammad Ali cut your face, was your nose broken as well?
Chuck Wepner: I'm not sure if my nose was broken, but I had serious breaks and minor breaks. My nose was bleeding, but I only took seven butterflies in the Ali fight. I took no real stitches. Al Braverman was a master with cuts, butterfly cuts, which were slight cuts. There wasn't a serious cut except for the abrasions and what he calls 'butterfly stitches'. To tell you the truth, I had a lot of fights where it was a lot worse. So, there was no problem.

Q: What were Muhammad Ali's strongest attributes, which you found exceptional, and in what way did he surprise you?
Chuck Wepner: Everything was exceptional! I was a big fan of his before the fight. The first four years, when he was twenty-five when they took four years off him for not going in the service, he lost four of his best years. He was so great in the beginning nobody could beat

him. When he came back after the four years, he wasn't the same fighter. He was so great he won back the title a couple of times.

But the thing that impressed me about Ali was his ability to take a punch. I mean, I hit him with a lot of shots up close and I pressed him. And his condition. We thought after the Foreman fight he'd take this fight lightly. And I thought I'll cut this guy up real early. We thought maybe by the tenth or eleventh round we would catch up to him because he would run out of gas, so we'll have a chance of knocking him out. But his physical condition and his ability to take a punch were two of his greatest attributes, and that might be why he was like he was after his illness, because he took punches and the rope-a-dope he did and all the shots he took. It was terrible. I saw him at the Yankee Stadium some years ago and it was terrible [his condition], but he was such a great fighter. Everything impressed me about him: his hand speed, his ability to take a punch and his conditioning.

Q: Your thoughts after the fight?
Chuck Wepner: Well, after the fight I came home. As a matter of fact, the night of the fight they had a big party for me at the Holiday Inn, which was where I was staying. I was tired, very tired. But you know what, I had over 300 people from Bayonne and surrounding areas who flew in for the fight. And I just felt I owed them and at least go downstairs and say hello. So I took a shower and got dressed, went downstairs and had this big party. I stayed about an hour because I was physically exhausted. Like I said, I went fifteen rounds, it was a lot. I stayed an hour and thanked everybody for coming and then got back to Bayonne. They had almost 300 people at New York airport who met me there.

All these years later it feels like it was just yesterday. Right now I'm probably more famous than I was then because Stallone wrote the movie about me called *Rocky*, a year after in 1976. I've done so many television and radio things. Right now they have a movie called *The Bayonne Bleeder*, which stars Liev Schreiber, who co-starred in *Wolverine I* and *II* with Hugh Jackman. He was going to be playing my part. He's done fifty-one different films and, as a matter of fact, a while ago I was over at where he was appearing on stage.

He's a serious actor and he did a play over there called *A View from the Bridge* with Scarlett Johansson. We went over and we went backstage. He must have had twenty people standing lined up outside. He said give me a couple of minutes with Chuck, and he took me right in and we sat and talked. He said he was so looking forward to doing this movie because he always wanted to do a movie of an alive person – and he loves boxing. He was just so nice to me. He's such a nice looking guy, a big guy, 6ft 2, about 250–220, very close to my weight when I fought for the title. I'm 6ft 5, he's a little shorter, but he's a great actor and a terrific guy. It was just such a nice experience just to sit there and talk to him and have him say how excited he was about doing this movie. It was my nickname when I was fighting.

Q: After the fight Muhammad Ali appeared on ABC *Worldwide of Sport*, he made comments saying referee Perez allowed you to employ roughhouse tactics. Is this true?

Chuck Wepner: You know what, that's my style. Like I said, I wasn't a great fighter; I was a tough guy who could take a real good punch and I was always in condition. For this fight I was in super condition. Tony Perez came in the dressing room before the fight. He told me about the roughhouse tactics and said he wasn't going to allow them, and if I did he was going to take points off me. But if you saw the fight, in the second round Ali punched me on the back of my neck sixteen times consecutively – in the back of the head. It was to more or less show what he said I was doing to him. But I might have landed some punches, but Ali has a habit of ducking into you when you threw a punch, pulling in and ducking in.

So some of my punches, you know what, believe me if you look at that fight closely, I threw five or six punches that were illegal in fifteen rounds. Which was nothing compared to sixteen continuous punches he hit me with behind my neck. So we were going into the fight trying to get Ali mad, trying to get him out of his game. I didn't want Ali to box me. I knew I couldn't outbox him. He was one of the greatest boxers that ever lived. I wanted him to go toe-to-toe and try to make it a brawl. That's what I was trying to do, that's my style.

Q: Can you tell me how Sylvester Stallone was inspired to make the *Rocky* movie?

Chuck Wepner: Stallone was down and out, really. He was an actor for quite a few years but he never got his big break. He just didn't get a big part or a lead part in a big movie. According to Stallone, and this is his own words, he had forty dollars to his name and he lived in a small apartment. He went to see the fight. He paid for a ticket to see the fight in Philadelphia. And he sat there and he saw the way the crowd would change from cheering for Ali to cheering for Chuck, shouting "Chuck! Chuck! Chuck!" after the knockdown. They knew I was in the fight to win. I wasn't just going in for a payday. He just got the idea, *You know what, what a great idea for a movie: a forty-to-one underdog going the distance with Ali and having him down.* So after the fight he went up to his apartment, locked himself in the apartment three straight days and wrote the entire script of *Rocky*.

Q: When did you actually meet Sylvester Stallone, did you communicate and liaise with him?

Chuck Wepner: I got a call from one of his producers telling me that he was writing a movie. It was going to be called *Rocky* and that I was the inspiration and that he'd seen the fight. He wanted me to know he was writing the movie. I went to the premier and saw *Rocky*. The tickets were mailed to me to the New York premier and I went to the premier. I was amazed. I thought it was going to be just like everybody else – it was just going to be another fight movie and poorly done because Stallone had never had a 'name' as a writer or producer. I sat in the theater that night and it was mad. It was a sell-out. There were some big celebrities there, too. It just amazed me, people were jumping up and down and screaming. The movie was such an inspirational movie. When it was over, I was sitting in my seat and people were coming up to me and shaking my hands and hugging me.

If you read all the articles, it said I had inspired the movie. It just amazed me. After that, a few months later, about five months later, I got a call from Stallone himself asking me to come over to New York and he wanted me to read for a part for *Rocky II*. I was going to play a guy named King Weather – Chuck Wepner, King Weather – one of his sparring partners. He sent me the script. I studied my part and I went over to New York and read for it. As a matter of fact, I read for it twice. He asked me to come back for a second time to see if I could do better. Between you and me, I never had any acting experience, or anything else like that. But I should have gone to somebody who did and got some coaching, but I didn't. And I was still high from the fight. I was still the high Chuck Wepner. I went fifteen rounds [with Ali] and they made *Rocky* about me. I didn't get the part but Stallone and I stayed friends for all those years. Then many years later I sued him. But you know what, we're still friends. I think Sylvester Stallone is a terrific actor and I think he's a terrific writer, and I love the guy! He made me Rocky, how can I not like the guy!

Q: Any interesting stories pertaining to Sylvester Stallone?
Chuck Wepner: I've been with Stallone five, six times since then. As a matter of fact, when *Rocky* first premiered he threw a big party down in Atlantic City at Caesars. He opened up those clubs called Planet Hollywood and he invited me down and I stayed in the next hotel, The Claridge, that weekend. I came down with about four or five couples. I brought them down, we were players – me and my wife – in those days, and we still are. We would come down at the hotels and gamble. I went to the opening of Planet Hollywood. They had 1,000 people walk in front of Caesars Palace at Planet Hollywood. When I came down the headlights hit me. They started yelling and screaming and the bouncers came out and escorted me to Planet Hollywood with Stallone, who was with his girlfriend then, who was a beautiful redhead who is a big-time model now. Anyway, he gave me a big hug, and he said to the crowd, "Hey,

guys, here is the real Rocky. The guy who inspired the movie." We were together a couple of times after that. The last time we were together was at the TV Show. I was in the audience. They were going to do a little surprise.

First, they talked to Stallone about the movie and said, "I understand Chuck Wepner inspired it." But at that time the suit was going on. Stallone said yeah, Wepner inspired it, blah blah blah, but there's a suit going on so I can't talk about it now. Anyway, the suit went through. It was a Federal Court and in a few months I won it easily. I sued Stallone and my lawyers sued Stallone because he made over two billion dollars using my name as the inspiration for the *Rocky* movies. During these movies he kept saying Chuck Wepner inspired me, Chuck Wepner this, Chuck Wepner that, and used my name without giving anything for it all those years. That's what we sued him for and we won it in the Federal Court. It was a no-brainer, really. And between you and me, I don't think Stallone really worried about it. It was settled very quickly. We resolved it between the both of us and we went on from there.

Q: What did Sylvester Stallone think of Muhammad Ali?

Chuck Wepner: He loves Muhammad Ali – everyone loves Muhammad Ali. I am so fortunate because I got to spend almost four months promoting our fight [with Ali]. Me and Ali did things together, we made appearances together. We made some appearances afterwards. And he is so funny and so sharp. He's an intelligent man even though he never had a lot of schooling. He's an intelligent man and he told some great stories. We were together five or six times. During that time face to face we made appearances together. He's just a treat to be with. I love him. I count that as one of the great things in my life being a personal friend of his. Every time he saw me he hugged me and gave me a kiss. I've met a couple of presidents of the United States. I've been in their company, and many governors. Here in New Jersey, I've met every governor since 1976. When he presented me with boxing gloves, I still have them. Ali is the greatest celebrity that I've ever been with by far.

Q: Like all fights, you and Muhammad Ali endeavored to promote your fight. What platforms did you utilize?

Chuck Wepner: We did the *Mike Douglas Show* before we had the fight. He wanted me to say some things to hype up the fight. He wanted me to use the 'N' word, which I wouldn't. But to him it was just another word in his vocabulary. When you're black and you use that word, it's OK. I understand that. But I never used that. I don't think it's a nice word and I wouldn't use it. Anyway, he said alright then, I'm going to get up here when we're doing the show. The story was that he said if you even dream that you can beat me, you'd wake up and apologize. That was one of the things he said on the show. He used to make up poems and during the promotion of a fight everybody read his poems.

I wrote two poems. The first one was 'Goodby Ali, Hello Chuck', and the other one was, 'What's in a Word'. If you look it up you'll see the poems in their lengths. One of the lines of the poems was: by March 24 there will be a new king and his name will be Big Chuck. And he said on television, "Now you know why I like this man, this man's intelligent. He can write poetry, too." A lot of the guys he fought were tough guys, but they weren't scholars, between you and me. So it's the way it is in boxing, you don't get too many guys with PhDs in boxing. The guys who are boxing usually come from the ghettos and poverty, and they fight their way out of it by becoming boxers. But Ali always liked me, we always got along great. I met his daughters at dinners and I met two of his wives. He's always been very kind to me and I consider that a great attribute of his. And it's a great honor for me that he is kind to me.

Q: Is it true he received $1.5 million and you received $100,000 for the fight?

Chuck Wepner: That's exactly right. I got $100,000 and he got $1.5 million. You know what, I got the chance to go to camp and train full-time. To me, that was worth it. I got a chance to show what I could do with the proper training.

Q: Don King financed this fight. It's a common known fact that he financed it from the Cleveland Mob money. Is this true?

Chuck Wepner: You know what, there was a movie called *Only in America* and it was about the fight, and they said that. But you know what, Don King in them days didn't have a lot of money. I don't know where they got the money from to finance it, but he financed it. Like I said, Don King was very good to me, we're still friends and he never cheated me out of a penny. All of these fighters don't do anything but box, so they borrow money off Don King before the fight – maybe $150,000 or $200,000 – so they can keep living high and everything else and do their training. When the fight's over they owe Don King that money, but they don't want to pay it back. So Don King takes it out of their purse, which he should do.

It's silly when these guys complain and say Don King ripped them off. How about the money you borrowed from Don King? You know what I mean. I probably know ten guys who fought for the championship under Don King as a promoter. And probably I'm the only one who said Don King never cheated me because I never borrowed money from Don King. I always worked a job. I had a job then. I was working for a liquor company and I have the same job now. It's forty years since I've been with the same company.

Q: After you fought Muhammad Ali you went back to your day job. Is this true?

Chuck Wepner: That's right. I went back. I fought Ali, got home and four days later I was on the road selling liquor. And I'm still doing that today.

Q: When you came back home from fighting the legend can you describe the atmosphere in your hometown?

Chuck Wepner: There were 300 people at the airport. They picked me up by limo and they took me back to Bayonne. That day was Chuck Wepner Day in Hudson County. It has been ever seen. It was a great experience in my life.

Q: What was the best and most grueling fight you saw Muhammad Ali in?

Chuck Wepner: Thrilla in Manila with Joe Frazier. A great, great fight. It was just an awesome fight. I've seen it ten times. I remember what a great fight it was, they went toe to toe. All three fights with Frazier were great fights. Joe had a style of coming in and Ali would box him. They didn't like each other. Joe didn't like Ali because Ali had said some stuff about him. Ali didn't mean anything about it. He was just trying to pump up the fight.

Q: How would you compare Muhammad Ali to heavyweights of a new era such as Mike Tyson?

Chuck Wepner: Mike Tyson in his prime is one of the greatest, but I would have to put Ali on the top as much as I think about Jack Dempsey and others like Rocky Marciano. Rocky was 5ft 7, weighed about 190 pounds, Ali was 6ft 3, 225 pounds. I guess Ali would have been a little too big and a little too fast. I think Marciano was a great heavyweight, but he didn't have the competition when he fought the size of the guys Ali fought in Ali's career.

Q: After Muhammad Ali retired did you see him and interact with him?

Chuck Wepner: I saw him in an appearance where we did an autograph signing together over in New York. To tell you a story, I was sitting in a room with Sandy Koufax, the pitcher for the Dodgers, who was a great, great star. Sandy had about ten people in the line and I had a few people in the line. Ali walked up into the room and everybody disappeared from our lines and went over to his. Sandy looks at me and says, "I guess I'm done signing autographs, the champ's here now." He picks up his bag and walks out. That's how famous Ali was. Even the great Sandy Koufax, people who wanted his autograph, as soon as Ali walked in everybody ran over to Ali including me. We were both sitting there, me and Sandy, with nobody in line because everybody ran over to get Ali's autograph.

We made a few appearances together and we did the same up

in Washington D.C. Don King promoted this also. I played Mr. Tooth Decay and I was going to be fighting Ali. It was for the kids in Washington D.C. to make them brush their teeth. I played Mr. Tooth Decay and I had a white outfit with a hood with TD on my chest. Ali would come out and I would run across the room and throw my punch and he would fall down. Then we would jump in the ring and he would brush his teeth and he would jump back up. In other words, telling the kids if you brush your teeth you're like a Superman. And finally he knocked me down a couple of times. We had such a great time over the weekend. He was showing everybody magic and everything else. He wasn't the same Ali when I fought him, but he was still great enough to draw a huge crowd wherever he went.

Q: How would you define his personality? He treated everybody the same whether you were a prominent celebrity or any normal person.
Chuck Wepner: Yes, he did treat everybody the same and he loved kids – he loved children. Anytime you saw Muhammad Ali do anything you'd see a big crowd of kids around. He would do little magic tricks for them and that was his hobby – magic. He just loved children and children loved Muhammad Ali.

Q: Any final words on how Muhammad Ali has impacted your life?
Chuck Wepner: The most amazing experience in my life was fighting Muhammad Ali. All these years later, like I said, I'm still here, I'm still Chuck Wepner. Everybody calls me 'Champ' because I held a few different championships. I owe all this to Muhammad Ali because if I had fought anybody else except Muhammad Ali, I would never ever have got any exposure and the adulation that I get right now. I can thank Ali for this. I love the guy. I think he's one of the greatest human beings that was ever born.

RICHARD DUNN

Richard Dunn had British, Commonwealth and European titles to his credit before he pursued his biggest challenge: facing the most compelling boxer of our time in 1976 in Germany. The British boxer came in as a heavy underdog, but he gave all he had in a courageous performance much appreciated by British fans. After all those years, he believes fighting Ali was the most memorable and proudest moment of his life.

Q: Can you tell me how you managed to secure a fight deal with Muhammad Ali in 1976?
Richard Dunn: In 1975, September 30, I won the British and the Commonwealth championship and I went on to defend it. Then in 1976, I won the vacant European heavyweight championship, which then gave me a right to fight for the heavyweight championship of the world. And there's only one fighter who was the heavyweight champion of the world, wasn't there? The great Muhammad. I won the vacant European championship on April 6, 1976, and the fight with Muhammad Ali was on May 24, of the same year. So it was just seven weeks later. I was already fit after fighting for the European title; it was just a matter of me keeping it up.

Q: Can you express your thoughts before the fight – he'd fought Henry Cooper twice and had beaten him?
Richard Dunn: I wasn't even boxing when Henry Cooper fought him. I hadn't started boxing until I was twenty years old. Cooper fought him in 1963 and 1966. I was an amateur in 1965. I never even thought about fighting Muhammad Ali. In fact, I never even thought about turning professional until 1969. So, that was nowhere in my mind. Obviously, every fighter wants to fight Ali, but I never thought in a million years it would be me. Winning the British, European and the Commonwealth championship was the only place to go, but that was for the world title.

Q: Can you tell me when you met Muhammad Ali at a London gym?

Richard Dunn: We weren't training, but I was there because he was going to be down there. That's the only reason I went there. I'll tell you who was training there, John H. Stracey. He was defending his welterweight championship in Germany. I came in and we had a conference and a bit of a slanging match. We had a press conference in Germany as it happens, in Munich, where the fight was going to be. I was sat on one side and he was sat on the other side. So we never actually shouted or balled each other because he was being interviewed by one person and I was being interviewed by another person. We kept looking at each other and shaking our fists at each other, things like that. It went very well.

Q: What was the atmosphere like in Germany?

Richard Dunn: It was very good. As you know, Ali fought Karl Mildenberger in Germany, who was also a southpaw fighter like I was. So they tried to compare us, but there was no comparison because we're two different fighters.

Q: Before facing Muhammad Ali, what was going through your head in the dressing room?

Richard Dunn: What it was, obviously I'm always nervous – everyone's nervous before a fight like this. My thoughts were, *This is my chance, this is probably the only chance I'll ever get to win the heavyweight championship of the world. So I must go out there and give it 250 percent, and even 500 percent.* I tried as hard as I could, that's exactly what I did. I came second, but that's not the point. I was there and I was trying my hardest.

Q: Did your trainer give you any specific advice before the fight?

Richard Dunn: Just to go out there and do your best and enjoy yourself, which I did. As I said to you, I tried my best. They just said to me to keep it up. I mean, for the first three rounds I was doing really well. I'm working on it, banging away. They said keep doing what you're doing. So that's what I tried to do. In the fourth round, I made a mistake and got caught with that beautiful right hand, and it was downwards after that. But I enjoyed it, every single minute of it.

Q: Is it true that although you were knocked down five times you got up all five times, and did you say something racist to him?
Richard Dunn: Yes. I got knocked down five times and I got up five times. His speed was the main thing, he was extremely fast. I can't say to you what I said because it's racist. We had some good banter, let's put it that way.

Q: He said, "Boy, you gotta work harder if you want my title!"
Richard Dunn: That's exactly what he said. As I just said to you, I can't tell you what I said back. I've met up with him when he's come back to England and I hope we're still friends.

Q: Do you think Muhammad Ali's taunting got to his opponents?
Richard Dunn: It depends on the fighter. It didn't get on my nerves. It's all part of the build-up to the fight. Because the more he taunts, then the more people go see it.

Q: Any specific moments come to your mind in the fight?
Richard Dunn: The first three rounds. The first, second and the third, I was in the fight all the way. I was really into him. But then in the fourth round he caught me with the most beautiful right hand, and after that I think it was just . . .

Q: Did you find his footwork different to most boxers?
Richard Dunn: He was extremely fast on his feet. He was very good. He was a great mover. I think he would've been a good dancer, don't you? He would have been a great dancer I think because he was so fast on his feet.

Q: Would you say this fight was your fondest boxing memory?
Richard Dunn: Yes, I would. You don't get higher than that, do

you? Fighting for the heavyweight championship of the world against the greatest fighter of all time, it was the pinnacle of my career to be quite truthful. As I said before, I didn't start boxing until I was twenty. So I think I did alright.

Q: After the fight Muhammad Ali actually complimented you, the interviewer was asking him questions and you were standing next to him.

Richard Dunn: I can't remember it too much because after the fight it was just a blur. There was that many press and people and photographers climbing all over you, you couldn't actually hear what he was saying half the time. But I was very grateful that he said such nice things about me. He said that I hurt him, in probably the third round, with a beautiful left hook. I suppose that's my claim to fame these days.

Q: Some people thought it was a mismatch?

Richard Dunn: That's right. Everyone says that. But so what! They weren't in there; I was in there. I had earned my right to be in there. I'd won the British, the Commonwealth and European heavyweight championships. So the only thing to go for after that is the world championship. So I had earned my place! And I don't give a monkey's what anyone else says. I'd earned my place to be in there and I took it with both hands and I came second. I'm not bothered at all.

Q: When you got home in Bradford you received an amazing reception . . .

Richard Dunn: It was fantastic. I've not seen anything like it, to be quite truthful. I expected a few people to be there, but they were lining up the streets all the way from the 606 down to the town hall. There were 10,000 people there. I watched it on tape the other day, it was phenomenal. I'd never known anything like it in my life. I'm extremely proud of it.

Q: Did you ever come into contact with Muhammad Ali after the fight?

Richard Dunn: Yes. I went to see him in Birmingham in 1985, when he opened the Muhammad Ali Center. I was invited. It was on a weekend. I saw him more recently. I'd not want to see him again like this, it was awful. It was at Old Trafford. It was a tour to publicize the Muhammad Ali Center in Kentucky, his hometown. He was fundraising for it. I was sat with Brian London and John H. Stracey and a few of the other fighters that night. It was a dinner event. Seeing Muhammad in that state really, really upset me. I didn't want to stay to be quite truthful. I wanted to go home because I felt so sorry. Plus the fact he's got the Parkinson's disease, which you know about. I am the president of our area for the Parkinson's disease society. I didn't want to see him like that. I don't think it was nice. They were dragging him all over the world. I don't think he knows where he is to be quite truthful. Sooner they find a cure for that the better.

Q: Any last words on Muhammad Ali?

Richard Dunn: I will never ever forget it. It was one of the best nights of my life. Then I met a legend and enjoyed every minute of it.

FOUR

FRIENDS AND ASSOCIATES

Ali loved to have people around him. It gave him a sense of joy and energized him, especially after he retired from the sport of boxing. He was at times ruthlessly exploited, with many so-called friends taking liberties with his generosity and mellow attitude, but his giving, and forgiving nature, also allowed him to make a positive difference in many people's lives that endures to this day. Ali's relationship with his trainer Angelo Dundee was exceptionally professional. Dundee had a tendency to focus on the job at hand, refraining from broaching the subjects of religion or politics with his fighter.

Ali was a people person and would talk to anyone; although he was associated with famous and high-profile personalities, Ali had an open-door policy in his home. When a complete stranger or fan turned up at his door he would rarely turn him away. If Ali had a weakness it was that he put a huge amount of trust in people, and if anyone, including friends, took advantage of him, he didn't make an issue out of it.

In today's sports world the amount of money high-profile sportsmen are making is incredible. The avenues athletes can pursue to help people and causes are potentially huge. Yet, despite their ever-growing wealth and profound influence, they refuse to use their star power to gravitate toward helping. Many of these personalities turn a blind eye particularly when it comes to political issues because of the possibility of damaging their own image, which could hit them financially. According to those who knew Ali well, money meant almost nothing to him. Of course, he made a lot of money during his illustrious career, but was seldom a lavish spender on himself. Much of the money made its way to the tax man, to his management and to a black organization he backed. On the other hand a huge amount was given away to friends, family and strangers by Ali and pumped into business deals – some of which were good, but most of which were completely disastrous that led to dire financial straits. Coming from a lower middle-class background, Ali always vowed to remember his roots and was humble. As much as he craved to be famous growing up, fame and money didn't go to his head, nor did it change him as a person. President Obama expressed as much in a *USA Today* article:

"We admire the man [Muhammad Ali] who has never stopped using his celebrity for good – the man who helped secure the release of fourteen hostages from Iraq in 1990; who journeyed to South Africa upon Nelson Mandela's release from prison; who traveled to Afghanistan to help struggling schools as a United Nations Messenger of Peace; and who routinely visits sick children with disabilities around the world, giving them the pleasure of his presence and the inspiration of his example."

Of course, millions idolized him and continue to do so, not just as a great sportsman but as a great man. Those who don't enjoy the sport of boxing admire the man because of his celebrity status and humanitarian work. Ali was also a celebrity's celebrity. In this section many of the prominent people associated with the legend give their sides of the story: from boxing promoters and celebrities to personal friends and associates. They reflect back on the Muhammad Ali they knew, with their first-hand accounts and their personal opinions on the man they ate with, traveled with, did business with and socialized with behind closed doors. What emerges is the portrait of a man who often appears very different from the one who basked in the public eye.

ANGELO DUNDEE

Angelo Dundee is arguably the greatest boxing coach of all time. After working with Ali for much of his career, he also coached Sugar Ray Leonard and George Foreman, alongside several other well-known fighters. After his retirement Dundee was hired to train Hollywood actor Russell Crowe for *Cinderella Man*. He also appeared in the movie. Dundee and Ali's relationship was extremely strong, with both men showing mutual reverence toward each other – and Dundee was widely respected as a decent, honorable man in an often corrupt sport, with Howard Cosell noting, "If I had a son who wanted to be a fighter and I couldn't talk him out of it, the only man I would let train him is Angelo Dundee." During his illustrious career, Dundee trained a total of fifteen world champions.

Q: Angelo, when did you pursue coaching boxing?
Angelo Dundee: I started in 1948 when I came back from the military. I was overseas in Europe and I met Joe Louis in 1944. I went to a lot of boxing tournaments in the United States.

Q: Tell me how you first met Muhammad Ali, who was back then known as Cassius Clay, and how you both embarked on a journey working together?
Angelo Dundee: I met Muhammad Ali when he was sixteen years old. He was in Louisville, Kentucky. I had Willie Pastrano fight Alonzo Johnson, and he came to see me. He was just a young man and he was very curious about how I trained my fighters. I had quite a few fighters who were fighting on national television all the time. He wanted to meet me and he met Willie Pastrano. What happened was he won the Olympics and came back and trained

with Archie Moore for a while. And the relationship wasn't that good because you can't have two stars working with each other; you've got to have a star and you've got to have somebody to train you. So it wasn't long before the Louisville Group sent him to Archie Moore who had him sweep the kitchen. So he said, "I haven't swept the kitchen for my mother." He wanted to fight but Archie was too busy with his own career – he was a champion. So, you see, you can't have two stars working with each other.

Q: What was Muhammad Ali like as a young man in the initial phases when you first started coaching him?
Angelo Dundee: I found out one thing: when you work with a superstar like Cassius, Muhammad Ali, you 'work with him' only; you don't try to press things on him. I made him feel he's the innovator and everything I taught he felt he did it himself.

Q: What was the first fight that you took him to?
Angelo Dundee: The first fight he had was in 1960. I didn't work the first fight because he was training in Louisville. The Louisville Group wanted me to go up there and work with him, but I said there was someone else who was training him. So I said after the fight let him come down. What happened was it was October and the Louisville Group wanted to send him down. I told them to send him down after the holidays. What happened was I got a call the next morning saying Cassius is coming tomorrow because he wants to fight. He didn't worry about the holidays.

Q: When he won the heavyweight championship from Sonny Liston, before facing Liston how confident were you and your fighter?
Angelo Dundee: One thing you must understand: each and every fight is a different situation. Ali was a special situation. The first fight with Liston was when nobody gave Muhammad a chance to win. It was remarkable the fact that they thought Muhammad was scared of Liston, but that wasn't the case; he was just terrorizing them. And

then when the fight came, he beat Liston and became the world champion. We just got along good together. We never beat on each other. After every fight he thought he was going to a birthday party or something. He was always in great shape, he loved to train. The gymnasium was where he was happy – in the gym. Muhammad was a very special human being and he enjoyed what he did. He worked as hard as he talked. He was always in great condition and I had an easy time working with Muhammad. We never had an argument, we just got along. It was a pairing which was meant to be. Even now I'm Muhammad's friend and he's my friend.

Q: Is it true Sonny Liston tried to cheat by blinding him?
Angelo Dundee: Liston didn't realize how good Muhammad was. Liston thought he would have an easy time with Muhammad. But what happened was he found out Muhammad was for real. Muhammad was a gifted athlete and full of energy. He was taller than Liston. Muhammad was 6ft 2, and he stood up tall. Liston was 6ft and tried to make himself big, but Muhammad just had too much speed and too much talent for Sonny Liston.

Q: When he won the heavyweight championship for the first time, how did he feel?
Angelo Dundee: To Muhammad it was nothing. In a way it was like an ice cream or something. He didn't smoke and he didn't drink. He was a very special man. He was meant to be a world champion.

Q: Can you tell me about the training routine you used to put him through?
Angelo Dundee: A lot of people didn't know that in the gymnasium where he used to work out, the ring was not the actual format. He worked very hard behind closed doors. He'd do a lot of calisthenics. I was very fortunate to have a great trainer work with me by the name of Luis Sierra, a Cuban. And I recognized the talent of Luis Sierra, a great trainer, and he would put Muhammad through a regimen of calisthenics to get Muhammad going for a long time

to condition his body. Muhammad loved working. He loved going through the exercises, but never lifted a weight but he ran. I told him how far to run. He didn't run more than three miles. Then he would come into the gym and work out for a few hours and then he would rest. He was a gifted athlete.

Q: If there was one thing you would have Muhammad Ali improve on what would it have been?
Angelo Dundee: The thing with Muhammad was when he first started off the critics thought he would be an easy beat because he moved too much and would tire. But as he got older he moved less and was more effective. I had no problem with Muhammad and he was very easy to teach. I made him feel he innovated every punch. We got along so well; we never had a problem.

Q: Roadwork . . .
Angelo Dundee: To get the muscles worked and tune his legs up, he didn't overdo it.

Q: Your relationship with him was very cohesive. What was Muhammad Ali like taking instructions from the coach?
Angelo Dundee: He was a great student. The mark of a great fighter is in the middle of a fight he can change his tactics and win the fight. Great fighters do that, and you have to be gifted to do that.

Q: Second Sonny Liston fight . . .
Angelo Dundee: What happened was in Liston's second fight, I made Muhammad, in the very first round, hit him with a one-two to bring back the memories of the beating Liston took in the first fight. And Liston was a great fighter. But, you see, in boxing a fighter will give another fighter trouble. And Muhammad could beat Liston every day of the week.

Q: Can you recall any unusual incidents in the gymnasium?
Angelo Dundee: The gymnasium was Muhammad's theater. He had

a good time in the gym. He would talk to the fans, when he was sparring he would kid around with the people. Muhammad had a good time and enjoyed what he did. We just had a great time. In the beginning people thought he was a gobby kid and that he wasn't for real – he was real. Muhammad always played tricks on me. One time when we were in Los Angeles, I was out with some newspaperman and when I came in Muhammad jumped out of the closet with a shield over his head, he shouted boom! He scared the hell out of me. Muhammad used to play tricks on me all the time and we always had fun together. My whole experience with Muhammad was fun.

Q: When you were on the road with him, was it hard to be away from home?

Angelo Dundee: It was easy. All we did was train. We went around and we would meet all the people, do all the publicity. Muhammad was a gifted man because he kept a lot of people happy. He had a lot of people around him and he liked having people around.

Q: Is it true Rocky Marciano didn't like Muhammad Ali?

Angelo Dundee: Oh, they got to be friends. I was very friendly with Rocky Marciano. He came to live in Miami Beach and we did that computer fight. Rocky didn't talk that much, and he said to me, "Man, your guy talks too much." I said, "Well, listen, this is different. The fans want to hear from the star." But Rocky and Muhammad got to be dear friends after they did the computer fight. I'll give you a great story about Muhammad and Rocky Marciano. After they did the computer fight Rocky said, "You're right, Angelo, Muhammad's a nice guy." Because I always told Rocky that Muhammad was a nice guy. And Muhammad was that kind of a human being who liked people, and today he's the same way. He has not changed. Muhammad is a tremendous human being. We were very lucky to have a superstar like him.

Q: Can you tell me about the build-up to the first Joe Frazier fight? He was a very good boxer, did you have any conversations

with your fighter regarding Joe Frazier before the fight? Any behind-the-scenes stories which you would like to share?

Angelo Dundee: The stories were such it was the biggest event of its time. Joe Frazier drew all the big stars and the luminaries. Sinatra was there snapping pictures for a magazine. All the big stars from around the country were there for that fight. It was happening. It was a fight that people wanted to see. The fight was a very close fight. I took Muhammad to the hospital after the fight because I was afraid his jaw was broken. He had a lump on his jaw. The doctor said he wanted to keep him overnight for observations. Muhammad said no way, he had to go back to talk to the press. So we didn't stay. But Joe went to the hospital and stayed there for a few days. It was a tremendous fight.

He knew how to talk to people, and all these gimmicks with the poetry. These were things utilized to publicize the fights. It was something that helped to fill the arena. Muhammad always had fun in the ring and out of the ring. I honestly felt Muhammad would beat Parkinson's, but evidently a big guy has a lot of trouble kicking Parkinson's. I notice a lot of younger people who have Parkinson's can beat it. There was an actor with Parkinson's, but he's beating it. He's a smaller guy. But evidently a big guy like Muhammad has difficulties knocking off the symptoms.

Q: Why was there a third Joe Frazier fight?

Angelo Dundee: The first Joe Frazier fight, people didn't realize that Muhammad Ali was doing a photograph session with one of the magazines the night before the fight till midnight. Also, what people don't know was that we had to weigh-in at Madison Square Garden and we couldn't leave the Garden because there were people around the Garden. We stayed in Madison Square Garden from the weigh-ins till the fight. We never left – me and Muhammad. I sent everybody else away and told them to bring his boxing gear that night. We stayed in Madison Square Garden from the weigh-ins, which was at noon and the fight didn't take place till 11 o'clock that night.

Q: He was taken to the brink by Joe Frazier before triumphing. What is your personal take on the third Joe Frazier fight?

Angelo Dundee: Joe Frazier and Muhammad could've fought a hundred times and it would have been a great fight, their styles blended. And every time they fought it was exciting. And the last fight in Manila was fantastic. I don't know how two guys fought that long. You see, the fight was indoors at the Araneta Coliseum and there was a roof and a tent with lights from the television cameras. I don't know how the two guys fought such a great fight in that kind of condition. The Thrilla in Manila, they were two remarkable people and Muhammad was [all about] survival of the fittest. He was the fittest and he survived. I don't know how they did because I got extremely exhausted just climbing up the stairs.

Q: Any interesting stories outside the ring?

Angelo Dundee: We had so much fun wherever we went, like when we went to Zaire, the people there adopted us. When we went to Manila the people adopted us. When we went to England . . . Muhammad was a kid that could be adopted anywhere because he was a warming individual, and he still is. He gets more from the look than you and I would get from the whole conversation. He was just a great kid and it was an honor for me to work with Muhammad Ali.

Q: At the 5th Street Gym which other boxers were you training?

Angelo Dundee: You have to realize that I had fifteen world champions. When Muhammad was training in the gym, I had Luis Rodriquez, Luis Pastrano, Fortino Hernandez, Sugar Ramos. I had so many great fighters, but Muhammad is heads and shoulders above all of them because he was really special. They all became friends. All those fighters were Muhammad's friends.

Q: Did you implement any psychological methods to get Muhammad Ali to accelerate beyond the limits?

Angelo Dundee: With Muhammad, it was all psychological. I made him feel he innovated everything. Angelo Dundee was just there to keep him company, let me tell you. We had a great time.

Q: Can you shed some light on the first Henry Cooper fight?
Angelo Dundee: The first Henry Cooper fight, you see, the people there in England didn't know Muhammad's personality. They like the quiet type. Because I had been to England before with Luis Pastrano and they loved Luis because he was a nice gentle type and wasn't that talkative. The closed mouth of a person the more they respect him in England. But, you see, with Muhammad, he was the first superstar to talk and they didn't know how to handle that. When we went there the first time, we could walk the streets, go to restaurants and do everything. But with the second time we couldn't walk the streets because it was a different atmosphere. People there were tremendous. The English are great boxing fans. I was there during the war. I was there in '43, '44, '45, that's where I met Joe Louis. He was there entertaining the troops. And I had no idea that I would end up getting into the boxing profession. Actually, I was an airplane inspector at the naval aircraft factory in Philadelphia.

And when I got to England they were very, very nice. I landed in the Manchester area and I wound up in Newbury, which was outside of London. I tell you I was very respectful of English people because they were so nice to us – the American troops. Into the fight, everybody thought I had cut the glove when he got knocked down. I really didn't cut the glove; the glove was split right from the beginning on the right glove. Muhammad was winning easily so I didn't say anything, but when he got that knockdown there was still time. I told the referee the glove was cut and it was split. The referee told the commissioner, the commissioner went back to the dressing room to get a glove but there was no glove. He came back and the referee said there's no glove. I said, "OK, we'll use the same glove."

Q: Henry Cooper was well known in England, how big was this fight?
Angelo Dundee: Henry Cooper would've been a big star in any

time. He was a good competitor, he was a great puncher. I see Henry at the Hall of Fame every year, we're friends.

Q: Ken Norton and Muhammad Ali fought three classic fights. Muhammad Ali won two and Ken Norton won one. Can you talk to me about the first fight where Muhammad Ali got his jaw broken?

Angelo Dundee: The first fight, I couldn't get Muhammad emotionally up because he didn't know who Ken Norton was. Ken Norton is a very good fighter with a very difficult style. He was a big man, he would bend and crouch and he would give Muhammad trouble any fight. None of the fights were that easy, but in the first fight Muhammad got his jaw broken in the very first round and he went the whole distance. I wanted to stop the fight but Muhammad wouldn't let me. He said, "No, no, I could go on. I could take care of this guy." But it was a very difficult fight, and all these fights were difficult because that style gave Muhammad trouble. I told him, "Muhammad, I think I'm going to stop this, it's bad." He said, "No, you ain't going to stop this or I'm going to knock you out." I said, "Don't worry about it, Muhammad, you're not going to knock me out." I had to take him to the hospital and he had to get his jaw wired. So what happened was I went to see him in the hospital and he was on the table and I was crying. I felt terrible. Muhammad said, "This is wired. Don't worry, Ange, we will return!" And we did.

Q: If Mike Tyson and Muhammad Ali fought in their prime, what is your personal opinion on the outcome of such a fight?

Angelo Dundee: Tyson would not have beaten Muhammad because he's shorter, he's slower and Muhammad would've outboxed him. Muhammad would beat that style. Joe Frazier was a tougher style because he used to shake, shake from the sides – Tyson didn't. So Muhammad would've beaten Tyson.

Q: I've seen a picture of you and Muhammad Ali with Stallone.

Angelo Dundee: I'll tell you something: I always thought the actors were drawn to boxing for the Ali star quality. But I did several movies including *Ali* where I trained Will Smith. I trained Russell Crowe for the *Cinderella Man*. The actors work as hard as fighters. That's why they're drawn to boxing. I'm happy to have met all these nice people and I got to be in another movie. I met all these nice people.

Q: How did Muhammad Ali take to fame?

Angelo Dundee: Muhammad is a people person and he loves people. Fame never went to his head. He liked people and if people were nice, he was nice with the people all the time. When he was a young man he was that way. Muhammad never changed at any time. He could handle fame. He just felt he was like any other human being. Muhammad was a great gift to the human race. I can't tell you more than that because I was with Muhammad for nineteen years and never had an argument. We got along fine and never had a problem. All I can tell you is I had a wonderful time being with Muhammad Ali.

BOBBY GOODMAN

Bobby Goodman, an inductee of the International Boxing Hall of Fame, was born and raised in the Bronx, a borough of New York City. As a public relations man, he spent a lot of time on the road working with Ali and other top boxing champions. In the 1970s, Don King promoted him to the posts of director of boxing and matchmaker. In 1996, he rejoined Don King Productions where he was the vice president of boxing operations and public relations. Then he became the chief operating officer for Roy Jones Jr. Square Ring Promotions.

Q: Bobby, Muhammad Ali did everything possible to help promote his fights, can you expand on this, please?
Bobby Goodman: At night he used to check in with me in my room. I'd always do a schedule for the next day of interviews, appearances and things we were going to do. And I'd be on camp with him for months on end when he was training up in Deer Lake. Sometimes he didn't think we were doing enough, so he would come up with things himself. Sometimes he might change an appointment to an earlier time or a later time. But he never turned down interviews, never turned down appearances that made sense. We were once in Houston, Texas, doing a fight with Buster Mathis. Every time he was in the presence of Ali, he would start laughing and smiling because Ali used to crack him up. We just weren't making the fight believable and just weren't selling tickets because Buster used to laugh at his idol every day.

It was not the fierce competition we were looking for. And after one day's workout I said to him, "Muhammad, this is no good, we're not selling any tickets. People don't believe there's any animosity. Buster laughs and smiles every time he sees you." I said we had to come up with something where we can help sell tickets and his eyes went wide. He said, "I've got it! I've got it. It'll make headlines all over the world." And I said, "What's that?" I couldn't wait to get the response out of his mouth. I said, "What's that, Muhammad?

What's that?" He said, "You can have me kidnapped. You can take me up in the woods and put me in the cabin, and just bring a couple of sparring partners and bring a ring. I can train there and show up a day or two before the fight." I said, "Yeah, but people won't see you and they think you're not going to be fighting. We will never sell tickets because they'd think it's not happening." He said, "OK, you're right. We'll come up with something else." It was just a fact he dreamed up something like that to come up with.

Then in the Philippines we were doing great with local media, but we weren't getting the push all around the world. So I talked to Ali and we spoke to his manager Herbert. Ali said he could say this was going to be his last fight. I said, "Alright! Well, listen, we're going to call a press conference up in the suite here, and you've got to be almost to the point of tears. It's been a great career and now you want to spend time with your family and you've made a decision. You've been fighting a long time." He said OK, great.

So we went through this and Ali pulled it off brilliantly. The room was packed with reporters and Ali had his head down. He said, "I can't deal with this anymore. I gotta spend more time with my family and home. I've got children growing up. I've got so much time . . . it's not right. I've devoted my whole life to the sport." We were in Malaysia, not the Philippines. Then somebody said, "What if you can get a third match with Joe Frazier?" His eyes lit up again, "Joe Frazier!! Where is he? Frazier!" The whole thing went out of the window after Frazier. He was lit up like a balloon. That was hard.

Q: Did Buster Mathis actually go to Muhammad Ali in the dressing room after the fight, and thank him for giving him a chance to fight him and express the adulation he had for him?
Bobby Goodman: He did thank him. Poor Buster is gone now. I remember we were in Germany. I think Ali was fighting Richard Dunn in Munich, Germany. He agreed to come onto the stage and the stage floor collapsed, which was about a seven or eight foot drop. Ali was sitting there on the edge on the splintered wood, sitting there with his legs dangling. He was alright. I was still

Ali – then Cassius Clay – and his brother Rahaman in a
mosque praying in Cairo, Egypt, June 1964. *Getty Images*

Ali making a speech at a Nation
of Islam rally, February 1968.
Getty Images

Promo shoot, October 1970. *Alamy*

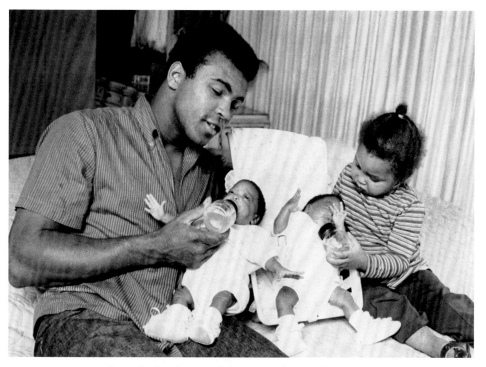

At home feeding his twin daughters Rasheda and Jamillah with some help from his eldest Maryum, November 1970. *Getty Images*

Ali and George Dillman at Deer Lake training camp in the 1970s. *Courtesy of George Dillman.*

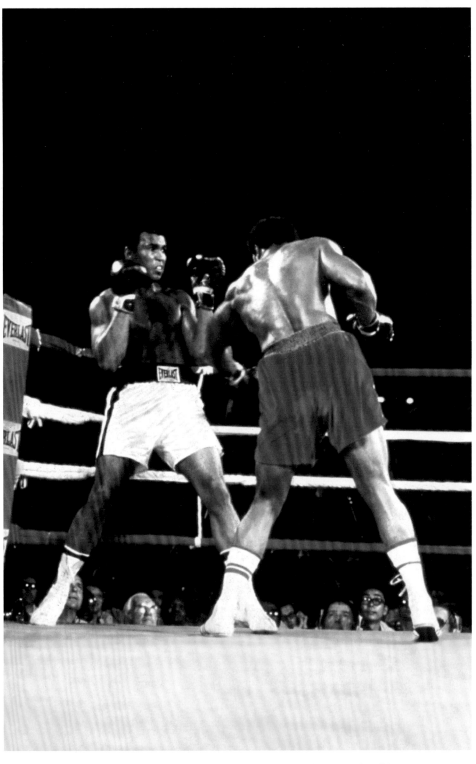

Ali and George Foreman's epic Rumble in the Jungle is considered by many to be the greatest boxing fight of all time, October 1974. *Alamy*

Ali at George Dillman's karate gym in the 1970s. *Courtesy of George Dillman.*

Ali has a pre-fight medical before Super Fight II against Joe Frazier in January 1974. *Alamy*

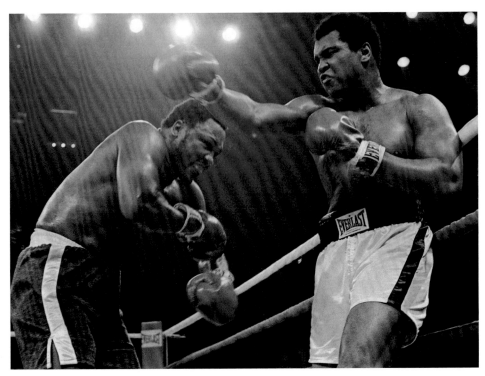

Joe Frazier and Ali battle it out in the ring in the Philippines, September 1975. *Getty Images*

The Thrilla in Manilla post-fight press conference in the Philippines, brother
Rahaman and Don King look on as Ali talks to the press, October 1975. *Getty Images*

August 1980, Muhammad Ali at home in Los Angeles
before his last fight with Larry Holmes. *Getty Images*

Ali with his friend, former-president Bill Clinton,
Lonnie Ali and Angelo Dundee, December 2003. *Getty Images*

Ali playing around with Will Smith at a book launch
as Puff Daddy looks on, December 2003. *Getty Images*

Ali with daughter Rasheda in 2005. *Getty Images*

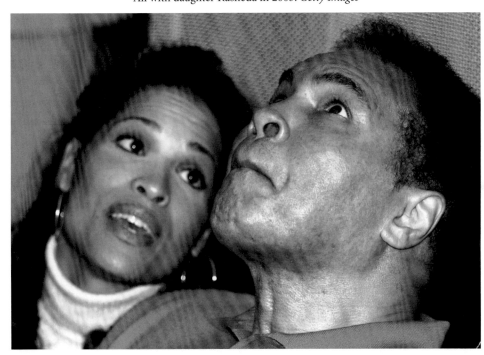

standing there next to the scale, everything beyond that collapsed and went in. And Ali says, "At least I hit my weight."

Q: What was Muhammad Ali like to negotiate with from a business perspective? Was he hard to negotiate with and did he want more money?

Bobby Goodman: No, Ali was a very fair-minded guy. He was certainly one of a kind. Don't forget when Ali, Frazier and Foreman were coming along the really crazy money wasn't around. We had closed-circuit television, but no pay-per-view like we have today where they can generate a hundred million dollars. They weren't pulling that kind of money. He had a big entourage that he always paid for. He tried to be firm sometimes. He might have fifty people with him. He said, "Here we are in Germany. I don't mind you calling home once in a while, don't stay on the phone and run up big phone bills." Because he was paying for everything, but he just couldn't find it in his heart to be that hard, cold guy. He said, "If you're hungry and you want to eat a steak, eat a steak, but don't order two steaks." He was truly a wonderful guy. To Angelo, me and Gene Kilroy, who ran his camp, through the years he showed nothing but kindness and love for everybody. He never exhibited any racial tendency to me.

Q: Do you feel some of the entourage took advantage of him?

Bobby Goodman: Ali welcomed it. He enjoyed having people around him. He enjoyed having a crew around him. That was all part of his negotiation which sometimes cost him a lot. He was realistic with it, he knew what it was. He truly loved the people around him as it used to keep him alive and keep him interested.

Q: What is the most remarkable story you remember when you were on the road with him?

Bobby Goodman: The remarkable story was how Ali could stay out those years and then finally come back in, of all places, Atlanta, Georgia, which had a racist governor named George Wallace. When we went to Atlanta to fight Jerry Quarry, he received death threats and even the Ku Klux Klan people came around. Muhammad won everybody over, with his great smile and his twinkle in his eyes. They became his fans. He was just a very unique individual.

Q: How did Muhammad Ali take racism in the early years?
Bobby Goodman: At the time, it was the Black Muslim movement and he took it seriously. That was supposed to be his position and the position of Elijah Muhammad was to talk about the white Devils, etc, whatever. But Ali never showed that side to us. I remember after Elijah had passed away and his son Wallace took over the Muslim movement. I hadn't seen him [Ali] for a long time. I decided I was going to take a drive up to the camp he was starting to set up.

He was in the kitchen by himself, it was a large cabin kitchen. When I pulled up and walked into the kitchen, he got excited and he ran over to me and we hugged each other. And he said, "Did you hear? Did you hear?" He was very excited. I said "What, Muhammad?" He said, "You know now Wallace took over, you can become a Muslim?" I said, "Muhammad, we love each other, right?" He said, "Yes. Yes." I said, "Well, then you keep on believing what you believe in and I respect that. And let me believe in what I believe in and respect that. And we'll keep on loving each other." He said OK and we hugged again and that was the end of that. He believes in what he does and he's been very true. Even today, he's in peace with himself and he knows what's going on around him. He's a wonderful guy.

Q: Is it true he got the concept of trash-talking from Gorgeous George the wrestler?
Bobby Goodman: He always loved Gorgeous George and the way he promoted himself. He always made people dislike him who wanted him to get beat. He got a lot of that from Gorgeous George. In fact, he had one of his robes. He had Elvis Presley's robes, too. He was always very into the showman and he loved the showmanship. He was an amazing guy. He could turn it on and turn it off. A lot of athletes can't do that. A lot of the boxers could never do that. When they get into that confrontation they don't know how to turn it off.

He had the sense of where he was in his set-up to start the attacks. I think he sometimes tried to press all the buttons until he hit the right button that shocked everyone. Then he would use that. He did this very much with Joe Frazier. He knew what button to press to get Joe upset. He was a pretty bright strategist.

Q: Throughout your career with Muhammad Ali, what were the highs and lows?
Bobby Goodman: The first Ali fight I worked with was against Doug Jones in 1963. In that particular fight, although I was around Ali, I was assigned to Doug Jones. So I handled that. It was a great fight. It was a very good fight and Doug Jones did very well in the fight. It was in Madison Square Garden. But the highlight, certainly for me, was when he recaptured his crown from George Foreman. At that point in George's career, he was not the most cooperative person to work with. He's since become a wonderful guy. But George Foreman back then was very difficult.

Q: How would you describe Muhammad Ali's relationship with the press?
Bobby Goodman: He was terrific. There was no one better than Ali with the press and he knew who they were. He knew Colin Hart, he knew those guys; he knew everybody; he knew them by name; he knew Dave Anderson; he knew Smith – he knew their tendencies. One of the things he used to do, when we were in camp where he had a dressing room, was he would sometimes invite the press, if there were a few in the camp, in his dressing room.

One day there was Milton Richman from UPI and a few others. When the press used to come to his dressing room, Ali used to have these long speeches painstakingly written down on handwritten yellow pads. He used to try his speeches on them. Sometimes they can be very long, so he went on and on with his speech. After a half hour nonstop speech, Ali went into a 'we've been in chains, we've been in chains'. Milton Richman said, "Muhammad, I don't give a shit, we've been in the oven." Ali started to laugh like hell and put down the pad. He was great with the press. He could never seem to do enough and was always trying to find ways to incite them and try and find ways to make them laugh, just as natural.

Q: Did you accompany him to talk shows and do you have any behind the scenes off-set recollections?
Bobby Goodman: We went many times to *The Tonight Show*, *The Merv Griffin Show*. Johnny Carson was the host of *The Tonight Show*. Ali was always a welcome guest because he always brought so many different things to the telecast. There was a time when I was handling a promotion with my father, and my father decided he would take Ernie Terrell, who Ali was fighting, to his place that day and I would take Ali. We tried to make sure we didn't bump into each other because they didn't really like each other. Terrell was still calling him Clay. So, as we were on our way to *The Today Show*, the worst place in the middle of 6th Avenue in New York, here we are bumping into each other. At the exact same moment on the exact same corner, Ernie getting out of the car and Ali walking. He used to like to jump out of the limo or car and see if he could create a crowd, which he always did. He had three, four hundred people walking down the street with him. It would cause a commotion and stop traffic right on the corner of the Rockefeller Center by NBC where we were going to for the show.

Q: What endorsements did Muhammad Ali get at the peak of his career in the 1960s, but in particular the 1970s as boxing was becoming a big business?
Bobby Goodman: During that time, when he made his comeback in the late 1960s, people stayed away from Ali because of his stand against the draft in 1967. He didn't come back until 1970 or 1971. At the time, sponsors were especially trying to pull away from him, staying at arm's length. Some were very supportive of him. One of those was Howard Cosell, who was with ABC at the time. It was a tough time. He would go and do some speaking engagements, but there wasn't a long line of sponsors waiting for him at that time.

Q: How much of Muhammad Ali's actual personality filters into promoting fights, or was it all an act, or was it a mixture of both?
Bobby Goodman: He was the real deal. He could find ways, he'd really think about it. He was the guy who named these fights. Sometimes we'd have these talk sessions and Angelo Dundee was always around when we discussed things like that. But Ali would come up with things himself. It was him who coined the words 'Thrilla in Manila' – when I get the gorilla in Manila – then 'Rumble in the Jungle' with George Foreman. He would give his opponents names. George Foreman was the Mummy. He'd do imitations of a Mummy chasing around. Floyd Patterson was the Rabbit. George Chuvalo was the Washer Woman.

Q: Boxing is big, of course, do you feel what Muhammad Ali had personality-wise could ever be replicated?
Bobby Goodman: He was one of a kind. There are others who have tried to imitate, but he was a natural – it was him. Nobody's been able to do it like him since.

Q: Do you feel he was an intelligent person despite the fact in school, he didn't have an aptitude for learning and obtaining high grades?
Bobby Goodman: Maybe he didn't want to sit and read books or study, whatever. But you know this man had some genius in him. He was a natural. He was a very bright person.

Q: Did you often go to his house for meetings?
Bobby Goodman: We did from time to time and, of course, we stayed together at the camp. Yes, I visited him from time to time and certainly spent a lot of time living in and around him in various camps, and I got to know him real well. He was very unique.

Q: What was one of the most intriguing and controversial incidents, going back to the 1960s, which made the headlines?
Bobby Goodman: When he refused to step forward for the draft,

which was an intriguing story and also a massive and courageous stand by a kid who believed in what he was doing.

Q: How much of an impact did this have on him and his career?
Bobby Goodman: It had a huge impact. Huge impact in sport and huge impact on him personally. That was a very courageous stand for him to take, which showed that he truly believed in what he was doing and the reasons why. I mean, him saying he didn't have any problems with the Vietcongs, it was him saying that was something he believed in. It was a tremendous stand and it had a huge impact on the sport! Then you saw Joe Frazier go on and capture some recognition of the crown. I think Jimmy Ellis got some recognition of the crown. Joe Frazier, of course, was recognized by the New York State as the champion. It had quite a bit impact in those days. When Ali did come back and fight Jerry Quarry, he then fought Joe Frazier for the crown. But to many people Muhammad was still the champion – the uncrowned champion.

Q: Can you recall the Cleveland Williams fight press conference?
Bobby Goodman: At the time, Cleveland Williams had just had some gunshot wounds and had survived. He was an amazing specimen physically. Hugh Benbow was his manager. Cleveland Williams was just knocking everybody dead, but here he had made a remarkable recovery from I don't know how many gunshots, but he did come back. But Ali's speed was just too great for Cleveland and those people around thought the Big Cat had a chance.

Q: How did you hype up this fight?
Bobby Goodman: Well, I don't really recall that particular press conference because at that time, I don't think I went to have a press conference in Texas – the fight was held there. I don't recall that one. I mean, I recall doing the fight, doing the press kits, doing the questions and the photos and all that stuff. But I don't recall that particular press conference.

Q: Why were people around the world mesmerized by him?

Bobby Goodman: Because he transcended sports. He was an international figure who was probably the most instantly recognized figure in the world at that time. Maybe it was something to do with his stand with the draft. Maybe it was the fact he did come back which showed the world he had that ability. So many people, especially young people, who were not in favor of the war in Vietnam, he was sort of a hero to them because he had taken such a great stance. Of course, the older Americans, until he won them over again, were against him because he didn't step forward for the draft. Throughout the world nobody was as instantly recognized as Ali. I credit Ali for making the world of boxing. Some places never heard of boxing and never really concentrated on boxing, then there were followers of Ali and he brought them into boxing. So we owe that to Ali – a great gratitude.

Q: Back in the 1960s, how imperative was it for you to garner mainstream media attention and what medium of media promoted fights?

Bobby Goodman: He transcended the sport, as I said. He was the one who took us from the sports pages onto the news side. He took us from the sports pages and onto the major magazines. Ali still holds the record for the most covers of *Sports Illustrated*. He's also on *Time, Newsweek* and *Life*. Ali took us to new places and really got a lot of fans, casual fans, who became really interested in the sport to the point where they became lifelong fans. And it was because of Muhammad Ali.

Q: How did Don King filter into promoting Ali in the 1970s?

Bobby Goodman: Through his wit and grit. He was a very bright person and figured out how to win over Ali and his manager at the time – Herbert Muhammad. Ali went down to do an exhibition for a hospital in Cleveland that was having a tough time. And Ali came in and they sold it out. They did well. And that was his first real full-time involvement with Muhammad. It carried over into further fights and he became a big promoter. He was always smart and creative. He wasn't afraid to gamble. He wasn't afraid to take that risk and go out and guarantee the money, and then figure out how the hell he was going to make it.

Q: When Muhammad Ali retired did you keep in touch?
Bobby Goodman: There were a number of occasions. I was then running the Madison Square Garden boxing. And they had called me from upstairs, the parent corporation, which at the time was Paramount, I believe. They were trying to create a Hall of Fame for the Garden and they wanted Ali to be part of it. When they contacted his representative directly, Ali said no because he had another engagement so he couldn't make it. So they called me and said, "Hey, Bob, they're having a big dinner on the floor of the Madison Square Garden. It's a charity and we wanted Ali here, but he said he can't make it." I said, "Why didn't you come down to me? I worked with him for so many years." They said, "Well, could you give it a try?" And I said I'd do what I could. And I did call. They got back to me pretty quickly and said, yes, for you we'll do that and he did come in. My wife and I sat at his table. That was when he started having problems with speaking. I was at the Madison Square Garden from 1985 to 1993. This was probably in the late 1980s.

We also had a reunion when we went back and visited the camp. They called a handful of people and said they were going to visit the camp, spend a nice afternoon at the camp one day – just a handful of us, six or seven of us. It was a wonderful day. A couple of times people would call me and say Ali was going to be in New York, and we were going to have a little private gathering in my apartment. So we would come in and meet there.

Q: At the press conferences were there heated moments, Muhammad Ali had a penchant for taunting his opponents?
Bobby Goodman: Absolutely! Joe Frazier and Ali, before their second fight in Madison Square Garden, I had gone to spend some time with Joe Frazier. They called Howard Cosell, who was going

to have Joe Frazier and Ali in the studio reviewing their first fight. Joe didn't want to go. He said no. Eddie Futch, who was training Joe, didn't think it was a good idea, either. He said Joe is really serious about his dislike... he feels Muhammad disrespects him. It was serious.

Howard talked to all of us on the phone and insisted he would control them and make sure it wouldn't get out of hand. Lo and behold we went up to the studio in New York and Howard didn't even sit in the middle; he sat Joe and Ali next to each other! When the rerun of the first fight was playing, Ali keeps poking him and saying stuff. He said, "You're ignorant, Joe. You wouldn't understand that." Now smoke is coming out of his ears. He called him ignorant one too many times. Joe just stood up and grabbed Ali and they went down on the ground. And Joe has his foot and tries twisting it. I run in and I tried to get Joe's hands off his foot, and I said, "Joe, if you break his ankle there won't be a fight." Then they stopped and we left the studio after that. But it was a scary moment – it was a concrete floor.

Q: Joe Frazier was a serious type of a guy?
Bobby Goodman: Joe was very serious! He could kid around, but his threshold level of being insulted wasn't very high, and Ali used to dig at him. He didn't like being called names. He didn't mind being called boxing names, but insulting him personally saying you're ignorant, that's something Joe wouldn't tolerate.

Q: Anything you would like to add?
Bobby Goodman: Other than the fact that I was with some great, great fighters through the years and very close to them. I was close to Joe Frazier as well. And I've grown close to George Foreman since that event, but there will never be another Ali. As far as his overall composition, his talents, his general wit, his understanding of the promotion, there will never be another one. It's sad for the sport because those kinds of people come once in a lifetime.

DON KING

Don King is the most influential and recognizable promoter in the sport of boxing, as well as being perhaps the most controversial. His flamboyant personality, trademark hairstyle and presence as the promoter of fights including the Rumble in the Jungle and Thrilla in Manila made him famous in the 1970s, and he continues to make regular media appearances while in his late 80s.

Q: Before you met Muhammad Ali, what was your impression of him?

Don King: Muhammad Ali was a special kind of a fellow, you know. He was a great athlete. He used to come into my club. I had a nightclub called the New Corner Tavern. He would come in there and he would sing on the stage and stand by me. He was in exile and was standing up for his rights as a conscientious objector. But I had known him long before because he was a hero in our community. We didn't have too many heroes you can identify with. Muhammad Ali was there, he was a fighter of the people. He was people's champion. This is a remarkable attitude and a fighter for humanity and example of Matthew verse twelve: do unto others as you have them do unto you. And he stood up for what he believed in, and that means he was willing to take the consequences of his actions as well as the rewards.

Q: When you started working with him and promoting him, what was your perception of him and his personality?

Don King: He was a promoter's dream. He was a guy that promoted the people, excited the people. He made the fights. And one thing, he never condemned other fighters. He always made the fighters look important that were lower, which many people would call 'tomato cans' and 'bums'. Ali would make them look very important and he taught me to put nobody down. Because if your major fighter got beat by a so-called lesser opponent, that means you did not achieve what you set out to.

Every now and again the so-called lesser opponent would make a major upset, that's the word: major upset. In the boxing ring when an upset comes, at least you have a tough guy and not a bum. So, he had a beautiful smile and he was young. At the same time, he had the wisdom and the understanding because he would not give in to putting down anybody whilst standing up for himself. He was with the masses and not classes. He could walk with kings and still ask you to come on talk to him. So he was the man of the people. He was a great friend of mine before I ever got into boxing. He would come into my nightclub, we would always meet and greet wherever we went to see his fights. And when he was in exile he was around all the time.

Q: What was the most compelling conversation you both ever had?

Don King: Well, you know, Muhammad Ali was very progressive. He was a guy who realized the reality of our situation in America. While we both loved America, he tried to get tested in America and he came out winning – with the Supreme Court upholding him and dealing with him. But it definitely was a phase a person can understand when he was fighting. He could relate and identify and edify to the masses what the struggle was. He was a conscientious objector and he was criticized. They were calling him all kinds of names. He pointed out and said you go to war and you come back, but my thing is with God and my religion. He said the Vietcong never called me Nigger. He brought it down to basic terms where everybody could understand it because people were overshadowed of the racial mentality they were prevailing on our community, and the different things that happened because of the indoctrination of our fellow Americans.

He would come up with statements that were able to relate to the complexion to get the protection. You've got to be able to look at that deep inside rather than this guy and that guy saying these exclamations. He would always coin it in a way where you could really relate, you could understand what the handicaps were. And the surmountable amounts you had to surmount in spite of being insurmountable. And he would come out with that golden smile, but he would be able to stand in a fight. This is something that I learned from him and I'm continuing to do so. It's much easier to die for America than it is to live for America. When you burn yourself you're caught up in a web of hypocrisy, prejudice and racism. And being a man of color he knew that this was the greatest country in the world. He knew it was the best country in the world, but he had awakening. You saw the civil rights movement as it came down. Everybody began to progress – the American people. And this is what he was motivating and getting people to do in the sports arenas standing up for their rights.

I remember about Muhammad as a sportsman. He put four years of his career – the height of his career – he sacrificed millions of dollars, and to carry his point. And his point was upheld by the United States Supreme Court. I mean, this was far from a crime. You have to understand the specifics of this, Fiaz. In 1886, when the Chief Justice Roger Brooke Taney said black man has no rights that a white man is bound to respect. To Supreme Court decision upholding a black man's rights in one of the most noble causes that you can be condemned about is being unpatriotic. They upheld his. I mean, it was just a remarkable dramatic situation for those who are really concerned about America, they want to treat the cause rather than just . . .

Q: How significant were the Frazier–Ali fights from an historical sense as far as the sport of boxing is concerned?
Don King: You know, the most significant thing about this fight is that Muhammad Ali shocked the world. He went out there and he fought. It was the most grueling fight. He said it was the closest fight he ever had. Joe Frazier was trying to continue but the corner stopped it. It was a remarkable feat of courage, perseverance, never-say-no attitude. My phrase for that was: you're in it to win it, you can't give in, you can't give up and you can't quit. Victory... and that's what Muhammad Ali did and that was a profound statement

as well as a great classic when he went in there and beat Joe Frazier like that. So, you know, these are the things people . . . every act in his life, it was always a message with Muhammad Ali. He was a people person. He would sit down in the lobby of a hotel, and instead of run away from people he signed autographs for them.

He was very concerned about the old-aged people and he was an attention for younger people. He acted like a child. So he was an exemple to children. He had this child-like smile and attitude. He didn't see color; he saw people. He recognized what it was and especially coming out of Kentucky, the South, the understanding where everybody had to suffer with racism in the wake of slavery. Muhammad Ali kept strong, and to overcome barriers then talk about how difficult it was and how difficult it must have been for those who were before him. And he stood up for the Muslims. At that time, the Honorable Elijah Muhammad was out there with the Nation of Islam, and you're talking about controversy. You had controversy within controversy. Then you had so much fun with him outside the ring. His personality was great. These are the things. Muhammad Ali was the personification of personality.

Q: You promoted Muhammad Ali and also Mike Tyson, what is the comparison?
Don King: They were both great heavyweights. Muhammad Ali had the blinding speed and he was a dancer in the ring. He was a fighter. He was a combination of things. He was emulating and imitating Sugar Ray Robinson, who was one of his idols. Ray Robinson, I think, was the best boxer of all time. Muhammad Ali made a heavyweight look like a middleweight the way he was fighting. Then he would coin all of his phrases and predictions. They would become exciting up to the countdown to see it. The people hated him or loved him.

Mike Tyson had awesome, devastating power. He was not the boxer that would be boxing and laughing – he was menacing. He was the guy that came in that they feared. You would be shivering in your bones. He would go out and seek and destroy. Ali would go another way. He would win with his skill, charm and wit. So these two guys were both great fighters. Mike Tyson, same thing – love him or hate him. But he was the menacing, devastating guy that wants to punch you so hard and put your nose up your brain. He was the kind of guy not to be loved like a guy like Muhammad Ali ended up being. But it was not that Ali wasn't in the beginning, because he was excoriated and vilified, but he was still at a time when he was making a move to become recognized by people.

Q: Do you feel ultimate fighting (UFC) is a threat to the boxing business?

Don King: I like ultimate fighting. It's a raw thing like street fighting. Ultimate fighting is raw, that's why you've got huge number of fans. I intend to promote that, too. The only really successful [person] in the ultimate fighting is Dana White. They've got the cage and all that. This was a raw type of barbarism, now it's become a sophisticated type of barbarism which the public loves. When you have these types of things you can bring people together. I think it's sensational and I have nothing but praise for those who have been successful and carved a niche out beyond. It used to be like when Clint Eastwood used to go around with his little ape, with the boxing movies which he was doing where he's going around and fighting [bare fisted].

Then you can look at the champions of the past where they used to fight forty to fifty rounds. Then as it began to get sophisticated the Marquess of Queensberry, guy from the United Kingdom, began to bring it down to where there were rules, regulations of that sort. Then you find in this era the WBC, under the leadership of the dynamic Jose Sulaiman, has been able to bring a lot of safety to boxers and establish the rounds by bringing it down to twelve and having a doctor at the ringside. I think ultimate fighting is good. With the ultimate fighting you have a mixture of arts and boxing. Nothing gets out of the Sweet Science because you're swinging, you're in a combat sport. So boxing is different because it's specifically boxing.

They both can survive and they both bring people together. So what you're doing is the younger crowd, which is coming up, didn't have the golden opportunity of witnessing a Muhammad Ali; George Foreman; Ken Norton; Roberto Duran; Sugar Ray Leonard; Sugar Ray Robinson; Joe Louis, all of those that were really carrying the banner for when other sports were not coming into plan as they are today. So I think now with the ultimate fighting, there are new kinds of fans, not as per se boxing fans, but as fans of a brutal combat sport with elbows, kicking, biting.

This is something which the youngsters love and is the younger attitudes of kids. I think one can help the other, and, you know, we did that with Antonio Inoki and Muhammad Ali. I used to have the ultimate fighting on one of my cards with Muhammad Ali. What's the guy's name? He named himself after Muhammad Ali fighting out of Orlando years ago. So we were doing that, and Ali fought the Japanese wrestler, as you know, Inoki. Inoki was an ultimate fighting champion and Ali was a boxing champion. They put them together and Inoki was kicking him all over the legs. But those are the things which are coming in and are harmonizing. So I think it's great. I have no quarrel with ultimate fighting because it's a people's sport and a lot of people and youngsters are coming to see it. It's exciting. Hey, that brings people together and that's what I'm about – promoting the people.

JIM BROWN

Jim Brown is the greatest professional football player in history and one of the greatest athletes America has ever produced. From 1957 to 1965, he played for the Cleveland Browns and was recognized as the AP NFL Valuable Player three times, winning an NFL championship with the Browns in 1964 and setting several rushing records. After retiring from football, Brown made the transition to Hollywood and appeared in films including *The Dirty Dozen* and *Ice Station Zebra*, while also working with the civil rights movement. He was inducted into the Pro Football Hall of Fame in 1971. Brown and Muhammad Ali were close friends from the mid-1960s until Ali's death.

Q: Jim, when did you first meet Muhammad Ali?
Jim Brown: Yeah, it was back in the 1960s. During the civil rights movement, I met him and we became pretty close. I had a lot of admiration for his position. He was a social activist. He fought for everything that was right about being a first-class citizen in this country. And I had great admiration for his stance and his courage. And, of course, he was a great fighter. I followed his fights and broadcasted a couple of them. I supported his position.

Q: Can you tell me about the historical meeting you and some of the elite African-American athletes had with Muhammad Ali during the time he caused a great uproar after his refusal to join the army?
Jim Brown: I was in England finishing up a film. There was a lot of publicity about Muhammad Ali that I thought was really propaganda. And I thought they were misleading the public. I ran an organization at the time called The Negro Industrial and Economic Union. I called the executive director, John Wooten, and told him we should meet with Ali, as top black athletes in the country, and have a discussion with him to determine what his true position was and what the facts

were. Then when I came back into the country, we would set a date for that meeting, and we did that. I came back and the night before I met with Muhammad Ali at my home, where me and him discussed the whole concept of what we were doing.

The next day, in my office in Cleveland, we were able to sit down with him and for about four hours discuss his position and his concept, his ideas and get the facts. And the facts were: he had a religion that did not believe in war and because of his religion, he wasn't going to go into the service. And we felt that was a valid position and that he was very sincere in that position. So we came out and had our press conference and made it known that as a unit we agreed that we would support his position. Because we believed that it was a genuine position and the correct position for him. So that is the basis of that story.

Q: Do you feel that he did a lot and paved the way for the black community and also the black athletes in the 1960s?
Jim Brown: Well, firstly, yes. He did great work for the black athletes, but more for the black community. He didn't concentrate on athletes; he concentrated on the black community because most athletes were living a pretty good life in America, and they were getting privileges that the black population did not get. So his concentration was on the so-called small people, the regular people – the citizens of this country. But I might add that Muhammad Ali, in fighting for justice for black people, was really fighting for all people because if one group of people do not enjoy democracy, then democracy is a sham. Democracy cannot just be for one group of people, it must be for all the people otherwise it doesn't work. So, his effort to help black people was an effort to help all people.

Q: Any deep conversation you had with Muhammad Ali that comes to mind – you were close friends for many decades?
Jim Brown: Yes, that's true. We had a lot of fun together and he was always joking. But there was a serious side to him. One day he said, "Come on, let's take a walk in the community." I said, "Take a walk

in the community? What are we going to do?" He said, "We're just going to walk in the community and talk to the people. And allow other people to talk to us. We will show them we care about them because we will take this walk." I thought it was a very simple thing, an elementary thing. I thought it was a very powerful thing for us to do because how many celebrities would think of just walking among the people saying hello, kissing babies, shaking hands and encouraging people that there is a better life than the worker was living, and we were thinking about them? I thought it was just a wonderful thing he thought of. So he started regularly walking among people, just saying hello, going in barber shops, hairdressers and the people loved it. He was the kind of a person that could talk to anyone and make people feel good. He was human and he was very kind.

Q: The Wilt Chamberlain fight, was Muhammad Ali going to fight him?

Jim Brown: Yes. It was an idea that we could do a fight together between Wilt Chamberlain and Muhammad Ali because Wilt was so big and strong. Herbert Muhammad was Ali's manager at the time. I was approached about the idea. I said it's a good idea and it might be interesting. We talked to Herbert. So what was going to happen, I was going to be the manager of Wilt Chamberlain and I think Cus D'Amato was going to be the trainer. And we went to New York and met at the hotel across Madison Square Garden. I put it together. But when Ali and Wilt got together Ali came up to about Wilt Chamberlain's chest. Herbert saw how big Wilt was. I think he decided it would not be a good idea because there would be a possibility Ali could not reach Wilt Chamberlain's jaw. So everything was called off. But it was a legitimate attempt to put the two of them together.

Q: Can you talk about your sparring experience with Muhammad Ali?

Jim Brown: Yes. Once Ali came to the house with Angelo Dundee and a group of people, and he brought me a pair of boxing gloves as a gift. Then he said, "Come on, put them on and let's spar in the yard!" I had a house in the hills with a deck that overlooked the city. So, I put the gloves on and we started to spar, and he said, "Come on, hit me!" I kept trying to hit him but never could hit him. He was too quick, too fast and he wouldn't even punch me. And for about three rounds, I kept on trying to hit him and never could hit him and I got tired. When I got tired he started to jab me, and show me how he would then get his opponent tired. When they got tired he would do a jab and right cross, and that's how he won a lot of his fights. We had a big laugh about it because I never thought I could fight Muhammad Ali. So everything was in fun and jest. He always had a twinkle in his eye, always having fun and making a point. So he made that point very clear that day: that a football player would not have a chance against him as a fighter.

Q: Did he ever come on the set of any of your movies?
Jim Brown: Yeah. When I was in London he came on the set of *The Dirty Dozen*. He met a lot of the stars and said hello to a lot of them. He clowned around with some of them and enjoyed it. We were shooting there at the time and he was training in England.

Q: Do you think Muhammad Ali eventually moved away from the Nation of Islam and made a transition into mainstream Islam, what's your opinion on this?
Jim Brown: Actually, I don't know the whole story, but I know that Muhammad Ali believed in Elijah Muhammad. I think when Elijah Muhammad died everything changed for him. I think he did become a more mainstream follower of Islam. I don't think he really turned his back on Elijah's people in the Nation of Islam. I think he just became more of a mainstream follower of Islam. He had a great love for Elijah Muhammad, because when he fought Sonny Liston in Miami, and I got with him after the fight, he pointed out to me that he did not plan to follow Malcolm X, but he was going to remain a follower of the Honorable Elijah Muhammad. And that's what he did.

Q: Which fights did you attend at ringside and do you have any behind-the-scenes stories?

Jim Brown: When Ali fought Henry Cooper I was at ringside. I was in Zaire when he fought George Foreman; I broadcast the fight with David Frost from Zaire, Africa, when he beat George Foreman. Well, a behind-the-scenes story is that the fight was postponed and the people were really behind Muhammad Ali 100 percent. But George was a favorite at the time. I think he took a couple of police dogs over to Africa, but the people did not like police dogs because the police use them just to arrest people. It was just a bad move on George's part not knowing that and Ali took full advantage of it. He created this Zaire language statement "Ali bombayi!" "Ali bombayi!" I guess it meant "Ali knock George Foreman out," to that effect.

Q: You were friends with Muhammad Ali for a long time, any final words?

Jim Brown: Muhammad Ali was a great man who believed in people. He fought for the rights of black people and had a great love for people. Arguably he could be called the greatest fighter of all time. But as good as he was in the ring, he was even greater outside of the ring because he stood up for what he believed in. He was a great man.

WALTER BEACH

Walter Beach III, born in Pontiac, Michigan to a hardworking family, played football for the Boston Patriots in the AFL and the Cleveland Browns in the NFL. He was one of the African-American athletes invited to the historical meeting in Cleveland, in 1967, by NFL Hall of Fame member Jim Brown to support Muhammad Ali's draft situation. He is currently the CEO of Amer-I-Can of New York, Inc, a company founded by his teammate and friend Jim Brown.

Q: You were one of the well-known African-American athletes who supported Muhammad Ali's draft stance. How did your own upbringing affect how you evolved as a person?
Walter Beach: The culture, in society at the time the Jim Crow segregation was prevalent and you developed a personal strategy to address it. Some individuals reflected more so than others. And some of them were, you know, acclimated to the system of Jim Crow segregation. It was a personal journey. I came from a race-conscious family. My grandmother and grandfather were very conscious of race. So I was always confronted with that. My mother, my father and grandmother were always addressing those particular issues. That was the essence of my development. Some individuals came up in a different environment, but I was always made aware in my community because it was a small community in Pontiac, Michigan. We had an extended family type of a situation. I was always very conscious of what my race was and my responsibility, duty and commitment to my family. That was just my upbringing.

Q: Can you shed light on the historical meeting organized by your friend and Hall of Fame inductee, Jim Brown, to support Muhammad Ali's draft stance?
Walter Beach: The first time I actually met him was at that meeting. That was developed basically by Jim Brown. He was a member of the Cleveland Browns, the same time I was. Jim had

contacted Lew Alcindor (Kareem Abdul-Jabbar), Bill Russell and some of the individual athletes. At that particular time, I was a member of the Cleveland Browns. So Jim brought us together and we had discussions, and Ali shared his views with everybody about commitment to his religion and the Nation of Islam.

I don't think, to the best of my knowledge, any one of us were Muslims. Well, I know I wasn't. I thought most of the people in the group were not Muslims, but we supported the principle. The principle he had, we agreed with. We agreed that was the way he felt exercising what I would call 'his inherent validity of what he wanted to do'. And I think that's what we all supported. It was one of the things when you're confronted with those kinds of situations, situations of your personal belief and faith. And his belief and faith was that he shouldn't go to war. He was a conscientious objector, he didn't believe in going to war. He especially didn't believe in going to war against individuals or people he thought he had no particular argument with. Based on his religion and political beliefs, I agreed with that. I wasn't a conscientious objector. In fact, I did serve in the military.

Q: Did Muhammad Ali clarify anything specific?
Walter Beach: Ali was very clear he was a conscientious objector. He didn't believe in going to war. He also supported the Nation of Islam in terms of what the minister was articulating. He also believed in being a member of a community. There were a lot of people in opposition to the Vietnam War, not only Ali. And Ali was very clear about the fact that he didn't want to be associated with that kind of behavior. I think our group of athletes at the meeting all supported that: his right to express himself. We were not speaking for anybody else other than ourselves. That was what the Negro Union was about. We tried to organize to bring athletes together, that we have a bigger responsibility and not just play sports. It was a discussion with all athletes who were in that particular meeting. We shared our philosophy and conversation and no one was more important than anyone else. We respected each other and we acknowledged the fact that there could be a difference made.

But in that particular group there were no particular differences. And what Ali talked about was the black man, African-American man in this country being subjected to some of the same things that, what I would say to you, the imperialized and Communists were doing in Vietnam. But the principle is: why go to war with someone you have a battle with when your side is not really treating you well, anyway. It's kind of an interesting relationship. But those who have been in the field personally feel that if someone's violating your rights, and at the same time he asks you to come and join him to violate someone else's rights, it's kind of a stretch of someone's imagination that you'd be interested in doing that. I wasn't one of them and I don't think Ali was one of them. I'm not trying to equate myself with Muhammad Ali, because he's probably one of the foremost human beings I've come into contact with who I really respect.

Q: Was there anything specific that captured your attention that he propagated?
Walter Beach: Ali was interesting. I had a chance to talk with him when he was preparing for a couple of his fights. I remember we had a discussion when he was getting ready for one of his fights, somebody asked him, "Do you have a game plan or strategy?" He said, "Yeah. You always have a game plan and a strategy until you get hit." He said when someone hits you, you forget all about that. Ali was a very gracious, funny and comical guy.

He was very witty, but at the same time when he was serious he had a great deal of insight. And he was very critical and a very critical thinker. But it was a fact that social morality was something he was concerned about. He, like a lot of us at the time, wondered why there was no moral outrage at the injustice. It's similar to today. You don't have outrage about the injustices that certain people face. He was in a different level and the intensity of morality we were exposed to at that time. I think that the understanding was that we were involved in sports as entertainment. And entertainment is precisely that: to soothe the individuals, you entertain them.

But there are some real critical issues. The environment and culture are far more important than entertainment. I was personally brought into that by one of the individuals that I considered a hero – other than Jim Brown, Muhammad Ali and Bill Russell – Paul Robeson. Paul Robeson was a quality human being. He always talked about human issues. He was also a very talented entertainer, an actor, a singer and athlete. But there were always other things going on in his life other than just the entertainment. And that is something which I think might be missing a great deal today in present day athletes, which is, again, my personal opinion. I don't know any professional athlete who deals with any kind of social issues and cultural issues, which affect not only African-Americans but all human beings in a meaningful and relevant manner.

Q: Did you go to watch his fights?
Walter Beach: I didn't see much of his fights other than on television. I was a professional football player. I don't think I've been to a football game in my life – the Browns invited me down once. I'm not that type of a person. That's not the height of my entertainment. In fact, my entertainment comes from a great deal of reading. I just love to read and focus. And I play chess. That's where I find my comfort satisfaction. I don't attend fights, baseball games and basketball games, of that nature.

Q: Do you feel Ali was a naturally gifted athlete, and was this the reason behind his success in the ring?
Walter Beach: He was a superb athlete. He's probably one of the masters of the game. He studied, he trained and worked hard. People have a tendency to think, especially super athletes like today's Michael Jordan, Kobe Bryant, and they work at that! They have a God-given talent but they work at it. And Ali worked at it, he didn't just take it for granted. So he paid the dues. He was up in the morning doing the roadwork. Let me tell you this: the athletic ability and the God-given talent is necessary but it's not sufficient. So what you're given, you need that. But for it to be sufficient you need to work on it. You've got to put your time in. You've got to do

your roadwork, hit the big heavy bag and you have to watch the films and study. So it requires a level of commitment that takes you out of the normal, your average range to the level of being a superior athlete. And Muhammad Ali was a superior athlete physically and spiritually. And his spiritual development is another thing people don't address. Spirituality, he had to raise it, and his confidence and spiritual commitment to being the best thing he could be.

Q: Was there anything that Muhammad Ali said that you found edifying?

Walter Beach: Well, I heard several things he said that I would consider, you know, having some power on the mind. He quoted a lot of the times where he talks about oppression. He stated one time in my presence, it weren't his words but it were someone else's words from South Africa. He said, "The statement is probably the most potent weapon in the hands of the oppressor." Muhammad Ali said that the mind is the most important weapon. You've got to keep your mind clear and focused. You've got to be able to fight. That was basically going back to the aspect where I was telling you about planning everything, but then you get hit. The mind is the most important thing. That's one of the messages I got from Muhammad Ali: to have a clear, sharp and focused mind. And I think that's where a lot of his humor and wit came from because his mind was sharp and clear.

FRED WILLIAMSON

Professional football player turned actor Fred Williamson is most famous for playing a pivotal role in the 'Blaxploitation' movie boom of the 1970s. During the 1960s, he played for NFL Pittsburgh Steelers, AFL Oakland Raiders and AFL Kansas City Chiefs. He made the transition to acting in 1967, appearing in movies including *Black Caesar*, *Hell Up In Harlem* and *MASH*, becoming known as The Hammer because of his karate-based on-screen fighting style. In 1996, Williamson co-starred in *From Dusk till Dawn* and appeared in the feature film *Starsky and Hutch*. He continues to act, direct and produce.

Q: In the late 1950s and 1960s, how hard was it for African-American athletes and actors to make it big in the United States and break the racial barrier?
Fred Williamson: It's pretty hard to answer that question and combine those two because those are separate entities. Athletes always find a way to make it in any society because people want to win, it's an individual event. So obviously, to do that they want to get the best athletes and best athletes were black – that's just the way it is. So it was not so hard for athletes to have success. We probably were at the low end of the pay scale, but at least there were jobs available for good black athletes.

But as far as actors are concerned, it still comes down to the challenge: you bring something to the table and allow people to make money from your talent, then there's a way to overcome the barrier. You can't come asking for something, you have to bring something different. So you bring something different and something that is marketable, then you have a better chance of becoming successful because it's just not based on talent. There are a lot of people unemployed that are talented. You have to bring something to the table where people can make money off you. Everybody likes to make money, but that doesn't mean they want to come to your house to have dinner, nor do you want them to come to your house to have dinner. All you want to do is allow them to make some money, they make money off you and you make money. So it's all about dollars and cents.

Q: When did Muhammad Ali come to your attention?

Fred Williamson: I was looking at the man because the man was a mirror of my approach to the business world, my approach to society. Muhammad Ali was a manipulator like I have been in my career. I have been manipulating people without having them know that they're being manipulated. It's been over forty years since I played football, since I've hung up my shoes. I was known as The Hammer. Today, I'm still known as The Hammer by people who never saw me play, by people who only heard of me. So my nickname The Hammer has stuck with me and stuck with people's minds because I have allowed it to happen. Muhammad Ali had the same idea about the tough look, being the baddest guy on the planet is not the way to be marketable; you have to bring something different to the table like I said. He was a braggadocio whom everybody wanted to shut up. Everybody wanted to beat him up and put him down.

By doing that he put himself in a position where people went into him. Even though he wasn't a bad guy in the ring, everybody wanted to fight Muhammad Ali to shut him up. He was a master at doing this. He was a master at crowding people at the corner, getting them angry at him then backing off, showing a little smile and a little charm. People would say, "Wow, was he really serious? Is he really like that?" Nobody really knew because he never allowed you that opportunity. He would just do it that way for you. And it was based on your personality on how you accepted Muhammad Ali, which is the same way I played football. When I walked out on the field because of my braggadocio and me saying what I was going to do individually to the teams I was playing, fifty thousand people booed on one side of the field and fifty thousand people cheered on the other side of the field. That's a hundred thousand people looking at you. It doesn't matter because they're not going to influence your play. They're not going to influence what your ability is to get the job done. That's a hundred thousand people getting your attention.

Q: Do you feel Muhammad Ali did more than just elevate boxing? Would you say he was a spokesman for the black community, whose adulation for him stemmed from him standing up for their rights?

Fred Williamson: He was looked up to by every black person because he had something he believed in. He believed in his religion. He believed in his right, and took and suffered the consequences based on the fact his religion was in conflict with the American government. So people looked up to him because he was a man who stood for something. He stood for himself and he was not a sell-out. He was willing to go to jail and he was willing to pay the price for what he believed in. Any man who does that will obviously get a lot of following and respect from people no matter what color he is.

Q: Did the white man accept the blacks after Muhammad Ali's emergence on the scene, or was there mixed feelings?

Fred Williamson: No, no, no. White's never accepted us back then and they don't accept us today. It's about dollars. Again, it's about money. The difference between blacks and whites is: if you make people money they accept you. To make money for them, it doesn't mean they accept you socially. Then again, it's not important. Blacks who are striving for identity and to be respected on an equal level, that's really what blacks are trying to attain – economic equality and respect.

Q: So athletes and actors didn't get treated the same as the white actors and athletes on a professional basis in the civil rights movement period?

Fred Williamson: You can't put those two together. You can't put athletes and actors together because every athlete can't be an actor. When you look at the athletes who tried to go into the acting business, whether they were black or white, there are not many who made it. Jim Brown and I are probably the two prime examples of athletes who were top of their sports and were able to transcend into the acting business. That was a matter of timing and not so much black and white, but about marketability. Jim Brown, put him into a movie, people would want to see him. And it was the same with me. So we brought something to the table. We weren't asking for anything, we brought notoriety. After we got into the business, it was up to us to show them we had talent and to sustain the talent we had. Jim did well and I'm still doing well. Again, the difference between black and white is green, dude.

Q: Did you watch Muhammad Ali on TV or go to his fights?
Fred Williamson: I probably saw 95 percent of his fights. I think probably the most dramatic experience I had watching Muhammad Ali is when he was hit and went down for the first time in the Frazier fight. I think everybody in the room, where I was watching it, we all started crying. He went down and he lost the fight. That was a very dramatic experience for me and all of Muhammad Ali's followers.

Q: Were you friends?
Fred Williamson: Yeah, I was a friend of Muhammad Ali. Muhammad and I knew each other well because we have the same philosophy about success. So when we met we used to talk. I went to his home many times in Chicago, which is where I'm from, at the time he was living in Chicago. We used to have weekend things at his house. We'd put big tents up and he would have parties. Muhammad Ali and I were good friends.

Q: Would I be right in saying that the Nation of Islam was an avenue for black people to get together and help get the 'message' out?
Fred Williamson: No. I don't think you'd be correct in saying that. Islamic religion was never accepted because they thought,

first of all, Muhammad Ali was using it as an excuse not to go in the service when he was drafted. So a lot of people never really accepted the Islamic movement as a religion. They thought it might be something to unite black people against white people, so it was an organization that was always feared. It wasn't an organization that was respected. It was feared because white people had this fear about this unity between black people because we had never had unity as a whole. Here comes an organization, which is trying to unify blacks, so it created more fear than it brought positivity.

Q: What's the most compelling thing you heard him say?

Fred Williamson: It's not one thing. I think that when people really heard and listened to Muhammad Ali talk, they started to understand he was sincere in his beliefs and that he was not using his religion as an excuse to change things. He was trying to express himself that this is what he believes in. And you cannot discredit a man for his beliefs no matter what his beliefs are. If he believes hard enough you have to accept him or avoid him, you don't challenge him. And that's what happened to Muhammad Ali. He got challenged by the courts, by the government, by the law saying that his religion was not a real religion. But Muhammad Ali, if you listen to him speak you understand the man and the religion, felt that he was doing the right thing as per his religion. So I think that was his greatest asset. If you listen to him he knew well how to express himself.

Q: How would you define Muhammad Ali from the perspective of a great sportsman?

Fred Williamson: He was the greatest boxer of all time. His quote was 'float like a butterfly, sting like a bee'. He's probably the only heavyweight that boxed like a lightweight. The guy was fast, quicker than you can see. His footwork shows you that he was a stage fighter, not just a big clumsy lumbering heavyweight, which is what we have today. Today, we've got big clumsy guys throwing wild punches in the ring. We don't have anybody that's as good as him. The heavyweight division in boxing is dead! There's nobody interesting in the heavyweights today. He was able to accomplish things and make boxing into entertainment, all into one. Nobody's been able to do that in the heavyweight division ever since.

Q: Regarding the racial stigma, which has affected many people, how much of an impact did the Ku Klux Klan have on the American society back then?

Fred Williamson: Well, the Ku Klux Klan was the organization that was destined for failure from the start. You can't have an organization in America based on social conflict, which includes violence and crime and breaking the law. That's self-destructive right from the beginning. They have no real agenda except to kill black people and hang black people. You cannot have an agenda in America in society on hurting other people, no matter what color they are. Sooner or later a law is going to be broken. And if the laws are broken then the organization suffers a divide. There were too many things they were doing wrong in the Klan, it was destined for failure.

Q: What charity organization did Muhammad Ali support back in those days?

Fred Williamson: Ali knew what he was. He knew that he was a leader. He knew people followed him. He knew people listened to him. So he was very careful about getting in with any organization, which he would align himself to. There was an organization that Jim Brown had, which is helping black people in negative economic situations and helping them elevate themselves by finding jobs. That was an organization that Jim Brown had and Muhammad Ali was involved and was supporting him in what he was doing. So he was very careful about any organization he aligned himself with, but there were not many Muhammad Ali was involved in.

Q: Can you tell me about when you and your wife last met Muhammad Ali at an event?

Fred Williamson: We were in Vegas for an event. We did the whole hug thing. I was very moved by the fact he still knew who I was.

He remembered me and it was quite a moving experience that he wasn't so far gone as he physically appeared. His mentality was still working well and his speech was a bit slurred. And he was a little slow, but everything wasn't gone. I thought there's still a Muhammad Ali in there.

Q: Why is Muhammad Ali admired by people beyond the boxing and sports fraternity?

Fred Williamson: Muhammad Ali stood for something: he stood for a man who had beliefs and was willing to take the fall and go down because of his beliefs, on top of being a damn good fighter, motivation fighter. There's no fighter to have come along since then that brought that much entertainment inside the ring as well as outside the ring. There's no fighter today that brings that much excitement to their sport. It was most definitely entertaining.

Q: Would you say he had two personalities – outer and inner? He was a nice guy underneath all the bragging and the name-calling he did before a fight.

Fred Williamson: That was the beauty of the man – you never knew! He never told you! He never explained it to you. It's up to you to draw your own conclusions. This means that he put the pressure on you and on your personality and on your character to have you ask yourself, *Is this serious or is he just fooling around?* That was the beauty of it all. It allowed you to make the decision without him trying to explain himself, which he never did!

DR. HARRY EDWARDS

Dr. Harry Edwards is a professor emeritus of sociology at the University of Berkeley, California. He has been at the forefront of the intersection between race and sports in America for more than four decades, being a radical spokesman for black athletes in the sports world and an advocate for them taking management positions. He was a promising athlete before completing his degree in sociology, and served as a staff consultant to the San Francisco 49ers football team and the Golden State Warriors basketball team. He is the author of several books, including *The Revolt of the Black Athlete*, originally published in 1985 and now updated to comment on the Black Lives Matter movement.

Q: In the early days, how much of an impact did black athletes, such as Jesse Owens and Jackie Robinson, have on American society before Muhammad Ali rose to prominence?
Dr. Harry Edwards: In the years leading up to, and immediately after, World War II black athletes, black Americans overall, were fighting to gain access. They were fighting to break the shackles of segregation. That fight, of course, was highlighted in Jesse Owens' and Joe Louis' status of coming back from various athletic events. Jesse Owens from the 1936 Olympics, and the two fights Joe Louis had with the German champion. And that really kind of brought the black athlete to the fore on the mainstream stage, not just American society but the world.

Following World War II, for many black Americans themselves it was a war against racism as much as a war against empire. The black athlete role was actually accelerated, that was a tremendous push following World War II to integrate sports in American society. We all know about the great experiment by Jackie Robinson, but in professional football you also had Kenny Washington and Woody Strode integrating the Los Angeles Rams. You had players like Bill Willis and Marion Motley, who also came during that era into mainstream professional football. So there was this tremendous push for access. That was the struggle at that stage, the years immediately before World War II.

Then coming out of World War II, this tremendous pressure born out of blacks fighting in World War II as much as anything, war of racism, blacks had advances of being able to move the war into the street for somewhat of an equal footing with whites. And then the soldiers coming back from the war, who really fuelled the notion that if freedom and justice and so forth are good enough for the people of Europe, then it's good enough for the people of the Philippines, then it should be good enough for us right here. And black athletes coming out of the pre-World War II era, being the one that was really more than anyone else in the black community on the front stage, on the mainstream stage, there was this tremendous push to follow through after World War II. And that is how you got this tremendous pressure to integrate football and baseball, in particular Jackie Robinson; Kenny Washington; Woody Strode; Marion Motley; Bill Willis and all of these guys. It was a battle for access.

Q: When did you first come into contact with Muhammad Ali?
Dr. Harry Edwards: My first contact with Muhammad Ali was in 1960. I was a freshman track and field and basketball athlete at San Jose State. I had come out of junior college. I had set a national discus record and had transferred to San Jose State on a track and basketball scholarship. It just so happened the boxing coach for the United States 1960 Olympic team was Jules Menendez, who also happened to be from St. Louis – the same place I had come from to California to play. Jules Menendez was also from St. Louis. So when he brought the United States boxing team to San Jose to work out, I got a chance to meet Muhammad Ali. At that time, I was 6ft 7, 250 pounds, a discus thrower and a basketball player. He looked like this little 6ft 3, skinny kid. He may have weighed 175 pounds. But he was a boxer and he talked a lot and he was really fun to watch. That was my first contact with Muhammad Ali.

The second time I really became aware is after he won the Olympic gold medal in 1960. And he actually ended up fighting another guy who had roots in St. Louis, Sonny Liston, who we were aware of in St. Louis for a number of years, and more certainly after he beat Floyd Patterson. Then all of a sudden, I look up and here's Muhammad Ali fighting Sonny Liston. Nobody thought he could beat Liston. Liston was the biggest, meanest, baddest guy in the world. But the one person who really believed he can beat Liston was Cassius Clay. So that was my second really intense awareness of Muhammad Ali.

Then in 1967, at the time of his ban by the boxing world because of his refusal to comply with the draft, he came to Cornell University where I was doing the PhD work. As a matter of fact, I was asked to be his escort and guide for the day and so I sat next to him. We talked quite a bit at dinner that they had prior to him speaking to the student bodies at Cornell. So I've had some direct contact with Muhammad Ali going back over the years. And, of course, we've talked on a number of times over the years at speaking engagements, various events. One was a boxing exhibition event at San Quentin State Prison in the early 1970s when I was doing counselling for inmates. I saw him during that time.

Q: During the 1968 Olympics boycott, what role did Muhammad Ali play?
Dr. Harry Edwards: Ali in 1968 was, of course, battling to be reinstated as the heavyweight champion of the world, and in a more direct and urgent battle to stay out of jail. One of the things that we had demanded was justice for Muhammad Ali, in terms of that situation as a component of the Olympic project for human rights. We felt that stripping Muhammad Ali of his championship because of his refusal on religious grounds to comply with the military draft was a violation of his human rights. So there was that connection. But on a more fundamental level, Muhammad Ali was the godfather in many ways of the modern, more militant black athlete political movement. Jackie Robinson, Joe Louis and Jesse

Owens had battled for access. The generation that came up with and after Muhammad Ali struggled for dignity and respect, not just as athletes but as men.

We did not see it as sufficient to have access. To be 20th century gladiators in the entertainment service of American society, we wanted respect as men. We did not want to go and participate in athletic events such as the New York Athletic Club Games at Madison Square Garden when we could not join the New York Athletic Club because of our race. We did not think that it was right for us to participate in the Olympic Games when there was not a single black person on the United States Olympic Committee in 1967 when we started the movement. So Muhammad Ali was really the first to stand up more militantly for dignity and respect, as a man as well as an athlete in the post-World War II era. Those athletes who came before led the challenges of that generation, which was to break the shackles of segregation. The challenges of our generation were to break the mentalization of black athletes on athletic fields. But once we left the athletic arena we were just more colored people, more people confined to the status of second-class citizens.

So, Muhammad Ali was the first to really stand up and demand full, total, complete access and dignity and respect along with access. And to break the image of the black athlete as self-effacing, comfortable with his situation doing what he needed doing on the athletic field. Being grateful and thankful for the access then shutting up and going back to the ghettos, back to the segregated hotel, back to the status of being a 'boy' once he left the arena. Muhammad Ali led the way. And in the wake of Muhammad Ali and that direction he set almost single-handedly, Bill Russell was much more adamant and outspoken, which he was through his career. But Muhammad Ali kind of set the direction and tone for how Bill Russell was seeing, the same with Jim Brown; the same with Tommie Smith and John Carlos; the same with Arthur Ashe, at a certain level.

So, by the time Muhammad Ali had emerged, and moved not just from the outspoken: I'm black and I'm proud and I'm a beautiful guy, when he was in the 1960 Olympics, to Muhammad Ali who refused to step forward and submit to the demands of the draft, a new generation of athletes had emerged. So Tommie Smith and John Carlos were not Jesse Owens. Muhammad Ali was not Joe Louis. And, of course, Curt Flood, who is really the father of free agency in American sports, was not Jackie Robinson. What Muhammad Ali did and what he represented is a dividing line between the athletes between the second half of the 20th century and the black athlete of the first half of the 20th century. Muhammad Ali led the way for the modern black athlete to break with our fathers and mothers in terms of political, social and cultural ideology. He made it legitimate to be outspoken, to demand respect and dignity. He made it legitimate for black athletes to take their place as men as well as athletes of the modern social, political and popular cultural stage.

Q: Do you feel Muhammad Ali's persona made boxing a glamor industry and elevated sports in the United States?
Dr. Harry Edwards: Well, boxing had been a glamor industry at a certain level going all the way back to Jack Johnson, especially in the African-American community. What Ali did, in conjunction with television and the input, if you will, people such as Howard Cosell, is to make boxers more accessible – boxing ring celebrities. What television allowed Howard Cosell and Muhammad Ali to do was to glamorize and give a much greater profile in popular culture to the boxer. Jack Johnson had high profile in the African-American community, in the black community, and a very negative profile in the white community. Sugar Ray Robinson had a high profile. Joe Louis, of course, had a high profile. But they were fundamentally high profiles in the boxing world, except when they came to represent something more convenient for the broader society. So, Joe Louis came to represent the strong, right arm democracy against Nazism, the knockout punch of democracy against Nazism. But beyond those kinds of things, a boxer was basically a boxing entity, if you will.

With television, Muhammad Ali in conjunction with Howard Cosell, what they did was to make the black athlete pave the way for the black athlete becoming something broader and more significant than a major icon in the department of the human affairs, mainly sports. So Muhammad Ali stood for much more than just his status as a great boxer. Thomas Smith and John Carlos came to stand for much more than simply their status as great track athletes. Arthur Ashe came to stand for much more than simply his status as a Wimbledon champion and a great tennis player. Bill Russell stood for much more than simply winning the most championships won by any athlete of all times of any sport. Jim Brown came to stand for more than simply the greatest football player ever to play the game. They had a broader, political and social cultural status as a consequence of the role played by Muhammad Ali.

Q: How would you define Muhammad Ali from the perspective of a supremely gifted athlete?

Dr. Harry Edwards: From an athletic perspective, I think the way I have always looked at Muhammad Ali from a boxing perspective is: you take Sugar Ray Robinson and put another 60 pounds on him, and you put another seven or eight inches on him, then you have Muhammad Ali. He was literally a beautiful work of art to watch as an athlete. He pursued his craft of boxing as if he were a Picasso at painting, or Michalangelo with a chisel in his hand. You knew there was going to be something beautiful and memorable that was going to come out of it. You felt blessed to be there to watch him, his creation, whether it was Thrilla in Manila or the Rumble in the Jungle or Sonny Liston's first fight. You knew there was going to be something great that came out of it. There was electricity with the Muhammad Ali fight. And it was the way he approached his craft. When you see the rope-a-dope thing, it looked brutal.

Then when you look back in retrospect, then you understand that was knocking the corners off the block of granite George Foreman. And at the end he threw it all out. There he was standing over George Foreman – a work of art. At the end of it Muhammad Ali was the consummate artist. He always seemed to see something beautiful in every fight that he wanted to bring out, that he wanted to make manifest. It was like Michelangelo looking at a nondescript block of granite and seeing the clear top. There was something of that in every fight that Muhammad Ali fought.

And in some instances he just wanted to give a guy a payday. He would give this guy and his family the biggest payday of their career. He gave a lot of guys a payday. So there was always something intriguing, something that grabbed your attention and held it about the way Muhammad Ali pursued his craft. That ultimate mix of feel and power, craftsmanship, footwork, intelligence and just what he was able to do in that way was just a beautiful thing to watch.

Q: What is the most thought-provoking conversation you ever had with him?

Dr. Harry Edwards: It was at the dinner table at Cornell. I remember asking him what made him not step forward for the draft, and his statement was: I had no choice. I mean, it was at that point you know for the first time, I really felt the seriousness of Muhammad Ali, about what he saw as his mission on this earth. He saw himself as a champion well before he beat Sonny Liston. He saw himself as a serious person long before the world took even his name Muhammad Ali seriously. And leading into the draft situation, he saw himself as having no choice. That was the most compelling conversation of the very few direct conversations I had with him.

Q: In the 1970s Muhammad Ali fought in a number of high-profile fights and received big paydays up to the region of $5 million. Did he get commercial endorsements and did this change the boxing and the sporting world?

Dr. Harry Edwards: Well, in the 1970s Ali didn't get a bunch of endorsements! I mean, coming out of the draft situation a lot of corporations thought he was toxic. Ali was not really accepted and celebrated for the stand he took on the Vietnam issue, until well into the 1980s. Specifically, the Los Angeles Olympics and the Atlanta Olympics and so forth, a new generation emerged who were young people in the 1960s, who were college students in the early 1970s. As they began to really approach full stride as adults, they carried with them the image of Ali as heroic and iconic. And it was then that his status began to really blossom, emerge and be recognized, down to including lighting the torch at the Atlanta Olympics. The endorsement situation, in the 1960s and 1970s, was minimal for all black athletes. You had some black athletes such as O.J. Simpson who got to do endorsements. But they were always paired with somebody white, and that was going all the way into the 1980s.

So if you look at O.J. Simpson, he did a commercial with Arnold Palmer. You had other black athletes, even in the 1980s, like Magic Johnson who did a commercial with Willie Shoemaker, the jockey, or Larry Bird. It wasn't until the late 1980s, with the emergence of Michael Jordan that you really got a black athlete who did commercials and got endorsements with crossover appeal. O.J. Simpson finally emerged on his own with Hertz Rent-a-Car, running through airports. And to show you how racist it still was, there's not a single solitary Hertz Rent-a-Car commercial where you have black people commenting on O.J. Simpson running through airports. They wanted to keep them as far away from black identity as possible. You have all white women commenting. You have white kids commenting. You have white businessmen commenting, but no black people commenting on O.J. Simpson as he ran through airports in the Hertz commercials. That's how racist it still was even in the mid and late 1980s.

But Ali in the 1970s did not get any substantial number of commercials. I remember one commercial he did do, in the 1960s, I believe it was a commercial for Roach Motel. Bill Russell never got any substantial commercial work. Wilt Chamberlain didn't get any substantial commercial work. Hank Aaron didn't get any substantial commercial work. These things came later in the wake of broader acceptance of the dignity and so forth of black athletes off the field. These things came in the wake of the revolt of black athletes in the 1960s and 1970s and didn't really come to fruition until the 1980s. Ali didn't get a lot of commercial work.

Q: Do you feel, as the American society evolved and embraced different cultures and came to accept people from diverse races, that black athletes have come to be accepted more so than their predecessors?

Dr. Harry Edwards: The challenges are different. When we begin to talk about progress, progress is a lot like the concept of the profit. It's a very slippery concept. There's been tremendous change, there's no question about that. But the challenges of this generation are different. In Jesse Owens' and Joe Louis' days black athletes lived in the African-American community. There was a parallel black sports institution led, of course, by the Negro League. But there was black basketball, professional basketball league, such teams in New York as the Harlem Globetrotters and so forth. There was a separate institutional context within which black athletes literally performed and lived out their careers. That's what Joe Louis and Jackie Robinson broke out of. The challenges were clear: we needed to get out of segregation.

Then along came a second wave of Muhammad Ali, Bill Russell, and Jim Brown – that was for dignity and respect. We were being shut out from the full benefits of our athletic stars because we were not recognized as men in equal standing off the field. The challenge, again, was very clear. This generation can get the endorsements. In fact, often times leading athletes can get multi-million dollar endorsements, whether it's shoe endorsements, automobile endorsements or what have you. The money that the athletes make is phenomenal. A basketball player gets a $120-million contract. A black baseball player signing a $200-million contract. A black football player signing a $60-million contract.

The challenges today are a lot more subtle and the cost of standing up and meeting those challenges can be a lot greater. Because all of a sudden, your endorsements are gone, or your standing in the athletic community is impute. America has never had a tremendous problem forgiving sin. So Nike didn't drop Tiger Woods. America has not even had a phenomenal problem forgiving crime. The difficult problem in forgiving is unconventional politics.

So, today athletes are extremely cautious of any involvement of unconventional politics. When they do stand up and take a stand on some political issues, it will not be the way we did in the 1960s, in the same sense that we had to break with our fathers in terms of the way we approached the challenges we faced. This generation of black athletes will break with us. They will not be demonstrating from the Olympic podium. They will not be boycotting the Games at the colleges and universities. They might be making a statement the way the Phoenix Funds did on the immigration issue, which was a political stand and a political statement. But they went right out there and played the game.

So at the end of the day, this generation is going to have to find its own way. It's going to have to find its way to meet its challenges through the phenomenal amount of money and power that's at stake, when they make a statement through the phenomenal 24/7 media saturation that was not around in the 1960s. There was no ESPN; there was no Fox News; there was no Sporting News Network; there was no Fox Sports so forth and so on. So, all of that is in the mix for this generation of athletes. They're going to have to find their own political voice within that context. And when the right issues emerge, they will in the same sense every generation, going back to Jack Johnson, has found its political way. Every generation of black athlete has found its political way. Every generation of black athlete has found its political voice. I have full faith this generation will as well. But like us, it will not be done the way the last generation made the statements. We with our fathers and mothers in the 1960s made our own unique political statement and contribution to democratic participation in American society. This generation of black athletes will do the same.

Q: When the 1977 movie *The Greatest* was in production, were you in contact with Muhammad Ali when he was making this?
Dr. Harry Edwards: No, I wasn't. But I thought that . . . one of the great secrets of any profession is that the greatest in the profession make what they do look easy. And I think Muhammad Ali's

performance in that movie revealed that more than anything else, acting is not easy. But at the same time, I think that his story was important. And, of course, *The Greatest Love of All* that came out of that movie was an instant hit, especially the Whitney Houston version of it. So at the end of the day, more important than Ali's role, it was the story that every one of my generation and his generation most certainly knew. But as far as the artistic quality of his performance, I'm glad he didn't give up his day job.

Q: That brings me to the next question: was Muhammad Ali supposed to fight Wilt Chamberlain?

Dr. Harry Edwards: I think basically there were a lot of people who thought that there would be some monetary value, profit value, in having a Jim Brown or Wilt Chamberlain or some wrestler boxing Muhammad Ali. Muhammad Ali was arguably one of the, if not the, greatest boxer of the modern era – the greatest boxer of the last half of the 20th century. He made what he did look so artistically pleasing that it seemed easy. And if someone could get in the ring with him, who had huge, long arm reach that they'll be able to hold him off. And maybe even get in a couple of punches for six, seven, eight, nine rounds, it would only be a matter of time before – if it was a serious fight – Wilt Chamberlain got punched out. And at that point he would have to end up the same fate as George Foreman and any other number of big guys did. Muhammad Ali was a consummate professional artist. I remember Jim Brown telling a story about him walking with Ali. Jim said that he himself could be a pretty good boxer and he would like to take about six, seven months to get in shape and maybe have a fight with Muhammad Ali, which would make a lot of money. So Ali told him, "Are you sure you want to do that?" Jim said, "Yeah!" Jim Brown was one heck of an athlete, All-American lacrosse player, leading scorer on a basketball team, greatest football player in the history of the game.

So Ali told him, "OK. I'm going to stand here and you swing at me as hard as you can." Jim Brown said, "You really want me to swing at you as hard as I can!?" Ali said, "Yeah. Go for my chin. Go for my stomach, body, anywhere you can." Jim Brown stood back – and he was a great athlete – and swung and missed. By the time he could draw his hand back to swing again, Ali had hit him nine times. Just slapping him and punching him on the face. Jim Brown stood back and said, "Yeah. I see what you mean. That fight wouldn't be a good idea." There were a lot of people who felt that there would be a lot of money. The thing between him and Chamberlain was basically: hey, let's see if we could make some money on this. It would be interesting entertainment. We both have a fan base and let's see if we can bring them together and have some fun.

Q: Was Herbert Muhammad responsible for negotiating all commercial deals for Muhammad Ali?
Dr. Harry Edwards: Herbert was his agent. Certainly after Ali broke with the Louisville Group that had originally sponsored him in professional boxing. When he became a Muslim, Herbert Muhammad became his manager and negotiated a great many of his contracts. I have no personal knowledge of that relationship beyond what's in various biographies and so forth. So that's not one thing I can really comment on. But I do know that Herbert Muhammad had a role in his management team. To what extent that was a decisive managerial role, I couldn't speak for that.

Q: Did you witness any racist incidents against Muhammad Ali in the media or on a social level?
Dr. Harry Edwards: Just what you normally read in the media, and a lot of times it weren't necessarily blatant, it was subtle – different kinds of descriptions of Ali's attitude to disposition. That he was uppity, that he was associated with a black nationalist organization that advocated separation of blacks and whites. That he was a racist as far as white people are concerned. I mean, you get all that kind of stuff in the media. But that's typical in America, that didn't surprise anybody.

When you stand up and become a target, when you stand up and become a lightning rod in American society, as a black activist, as an outspoken black individual, someone who engages in unconventional politics, you're going to get all of that kind of commentary. There was nothing unusual about it. It's not like statements they wouldn't have made about me, about Smith or Carlos, about Jim Brown, about Bill Russell. That's American society. So, yeah, that was in sports columns. That was an ongoing constant thing. And I'm quite certain, just like Bill Russell, like myself, Smith and Carlos, he got the death threats. He got the hate mail. He got the racist assaults on his property and so forth, just like we did. I mean, that was part of the deal.

Q: Muhammad Ali is more than merely known as the world's greatest boxer; he's the greatest sportsman of the century. In your own words can you please elaborate on this statement?
Dr. Harry Edwards: At one point, Ali was the most recognizable face in the world. His influence, his confidence, what he stood for, what he had accomplished and what he had sacrificed spanned such a spectrum of issues and influences from athletics to domestic politics to global issues that he was easily the most significant and important athlete of the 20th century. There's no question about that.

I don't even know, other than maybe Jackie Robinson – and people throw in Jesse Owens, people throw in Joe Louis – how you would sort out that second group in terms of who would be second after Muhammad Ali. I think he is literally in a class by himself in terms of his significance in the 20th century as an athlete and an iconic figure. He changed sport and was easily the most significant athlete, if not sports personality, in general, including writers and all team owners and professional teams. He is the most significant sports personality of the 20th century.

Q: Do you feel the emergence of black athletes in athletics, sport and boxing in the 1960s heavily influenced the white man and changed his perspective over the years as far as acceptance on a more social level?
Dr. Harry Edwards: Oh, I don't think there's any question about it. I think if you go back and look at Dr. Martin Luther King and

the civil rights movement. Dr. King's movement and the concept, prescription and value sentiments were similar to Gandhi. But black people in American society didn't know anything about Gandhi. What they knew about was Jackie Robinson. Jackie Robinson in 1946, ten years before Dr. King even emerged, had undertaken non-violent direct action in the sense that he went on the field for the Brooklyn Dodgers and undertook all of the insults from people sliding in the second base with their spikes up, but he continued to perform. At the same time, there were literally thousands of black people who heard those insults, who saw those spikes, who saw pitchers throw at Jackie and who saw him run the bases and keep his mouth shut and get it done. They saw Jackie doing that, which kept the door open for sports for other blacks to enter that game. They saw that non-direct violent action worked.

So when Dr. King came along, ten years later, and began to talk about non-violent direct action and looking up to Gandhi, black people didn't look up to Gandhi. They looked up to Jackie Robinson, he was our Gandhi. So they had full faith in what Dr. King was saying because it had already worked in baseball. There's a direct line between Jackie Robinson, Dr. Martin Luther King and the voting rights act and all of that stuff that came out of the civil rights movement, the civil rights act, and Barack Obama. A direct line of attention between Jackie Robinson, Dr. King and Barack Obama. So there's no question that sports has had a phenomenal influence on the course of the developments of American society, in particular in terms of molding the basis of democratic participation across all institutions.

The emergence of Colin Powell came out of the contribution of blacks in American sports. If you go and look at the colleges and universities in this country that were integrated till this day, the most integrated grounds of campuses across this country is the athletic department. The first students often times were brought into a campus, or a major part of a first class of students brought in for an all-white campus was typically black athletes. University of Florida; Louisiana State University; University of Mississippi;

University of Alabama, all of those schools brought in black athletes who then because of their sports participation, eased the way for other black athletes and subsequently other black students and ultimately black faculty members to come into those institutional settings. But still black athletes represented in revenue producing sports on those campuses. So there's been no question that athletics, sports and the role of the black athlete has been seminal involving the basis of democratic participation in American society, right up to and including the election of Barack Obama as the forty-fourth president of the United States.

Q: Can you please conclude with final words on Muhammad Ali?
Dr. Harry Edwards: I think that he, as I stated, unquestionably is the greatest athlete and maybe the greatest sports figure of the 20th century. I think his iconic status is only going to continue to grow and expand. In future years he will be spoken of in the same company as Jim Thorpe, as far as being an iconic figure in American sports. But even bigger than Thorpe, because of what he meant in terms of broader, social, cultural and political issues.

JHOON RHEE

Jhoon Rhee, a world-renowned tae kwon do master, is one of the few people who worked with both Bruce Lee and Muhammad Ali. Master Rhee cultivated a friendship with the legendary boxer in the mid-1970s when he was brought in to be part of the team when Ali was training to fight legendary professional wrestler Antonio Inoki. Widely recognized as the father of American tae kwon do, he died in 2018 at the age of 86.

Q: When did you first meet Muhammad Ali?
Jhoon Rhee: It was in 1975. I was preparing him for his fight against Antonio Inoki in Japan. Prior to this, about a year before, he had a fight with Joe Frazier and Richard Dunn, a British champion, in Munich in 1976. I taught him how to block kicks. Besides, I had some good ideas of how to punch quickly. I called that accu-punch. When he used this punch in his fights, he won the fight both times. As you know, I started the Jhoon Rhee's Safe-T equipment for martial arts training. One of my students was in Philadelphia called Norman. Mr. Norman, who was a black gentleman, happened to be a very good friend of Muhammad Ali. Muhammad Ali was looking for a martial arts coach, so he asked if I would like to coach. And I said of course, I'd be honored to coach him. So that's how we connected. I visited Chicago and I visited Harrisonburg, Virginia, where he had a training camp where I visited him to teach him.

Q: Can you please tell me when you both met?
Jhoon Rhee: Mr. Norman asked me if I was interested. Of course, who wouldn't be! So I was invited to Deer Lake training camp in Pennsylvania and also Harrisonburg. That's how I met him. I think it was spring of 1975. The fight with the wrestler took place on June 26, 1976.

Q: How did you work out the training schedule?

Jhoon Rhee: I went once a week. Because he was very busy, he didn't have to train with me all the time. As you know, training is really one percent and practice is 99 percent. So I gave him some ideas on what to practice. Any technique you learn, you must really train it. In other words, when you have a good idea you have to get the idea to register in your head. Now you practice and repeat it over and over again and you will transform this idea into every muscle cell in your brain. When this becomes habit our skills will improve. To be able to perform anything you learn by repetition. By developing the muscle memory your brain then automatically directs the muscles. Those rules apply to other areas of life. I think everybody should develop a good idea, register it in the head and practice that over and over again to make it a living habit.

Q: How did Muhammad Ali conduct himself at the camp?

Jhoon Rhee: He was a very, very intelligent person and I think his IQ was very high. But everybody knows he didn't really have a formal education. But under the circumstances, he was very, very quick and spontaneous. He was very publicity-minded and when he was alone he was very quiet. As soon as any radio, newspaper or television personality appeared in the room, then he never stopped talking. He would make all kind of gestures to entertain all the media people. That's how he made himself so famous. Besides, he was the best fighter in the world, and in history.

Q: Were there any specific training methods or techniques you and Muhammad Ali discussed?

Jhoon Rhee: An accu-punch is a punch you execute the minute you decide to punch. In other words, the execution and decision is in one moment, there's no time gap between the two. When you do that, it's a mental punch. And when you perform like that you develop a tremendous acceleration. Force equals the mass times velocity. So we tried to develop acceleration. Whenever you increase the speed twice, force increases twice. If you have, let's say force is three times, so your square power becomes nine times – three times three is nine. So you can increase your force by nine times. In science it proves that whenever you increase your acceleration your power becomes really explosive.

Q: What did he think of kicking and your tae kwon do?
Jhoon Rhee: I tried to teach him kicking, but he really thought kicking was too hard for him at his age. So he was concentrating on his punching. He was very afraid of kicking. He thought that kicking was more powerful than punches, but it's not true! Whether you kick or punch, it's directly proportional to your body weight and also depends on how you execute them – like in accu-punch. So it's not really true that the kick is much stronger than a punch; it's how you concentrate putting your whole body weight into the target – that's it. I think a punch is so much more effective because it is easy to aim accurately to the target, whilst a kick is much more difficult to aim at the exact target you are aiming for.

Q: When you arrived in Japan for the Antonio Inoki fight on the first day, who else was part of the entourage?
Jhoon Rhee: I couldn't believe that so many media people were waiting at the airport. At least about a hundred media members were waiting in the airport. Of course, Ali and I were very close together. Ali was using publicity tactics to announce that he had a special Master Rhee's accu-punch. And that he learned techniques to block kicks so he was very confident. I forget the name but there was also the professional wrestler [Freddie Blassie] with us, it's been a long time. Professional wrestling is not real fighting, but they are real showmen. I'm not trying to criticize them. I mean, it's not easy to be a professional wrestling fighter, but he [Ali] recognized martial arts as the real thing, whereas professional wrestling is for TV show purposes. It's a business.

Q: Can you tell me more about the fight?
Jhoon Rhee: In Tokyo at the press conference I was sitting next to Ali

all the time. And as most Americans know, by that time I was already known all over the world as one of the best teachers and had many champions in the United States. So he was trying to scare Antonio Inoki by telling him he had Master Rhee as his coach and he was well prepared. He was so funny, he really stole the hearts of all the Japanese media and he had a lot of publicity. The fight was on, but it was very dull because Antonio Inoki was on the floor all the time. He was so scared to stand up. He was kicking his right thigh with his left leg. So Ali got bruised. I showed him something between the rounds and he was able to block it and stop him from kicking the same spot. I think Antonio Inoki was very smart to concentrate on one spot to paralyze his leg. But the next day, he was really bruised and we went to Korea the next day. But the doctor said he shouldn't go. Muhammad Ali said, "No. I can't break my promise to Master Rhee." He was very respectful of anybody he trusted.

Once he respects you, he's very respectful. Right after the fight on June 26, 1976, we went to Korea. We had a million fans lined up from almost about twenty miles from Seoul on the sidewalks. He was really welcomed by Korean fans. He had never had that kind of a welcome in his life. We stayed there for four days and three nights. When he saw so many beautiful Korean ladies waving at him, he said, "Master Rhee, Korean ladies are so beautiful." I said, "Yes, they are very beautiful." Then he said, "Can you find one lady for me?" I pretended I didn't hear him. Then a minute later, he asked me again. So I said, "Champ, I know I will do anything for you. You came here for me." There were about twenty other people from Muhammad Ali's camp. I said, "That's something I will never do for anybody." He was silent for a minute and then he said, "Master Rhee, I respect you." That's one of the conversations I had with him. Then the night before we were ready to leave from Korea, President Park invited us to visit him at the president's mansion. But it was very difficult to change twenty people's air tickets so we had to refuse and we just came back to America.

Then when he came back to Washington D.C. he stopped by me a month later. I said I'm going to call the press and talk about our experiences in Korea and Tokyo. He said go ahead. So we had about fifty media members come over. Someone asked, "What are you going to do when you retire?" He said, "I'm going to work for Allah." He used to say that all the time. Then he made contact with his eyes with my eyes, as soon as he saw me he said, "Oh, Master Rhee loves God more than I do." Then he said, "When I asked him to find me a beautiful lady, he refused to do it." I couldn't believe that he was saying it in front of all this press! The press was very inspired by his naïveté. That's very interesting.

Five years later, he came to Washington for some function. I didn't know he was going to be there. I was also invited to the function. Of course, many people lined up to get his signature, there were twenty other people lined up and I lined up to say hello to him in the line. Then one of his staff recognized me and he brought me to the front. He told the champ Master Rhee is here. Then he stood up and bowed to me. I couldn't believe he did that in front of all those people. But he's that kind of a person, and very serious when it comes to serious matters.

Q: Antonio Inoki couldn't speak English?
Jhoon Rhee: Inoki was very quiet. He is a real gentleman. He was a member of the National Assembly. He's a sportsman and a very successful businessman as well. In fact, from that experience he's the one who started K-1. I think he's sold it, but initially started it from that fight.

Q: The fight was all worked out. Did you know that?
Jhoon Rhee: I didn't know that. I thought it was real. But I think if it was fixed Inoki wouldn't stay on the floor all the time. Then when he went to Korea he said to the Korean press, when they asked, "What do you think of Inoki staying on the floor all the time." He replied, "I know many women make money lying in bed, but I've never seen any man lying on the floor making money." I think it was funny. He also said Korean people are very sensitive about the divide of North and South Korea. That time he made the Korean

public feel good, he said, "I'm going to use my punch and punch the chain and break the parallel line so you can all live together."

Q: Were there any interesting moments in Korea?
Jhoon Rhee: We were there about three days, but I don't think there was anything that stands out. Because the fight was so dull everybody was so disappointed. Again, the fight really triggered a lot of interest around the world because everybody was questioning who would be the winner between a wrestler and boxer. The fight ended in a draw. Other than that I didn't experience any excitement.

Q: Before the fight did Muhammad Ali express any nervousness?
Jhoon Rhee: Well, he was confident. In fact, when he knocked out Richard Dunn, the British champion, in Munich in 1976, I think it was in May, he knocked him out and an NBC sportscaster asked him, "What kind of punch was that, is that an anchor punch?" Ali said, "No. That's a different one. This is Master Jhoon Rhee's accu-punch." When he knocked Dunn out and he fell down, you can actually hear his voice say, "That was Master Jhoon Rhee's accu-punch!" That's what he said in the ring.

Q: Many martial arts and its exponents weren't really respected. What was Muhammad Ali's perception of martial arts?
Jhoon Rhee: Martial arts was hocus pocus because they [many] didn't really practice full contact. For me, it was punching and kicking, we really didn't know how it worked in a real fight. But I think the boxers now respect martial arts much, much more. Muhammad Ali really, really respected Bruce Lee.

Q: I was going to ask you about that! Can you tell me of any conversation you had with Muhammad Ali pertaining to Bruce Lee?
Jhoon Rhee: Oh, yeah. I talked about him. They are the same in that they have a similar personality, I'd say. And Muhammad Ali really wanted to meet Bruce Lee. When I met Muhammad Ali,

Bruce Lee was gone. I would have made the contact for two of the greatest to meet each other, but I was unable to do that.

Q: Muhammad Ali is more than merely a sports personality. His humanitarian works and attitudes seem to have impacted people on different levels.

Jhoon Rhee: I think he's a very much humanitarian person. He really had a passion for unfortunate people. He's really a special person the way he conducted himself and he was very courteous. He is not only a boxing champion, but was a human champion. And he's very well qualified to be respected by the world.

Q: After the Antonio Inoki fight, did you meet again?

Jhoon Rhee: I saw him at least six times. He was having problems with the Parkinson's disease. Then he could talk once in a while, but other than that he doesn't move around. It's a shame a great man at a young age cannot function physically. I think it's a good time to tell the audience that I am eighty years old. When I give my speech I do a hundred push-ups in a minute, break three boards dangling, twelve-inch distance punch. I'll straighten my leg to my stomach. I have tremendous energy and exercise to keep myself young. Because I want to really become a role model for all martial artists, plus everybody else.

Q: Did you talk to him about any of his boxing fights?

Jhoon Rhee: No, he never talked about boxing to me. I don't know the reason, but maybe out of respect for me not to offend me. That wouldn't offend me anyway, but maybe he thought so.

Q: Can you recall any humorous incidents?

Jhoon Rhee: I already explained to you when he asked for a lady, it was a very funny thing. Other than that, he was very religious. There were almost about five or six personal appearances each day in Korea and everywhere we went motorcycles led our car. It was really one of the greatest honors of my life.

Q: Any final comments?

Jhoon Rhee: I pray for his comfort under the circumstances. He has done a lot for humanity, for his fans, not only for boxing but the general public who love him. I hope that he does not suffer as far as his physical condition is concerned. But he seems to be very comfortable. One time when I saw him about ten years ago with my wife, he joked and – it was the first time he met my wife – he said to my wife, "Watch out! Master Rhee is very popular among women in Korea." He was still troubled with Parkinson's but he was able to joke like that.

LOUIS GOSSETT JR.

Louis Gossett Jr. was the first African-American to win an Oscar in a supporting role, awarded for his role in *An Officer and a Gentleman*. Born in New York, he had a penchant for sports but pursued acting as a career, declining an athletic scholarship at NY to concentrate on theatrical roles. As a social activist and strong believer in education, his Eracism Foundation aims to provide training for youth and adults by assisting them in setting the example for living a racially diverse and culturally inclusive life. Good friends with Muhammad Ali from the early 1960s onwards, he played a champion boxer in 1992 film *Diggstown*.

Q: How hard was it for you, black actors and athletes of the 1950s and 1960s, to overcome the racism barrier to pursue your careers?

Lou Gossett Jr.: It was quite difficult. Roles were few and far between and we were forced to compete with one another for little five-line roles sometimes. It was a very difficult time to stay friends at the same time. We call it 'crabs in the barrel', where we kind of pull each other down instead of helping each other up. We were starving and we had to make a living as much as anybody else. The people who were writing things were writing things that weren't for us. So we were stuck from time to time. Then Sidney Poitier came to the surface, and others. Even today, we're still doing this. We need to prove to people how many good people there are, good actors and actresses.

Q: When did you first hear about Muhammad Ali?

Lou Gossett Jr.: Muhammad Ali was Cassius Clay at the beginning when I first met him. He lived ten blocks away from me. He used to run the streets and stop by my house and tease my son – my son was a little kid. I was very close to him. We only lived a mile apart in Los Angeles. I met him just around the time he was going to fight for the championship. He was running the streets of Los Angeles and I lived in Hancock Park near Fremont Place. We got quite close.

Q: Did you go to any of his fights?
Lou Gossett Jr.: Absolutely! He was a remarkable athlete. I saw so many of them. I saw him fighting Jerry Quarry. I saw him fight Sonny Liston. I saw many others. He was so good that he hardly got hit. He was that pretty he hardly had a blemish on his face.

Q: Did you box yourself or come from a boxing background?
Lou Gossett Jr.: I knew Sugar Ray Robinson. I was an amateur. We [kids] did boxing, and basketball wasn't as strong. There was no place to play basketball so all the young kids aspired to be like Sugar Ray Robinson and Joe Louis. There was a thing called Golden Gloves and I competed in that in a small way. But those were the athletic things at that time, those were my heroes. Then later on it became Jackie Robinson and, of course, Elvis.

Q: How would you describe his personality?
Lou Gossett Jr.: It was excellent. Absolutely great personality, great charisma.

Q: When he took the stance against the Vietnam War, there was an imperious presence of black athletes to support him, including Jim Brown and Kareem Abdul-Jabbar . . .
Lou Gossett Jr.: It made sense that we should not go and try and kill somebody for certain things we don't have ourselves. We still hadn't equal rights in this country so it didn't seem to make sense to go and kill somebody else for their [American government] rights when we don't have ours. So it became a war like World War I and II, especially World War II where there was an obvious enemy and obvious doctrine which needed to be stopped otherwise it was going to be a global dominance.

Q: Did you ever have a conversation with him regarding his stance against the war?

Lou Gossett Jr.: Not really directly. The more he got famous he left the neighborhood, the more separated we got. But there was still a beautiful love and affection between the two of us. So I would hear what he had to say and I kind of quietly agreed. He said he had to fight his fight this way and I had to fight my fight my way.

Q: What about the Nation of Islam, he was attracted to this organization, some people thought it was a cult with parochial views?

Lou Gossett Jr.: There's no such thing because you don't have to be a Muslim to do this. But I think the African-Americans took a step which was to present to the overall American society what they can do for themselves. How they can keep people fed, get kids off the streets, how to make them well educated. So when the kid comes out into the mainstream, he has a basis of self-respect to respect the elders and culture and the way they present themselves. Nobody ever taught those kids that. Muhammad Ali, and others including myself, was pushing forward, we should take care of our own children so they are properly educated with knowledge of who they are and how to speak and present themselves. Then we can be responsible for those young people going to school and public, a place with respect. It's our job and that's what the Muslims began to do. They became a threat to the people who did things the old ways. Like you and I must agree, we always must change for the better. So if there's some freedom we have from generations before, we eventually have to change for something better. We never stop, change will always be inevitable.

Q: Muhammad Ali was more than merely an athlete, how would you define him? Even non-blacks started admiring and embracing him!

Lou Gossett Jr.: He was quite attracted to people and he encouraged people who were not black to have pride in themselves. So, when he said something was wrong, it was wrong. And people began to look beyond intrusively and improve themselves.

Q: What was your experience working on the *When We Were Kings* documentary?
Lou Gossett Jr.: It was fantastic. Boxers were my heroes back in the day. They are spectacular athletes, especially back in the day.

Q: Is there any significant conversation that stuck in your mind?
Lou Gossett Jr.: One thing that we have in common is how we take care of our children. They're going to be the future.

Q: Muhammad Ali was at the forefront of eradicating racism in American society. Can you tell me about your organization called Eracism?
Lou Gossett Jr.: There's always going to be racism one way or another. When we see a signal, God is erupting these volcanoes that were dead, making them come to life – these tsunamis and earthquakes. It's a way of him tapping on our shoulder telling us we can't survive without one another. We must clear up the air and get back into the cycle that was around when mankind started. Food, feed everyone and fresh air for people. But we kind of missed the cycle with our racist thoughts. One way or another we feel we have to get what we want and the other people don't matter. We have to change that. Our friends matter as much as we do. Our children matter and the most important thing is to make it better for the next generation. So that's the foundation and there are courses. So these kids come in and they learn. Most of the times when Ali did charity stuff he always called me. There are many of them including United Way, Save the Children. When they honored him it was for a charity.

Q: Do you think America has evolved as far as racism is concerned?
Lou Gossett Jr.: Racism will definitely change under the people

who run America. The better the people who run America the more racism goes away. But to guarantee it stays away, one needs an organiszed attempt at looking at what the problems are and change. It's happening as we speak. We've made history with our president. We must move directly, constantly towards peace and brotherhood. Always ride together and always stick together.

Q: What was the most impressive thing you saw Muhammad Ali do?
Lou Gossett Jr.: It was the rope-a-dope. His mentality was so strong and his physical fitness was so strong. He would stand and take all the blows. George Foreman could keep hitting him. George Foreman got very tired. He beat him in thirty seconds after that. Whatever fights I could go to, I went to. I went to his parties and barbeques and stuff like that where the whole family was there. He used to do a thing with his finger on your ear and it would feel like a bee stung your ear. He did that to my son a lot.

GEORGE DILLMAN

George Dillman is famous for his pressure point fighting and was one of the few men who was associated with and worked with both Bruce Lee and Muhammad Ali. Dillman, who bought Ali's Deer Lake training facility, became friends with the heavyweight champion and trained together when he set up camp in Pennsylvania. Dillman has a strong personality and is an intriguing man who always offers great insights. In this rare and exclusive interview he offers some revealing and interesting insights.

Q: George, when did you first meet Muhammad Ali?
George Dillman: Muhammad Ali, I usually say this when I have camps, I own his training camp in Reading, Pennsylvania. We have three-day camps there. In the heat of the karate circuit competitions, I used to travel to all the big karate competitions all over the country and compete. I met Muhammad Ali in 1967. I believe it was on March 28. I have this date on a card. I've lived a very interesting life. I was poor and I became a boxer myself. Then I got into karate and then I got into the military. In 1967, I was invited to a sports banquet in New York City in a big hotel near Madison Square Garden. I think the name of the hotel has changed now, but back then it was the Hotel New Yorker. I met Muhammad Ali at that banquet. There were many sports celebrities there. It was a banquet to raise money for charity. They had Muhammad Ali from boxing. I was there from karate. There were several big names from tennis, golf, baseball and everybody paid a lot of money and the money went to charity. I just happened to be sitting next to Muhammad Ali and we started talking. I asked him to start training with me.

What I'm gonna tell you is an honest-to-God true story. I was sitting next to him and I said, "You know, I think we should start training together." And he said, "Why!? I'm heavyweight champion of the world." I said, "Yeah, I understand that. I know that completely. At this time, I'm a well-known karate person and karate champion, that's why I'm here at the banquet. I'd just like to train with you. We could do roadwork, whatever you want. And I can give you some ideas." Which by the way I wound up doing, but we'll get back to that. In 1967, I lived in Washington D.C. and I was an officer with the United States military police. Muhammad said why should we train together? I told him you're great at boxing. I used to box – I boxed for three-and-a-half years – and I said if we get in the ring you would beat me, there's no doubt about that. But I think I'd give you a good run for your money, but you would defeat me.

Then I said, "If we go out here in the alley, I'm going to be able to use my hands and feet and I won't have gloves on. I will kick the daylights out of you. I don't care what you know. I'll beat you so bad you won't know who you are." He said, "You think so?" I said, "I know so!" I said to him, "Should we go in the alley?" He said, "No, no. Let me think about that. I would like to work out with you, but what would you do for me?" I said, "Well, I'm going to improve your hand speed, teach you what we call a backfist, which would be a quicker move." So we got talking about that, about me beating him up, and we exchanged business cards. I have that card to this day and I got him to autograph it. I did write the date, I believe the date was March 28. So, when we finished the banquet we went outside and we did some talking, and the press was around taking pictures, mostly of him because of his fame and ability to talk. We separated company at that point. I went back to Washington D.C.

At that time, I believe he lived in Miami, Florida. But I really didn't know where he lived, I just knew he lived in Miami and was training at the 5th Street Gym. I was in the military, and actually two weeks from that day he was arrested for avoiding the draft. Then everything else, I had to watch on TV. I couldn't associate with him because of me being in the military and being an officer, I had a top secret clearance. I didn't even place a phone call to his business number place because if it ever was traced and anything happened, I would lose my top secret clearance because he was now against the United States Army. That's all history and everyone knows he went to court over it. So I'll cut to the chase. I just had to tell you that it was meant to be. It was just one of those things in life you don't get to change directions.

Q: Am I right in saying when you met him again in Reading in 1972 in a restaurant this was the second time your paths crossed?

George Dillman: Yes. In 1967, I met him in D.C. and in 1968 I transferred in the military to Reading, Pennsylvania. I opened my karate school in Reading, Pennsylvania, downtown on 5th Street. Across the street there was a really good restaurant, which is now closed, but I only went there maybe two, three times a year. We were over there – my ex-wife Kim and me – on the off-hour when nobody was there because you could not go in at lunch. So we went around 2 p.m. to eat because we had to come back and teach our classes in the evening. She had already heard about the story where I could beat him up. I had told her and I told my students the story. I talked about that story. Every time Ali was on the news, I would say, "You're not going to believe this, but I told him I could kick his ass." So, in he walks in the restaurant. I'm sitting there and my wife says to me don't turn around now, Muhammad Ali is behind you. We're sitting behind the door, and I say, "Yeah, right!" She says, "No, he is! He's with Bernie Pollack." When she said that, I knew that he was a fight promoter so I turned around and sure enough there he was.

I got up, shook his hand and said, "Champ, do you remember me?" And he said, these were his exact words, "I don't remember your name, but you're that karate guy who said he could whoop me!" I said, "That's it! George Dillman." He said, "That's it. You said you could whoop me. You still think you could whoop me?" I said, "I do." He said, "I'm going to be training in this area, where are you at?" I said, "My school's across the street. Right up this street from this restaurant, not even half a block." He said, "Look, we have to eat. I don't want you to get away from me this time. Can you wait around until we've eaten because I want to talk to you?" I said I'll be here. We hadn't got our food yet, we ordered but we didn't get it. So we sat down, we got our food and had a cup of coffee waiting for him to finish. Then they walked out and we walked out with him and walked up the street. I showed him my karate school.

We started talking and he told me, "I'm going to be training here. I'm getting ready for a big comeback with this guy. Do you want to work out with me?" I told him yeah. He said, "I don't have any sparring partners. I don't have anything. I don't really have any equipment yet. I'm starting training this Friday. I'm going to do roadwork and hang up a bag over a tree outside and I'm going to work on the bag, skip rope and maybe shadowbox. You want to do that with me?" I replied yeah. That was a Tuesday. He said, "Get Bernie Pollack's phone number. I'm staying at his house. You've got to call Bernie Thursday night to find out where we are. I'm new here. I don't know where they are taking me to train, but I know it's only a few miles north of this city Reading." I knew where it was – Deer Lake. We call it Deer Lake. He gave me Bernie Pollack's phone number.

He got curious and he said, "What would you do, what do you want to train me in?" I said, "Well, I want to improve your hands. The way you hit. I think I've got some good ideas for you. I've got some breathing to teach you, breathing that will help you. You'll be able to take punches for twelve to fifteen rounds. You'll be able to take punches and not get tired. And you'll be able to hit back at other people by doing proper breathing. I would like to teach you how to block kicks." He said, "I don't want to learn how to kick." I said, "I don't want to teach you how to kick." He said, "If I kick somebody in the ring I'm disqualified." So I said, "Well, I'd like to teach you how to block kicks when they're coming out to you, in case anybody ever tries to sucker punch you or kick you in the street. You're the world heavyweight champion. You can block that and don't worry about it and do what you have to." He said, "That's great. You're on." So that Thursday night I called Bernie Pollack, and he told me to come up to his farm that he had. Bernie has just passed away, but Bernie put up an outdoor boxing ring with a tent over it.

Then Muhammad Ali and me that morning – it was like 6 a.m., my ex-wife Kim drove the car – went for a couple of mile run. We did three miles and slowly increased it to get up to five miles. And we came back and did bag work and shadowboxed. We didn't put on gloves because he had no equipment yet. Then I worked with him on the combo action of a backfist. A boxer and a karate person can throw the same move, but he can get the move out a little quicker by the way he positions the elbow. But the boxers don't do that. He said, "I can't hit the back of the fist!" I said, "I know, we're going to convert it and you're going to do the same motion." So we started working on that. They called it an 'overhand right', but if you look at it on any film you'll see it is a martial art backfist.

I tell people that if you look at it in any fights, and there's this in many documentaries, if you look at any Muhammad Ali fight before 1972 and you look at any fight after 1972, you will see without a doubt my influence, especially if you're a martial artist. You'll see he's moving different, he's breathing different.

In fact, in one of the fights, I think it was the George Chuvalo fight, he went over to the corner and did a martial arts breathing exercise and then came out and stared his man down. He didn't even take the two minutes in the corner. He came over and stared the man down waiting for him to get up to psych him up. He did a karate breathing exercise to recoup his breathing. He got all this influence from me. We trained for three-and-a-half years on a regular basis. I worked with him on the second Frazier fight; I didn't work with him on the first Frazier fight, but he lost that. I have pictures of Muhammad. If you see him looking down, looking a little depressed, I have my hands on my hips yelling at him because he was not going to fight Joe Frazier for the second time. Because the first fight was so tough, so bad, he said I'm not going to do it.

He said, "You don't see the press here." I said, "What?" He said, "The press is all at Joe Frazier's camp. They don't cover losers." I said, "Muhammad, you're not a loser. If you think like that then you will be a loser. If you think like a winner, you're going to think positive. We can train you and you can beat him, there's no doubt about that. He's slow. He throws punches in round circles. We're going to shorten that distance and you're going to outbox him." We did some serious training for Frazier II, Frazier III, George Foreman, George Chuvalo, Jerry Quarry and Floyd Patterson, and he won all of those. When he beat Floyd Patterson, he gave me credit in *World Boxing* magazine for being the man that taught him the move that closed Floyd Patterson's eye. He didn't say it was a backfist, but he said it was a move he used to keep hitting with that move on the same spot of the eye that it popped out. Patterson couldn't see so they stopped the fight. That was my involvement.

After three-and-a-half years he started to change wives. The wife Belinda was a real good friend of my wife and we went together to functions with them. While I was with Muhammad Ali, my wife at the time and myself and two of my students were the first ones to go to a Black Muslim rally – the first white people ever! It was Louis Farrakhan. They were talking in 1973. They were talking about the show that was going on and Nancy Wilson was going to be the main singer. I don't know if you've heard of Ben Vereen, but Ben Vereen and The Delfonics were going to be there. It was the greatest rock and roll show ever put together. And they were using Ali to recruit black people in the Muslims.

When I asked Ali if I could go to that meeting, he said, "You can't go to that meeting!" I said, "Why?" He said, "It's all black people! They're trying to recruit black people." I said, "Ali, you know I'm open-minded." He said, "Besides, they're going to be talking bad about white people." I said, "I could put up with that. I want to see Nancy Wilson. I love Nancy Wilson and I love The Delfonics and I want to go to that show." He said, "I'll tell you what, I'll ask. But I don't think you'll be able to go." He came back a week later and he said, "Well, they said you can go."

I said to my wife it's only because Muhammad Ali asked. If anybody else asked if I can bring four white people, they would have been told no. Because Muhammad Ali asked, they said yes because he was their money bag. We went and sat down at the table with Ali and Belinda. Four white people and there were 4,000 black people. Louis Farrakhan spoke for about a half an hour, yelling and screaming about the white people. Every time he would say white people are devils – this is a true story – he would yell that white people are the devils, and 4,000 people looked at my table as I sat there being humble. In fact, Ali had told me when you go in there they're going to be talking bad about you, you can't do any of your karate. I said I won't do any karate, I'll be way outnumbered. So we went down and they talked about us. And I've got to be honest, what Louis Farrakhan said, everything he said, I have to own up.

Ali and I talked about it later. I said about 80 to 90 percent of what he said was correct! He embellished on a few things. I think one or two things I brought up when I was with Ali, and he said, "Yeah, I thought that, too." But I said the rest was cool because we were prejudiced at the time in this country. We were putting the black people down. We were making them eat in different restaurants. He went through the whole thing. I had to admit that he was right. I went to Muhammad Ali's house and he went through the whole thing. I had to admit that he was right. I went to Muhammad Ali's house in New Jersey and I had dinner with The Delfonics and Nancy Wilson. Then it was back to training the next week.

Q: Can you tell me more about visiting him at his house?
George Dillman: I went to his house about twenty times. I didn't have to be invited; I could just show up. Every time we went to martial arts tournaments over in New Jersey, Atlantic City or near Philadelphia, we would stop over his house. I would take my students. On one particular occasion, Muhammad Ali was training with me so he knew what katas and forms were. One student of mine took second place in forms. He didn't do the form the way he should have, but that happens. He could've taken first place. So we show Muhammad Ali the trophy. He said what form did you do and the guy told him the name of the form. He said let me see it, and the student got pale and he said, "What?" He said I want to see the kata. I want to see the form. He said you can do the form in the living room. The student did the form like perfect.

And Muhammad Ali gave him a little applause. I said to the guy, "Why didn't you do the form that way at the tournament? You would have got first place." He said, "Well, Muhammad Ali wasn't watching me." That's a little story there.

We'd go to his house at anytime. I was out for dinner with him and his wife. He had a German shepherd dog he loved. When he was out his dog had got in his swimming pool and couldn't get out so he drowned. And we left and Muhammad Ali was crying like a baby. I said we'd better get out of here and just leave him alone. He was crying like a baby over the dog. Everybody has had that happen, but I was with him when that happened. I told him how sorry I was and told his wife we're going to leave. I told my wife we better leave him alone.

Q: Another interesting story you once related was when you were having a conversation you challenged him. You said you could kick him in the groin.

George Dillman: Yes. What happened was that took place when we met at the restaurant when he first came to Pennsylvania. We went up to my karate school. We were out on the street. Actually, he was still curious so he said, "What would you do to me if I threw a jab to the face? What about if I shot a left jab at you?" I said, "Well, you can go ahead if you want." He threw a left jab at me and I took my right hand and parried it. I just didn't parry it. I did that strong and I did a left roundhouse kick – I tapped. I didn't kick his groin hard, but just tapped his pants just enough that he doubled over. When he doubled over I stepped in with a right hand and I said, "Now do you want me to finish the job?" He said, "No, we're going to start training." That's when he actually told me to call him Thursday night and that we were going to train Friday. That's in the middle of that story I related to you before. I didn't know you knew about that, but yes, it's an important part of the story.

Q: Any unusual stories?

George Dillman: He called me all the time. One time he called me at 4 o'clock in the morning. My wife says to me someone wants you on the phone. I said it's 4 o'clock in the morning. She said I know but it's Muhammad Ali. I said what? She said it's not anybody, it's the heavyweight champion of the world. You better talk to him. So I get the phone and I wound up just listening to some of his ups and downs and complaints. Just like anybody else, he just wanted somebody to talk to. He didn't realize he was on the other end of the world and the time difference. But we mostly met at the camp. He would call me to tell me when he was coming to the camp. Then he would leave. I was around when it was being built. There are pictures in the gym of the camp being built. And I love that camp, it's a part of me.

By the way, if I can interject, he's in a bad state now. It's pretty bad. He can't really talk now, his voice is gone. He only blinks. The moment I was with him I took many pictures of him training at the camp. The pictures photographer just called me the other day, he said, "George, he can't talk, but I showed him some pictures of you with him training at his camp. He kept blinking 'yes, yes, yes' and smiling." He liked the camp.

Q: At the camp what training methods did you integrate with Muhammad Ali?

George Dillman: Most of the training we did was his training. And I did it with him. Anywhere from 5 a.m. to 6 a.m. depending on if he had a press conference. He tried to get it all in before people could bother him because he couldn't interrupt his training. We used to go running three miles and built it up to five miles. We would do this 5 a.m. or 6 a.m. in the morning. He would come back from that and we would do sit-ups and work on our abs. We did sit-ups and stretching, then he would jump up and work out and then actually get a rubdown. He did bag work, timing bag and the heavy bag. There were two bags there and we did them side by side. Then he would go out in the ring where they had sparring partners. He would usually use three different sparring partners. For three years, Larry Holmes was one of them. He had a bunch of sparring partners. He had Billy Daniels, who I really became friends with, who I don't think got any higher than third rank in the world. But Billy was a tough guy, had a lot of wins and losses. He had Eddie Mustafa Muhammad, who I'm still friends with today who I still talk to at least once a month. He's training boxers out in Las Vegas. Eddie Mustafa Muhammad was three-and-a-half-year light-heavyweight champion of the world and he trained at the camp. I met Sugar Ray Leonard. He started his whole career at that camp. Angelo Dundee was training Sugar Ray Leonard and Muhammad Ali. I met Floyd Patterson at the camp.

Q: Is there any intriguing story, which is very rare pertaining to you and Muhammad Ali?

George Dillman: One was about Elvis Presley. Muhammad came over to me, and he said, "You can't tell everybody. Tomorrow be here at 4 o'clock." He usually boxed at 2 o'clock – this is when he did his sparring. He says to me, "Tomorrow I'm going to train at 4 o' clock. Don't come at 2 o'clock, come at 4 o'clock. You can't tell your students, you can't put it in the newspaper. Nobody's to know that Elvis Presley is coming to watch me spar." I said, "Serious?" He said, "Yes. Elvis Presley is coming here and we're going to train, you and me. And I want Elvis to see what we do." Four o'clock came and we kept waiting and waiting. No Elvis.

I'm going to make a long story short. Muhammad Ali, at about 6 o'clock, said I've got to get my boxing in. So they started the boxing and he sparred with the sparring partners. Then after that we had dinner over in the kitchen and we sat around waiting for Elvis. I think somebody called to say he was coming late, he's coming late, he's coming late! No Elvis, no Elvis, no Elvis! It got late at night, it was 9 p.m. or 10 p.m. at night. I said, "I'm heading home. I doubt he's going to show." He said, "Yeah, I don't think he's going to show." So I went home.

I found out the next day that Elvis showed up 4 o'clock in the morning. They said he got lost. But he went to do other things and he showed up at 4 a.m. Ali woke up the cook and had the cook make some breakfast and coffee. Elvis, from what they told me, was a little high or drunk. I don't know how you want to say it but he was... and Ali gave him breakfast and they sat and had a chat. Then about 8 a.m. or 9 a.m. they went out shopping together. The people who own the store, their daughter was in high school and she loved Elvis. Elvis and Muhammad Ali go in the store to look for and buy some antiques. The parents couldn't believe that Elvis and Muhammad Ali were standing in front of them. When their daughter came home from school her parents told her what happened. She absolutely couldn't believe it. Two policemen guarded the store so nobody could go up. Elvis signed his signature on hundred dollar bills and gave each one of us as a gift. One guy sold his hundred dollar bill, I think for $3,000 within a week. Somebody said I'll give you three grand. He said OK and got rid of it. The other guy still has his and was in the papers not long ago.

Q: What did you think of Muhammad Ali's vivacious personality?

George Dillman: He was fantastic! He was nothing, nothing like people perceived or know him because of the press. He would turn on and off like a button. When the press came he started yelling and screaming, "I'm going to beat this guy and that guy! I'm going to do this to the guy!" The minute they leave, he'd say, "Well, that'd make me some more money."

In fact, one time he sat down with me before he was fighting George Chuvalo out of Canada. I believe Muhammad Ali was getting $3 million for that fight and George Chuvalo was getting $300,000. Muhammad Ali started screaming and yelling, what he's going to do to Chuvalo. Muhammad Ali sat down with me, and he said to me, "The man is pretty stupid. He won't yell and scream back." The only thing Chuvalo would say is, "We'll see how it goes in the ring." That's it. That's all he would say. He said, "If I can get him to call me names and I call him names, he'll be making $3 million and I'd be able to make $5 million! But he won't yell anything back and I'm calling him every name in the book! He's not saying anything." That's what Muhammad told me. You want to hear the greatest fight I ever saw?

Q: Yeah, go for it, George!

George Dillman: On Wednesday night, I'm not sure of the date but it has to be around 1975 when Muhammad Ali went to do a press conference in Pennsylvania. There were three sparring partners. One of them was Alonzo Johnson, the light-heavyweight contender at the time. The other two were somewhat famous. Alonzo Johnson was either light-heavyweight champion or was going to be. Muhammad Ali was to spar with each one of these fighters three times – there were three rounds for each fighter. He would fight nine. I was not at that event as I had to run my school. I went to train with Ali during the day because I had a karate school. That was my living so I trained at my karate school in the evening with my students, doing children's classes, just like everything today. The next day, I was to go up and train with Muhammad and do roadwork. He was going to train later. I got a phone call saying he won't be there at 5 a.m. because he'd be boxing the night before. So I was told not to come up until the afternoon about 2 o'clock. He said we're going to do a light workout because he has to do nine rounds for the press.

When I go up to the camp, my ex-wife was with me, we walk up to the gym as we always did, and the man named Bundini Brown was there, who was famous. He was Ali's cornerman, but he was more than that. He's the reason Ali won many of the fights. He used to give him inspiration when Ali was in the ring in real fights. He used to tell him he was losing, so unless he won the next two rounds, and things like that, to keep him going. Muhammad Ali would say, "How are we doing?" Bundini would lie to him and say, "You lost the first three rounds so you better start fighting." He would tell him things like that and Ali would go nuts and go out there and win the fight. I know if it wasn't for Bundini Brown, Ali would have lost several more fights. What happened was Bundini cuts me off going through the door, he says, "You better not go in there." I said, "What's up?" He says, "Muhammad Ali is pissed."

That's the words he used. I said, "What!?" He said, "I've never seen him like this. My whole life, as long as I've known him, I've never seen him like this. He's furious, he's lost it."

I said, "What's the matter?" He said, "Well, he's going to be fighting." I said, "Is he going to be working out?" He said, "Oh, yeah! He's going to be working out. But he doesn't really want people in there. I just thought I'd tell you you'd better head home because I've never seen him like this. He's pissed." I asked him what happened. He said, "Last night at the press conference, the three boxers who were sparring partners tried to take him. You know, George, sparring partner ain't supposed to show off. Well, the sparring partners tried to take him and tried to up him and get press because all the press was there and they didn't want to look bad. They were hitting too hard, almost making it like a real fight. Ali wound up defending himself. He thought it was just pictures for the press." Alonzo Johnson was the leader of this. He said he actually tried to knock Ali out! And Ali had to come out of the corner and hit back.

Sparring partners are supposed to train you for the fight, that's what they are paid to do. But they were there for photos and to look good. I said, "What's going to happen?" He said, "Muhammad Ali's going to take on all three of them and beat them up today." I said, "What!?" Bundini Brown said, "He's going to get them in the ring and beat them up, all three of them. They were told to be here at 12 o'clock." I said, "Bundini, I've got to watch this." He said, "No. Be quiet, just go in and don't say anything to anybody. Just go and sit and watch."

So I go in and sit down. Bundini goes over, gives Ali his gloves and wraps and Ali comes out of the locker room. He was steaming. His face was flushed. And the three boxers come in and everybody was so quiet you could hear a pin drop. People were putting the wraps and gloves on the boxers. Ali gets in the ring and starts bouncing and bobbing. Now, what I'm telling you, if I had it on film, which nobody filmed it, but it was the greatest fight I have ever seen – ever! And I've seen all of them. He got in the ring and started warming up, bouncing and jabbing and he went over to that corner. They were standing outside. He said, "I want you first! I want you second! And you, Mr. Big Mouth, you're last!" And he said, "Now I want the three of you fighting. You thought you were smart asses last night. Today you better be fighting. Now I want you to try to take me! I want you to hit me hard! I want to see what you got. Let's see what you really got. And you, Mr. Big Mouth, you better be fighting for your life!" I thought to myself, *Oh, my God*. He goes back in his corner, puts his mouthpiece in, the wraps are on. In comes the first boxer, he says, "By the way, you guys better use headgear." Bundini says, "You want your headgear, champ?" Ali replies, "No. I want to see what they got!"

The first guy came out, Ali actually beat the daylights out of him. And that guy was trying to hit Ali, tried to defend and hit him. Ali cut him, beat him, knocked him down and beat him bad for three rounds. The next guy comes in, Ali beat him, beat him bad, knocked him down on one knee. The guy got up and he beat him again. I'm sitting and watching this and I'm going, *Oh, my God*. The third guy, Alonzo Johnson, comes in. Ali says, "Give it all you got." Alonzo was a good fighter. He was trying to hit back, but Ali just hit him to a pulp, got him on the ropes and beat his head like a timing bag. He knocked him down on both knees, went to hit him again and they started shouting, "Stop, Champ! Stop, Champ!" Bundini went in between them and said, "You're going to kill him! You'll kill him! You don't want to kill him!" Alonzo couldn't get up.

Ali goes back, they take off his wraps. He throws his gloves on the floor and goes into his dressing room. The three boxers go off. Actually, they are helped to their dressing room. I don't even know if Ali knew I was present. Ali looked out of his dressing room. There's a two-way mirror that he could look out to see what was out there, but you couldn't look in because it was a mirror. He looked out from the two-way mirror, which I didn't know, and he'd seen Kim and myself sitting there. He opens the door and comes out over to us, he says, "Hey, what did you think of that? Was that an ass whipping or what?" This is an honest-to-God true story. I don't think I've ever told this story to the press.

Q: George, you were friends with the late Bruce Lee. Did you have a conversation with Muhammad Ali pertinent to Bruce Lee when he was still alive?

George Dillman: Muhammad Ali told me the one man he wanted to meet in the whole world was Bruce Lee because he met every celebrity. He even met kings and queens. I even believe he met the Queen. In fact, I'm sure he did, whether it was before or after that, but he did meet the Queen of England. And he met all kinds of celebrities, kings, queens and presidents. He said the one man I want to meet is Bruce Lee. This was in 1972, mid-1972. We were working out, and he said, "Look, do you know Bruce Lee?" I said, "Yes, I met Bruce Lee. We talk. I have his number and his address." He said, "That's the one man I'd like to meet. I've met presidents. I've met everybody you can think of, but the one man I'd like to meet in the whole world is Bruce Lee." I said, "Well, I can arrange that."

So I called Bruce Lee and we got talking, and I said, "Bruce, Muhammad Ali wants to meet you." He said, "Oh, I idolize him. I even try to bounce like him when I fight. I use the toes." And Ali said, "I want to meet him bad. Can you line that up?" I said I could line that up. So I had a conversation with Bruce, Bruce wanted to meet Muhammad, Muhammad wanted to meet Bruce. That was shortly after Bruce was gone to Hong Kong and never returned. And that's how that story went. They never got to meet.

Q: When Bruce Lee was catapulted to worldwide fame, just after his death, did Muhammad Ali ever have a conversation with you expressing any reverence towards the late star?

George Dillman: We spoke about Bruce many times and Muhammad actually told me at one point, he said, "You know I never met the man, but I've got a little depressed with Bruce Lee dying. That really hit home because I realized it could happen to me. It could happen to anybody. And he was so young." He said, "I was down in the dumps. I didn't even want to train for two weeks. I just realized I had to get back to training. But I just didn't have it. It just wired me out. I never got to meet the guy. That's the one man I wanted to meet." So we talked about it. That's one conversation. I was depressed also. I got depressed for a while. When everybody started to sell 'Bruce Lee everything' I was mad. I called them prostitutes. I said how in the hell can they do that? The guy's only been dead two weeks and they're selling the stuff and writing books about him. Writing stuff and saying he wrote it. He only ever wrote one book called *Gung Fu* and I have a copy of it here. I got the copy directly from Bruce Lee who handed it to me. I have a copy of the original book, not the one they reproduced afterwards.

But afterwards, any books that came out by Bruce Lee, he never wrote those books. He never even knew what was in them. That's that story. By the way, a book with direct quotes from Bruce Lee, it had Chinese sayings like 'the grass is greener on the other side of the fence', or whatever. He never said any of those sayings. They got that from his movie scripts. He said in the movies. He didn't write the script. A lot of things he said them in the movies, he was just saying the lines. You understand what I'm saying? He would give this talk about the inner self. He believed in all of that, but some of the quotes they gave were not his quotes. They were things he said in the movies, which were in the script at the time.

JOSE SULAIMAN

Jose Sulaiman was the president of the WBC (World Boxing Council) and the administrator of the WBC – commonly accepted as boxing's most prestigious organization – from the 1970s until his death in 2014. Currently his son Mauricio is the president. Sulaiman was an amateur boxer, trainer, referee and promoter and was good friends with Ali, a relationship which continued long after Ali's career ended. He was inducted into the International Boxing Hall of Fame in 2007.

Q: When did you first made contact with Muhammad Ali, and what was your involvement with boxing at the time?
Jose Sulaiman: It was when he fought Sonny Liston in Florida – the first fight. We became very close friends later when I was the president of the World Boxing Council. But we did not start off very well because later I criticized him fighting a wrestler [Antonio Inoki] in Japan. When he came back from Japan, one of the writers asked him, "What do you think of Jose Sulaiman?" And he said, "Jose who!?"

After that we became really close. I had sent a press release out as a form of communication saying that I thought his fight with Inoki will hurt his image. Also, it will ruin boxing with opposition from the boxing fans. But it was a sell-out. Of course, the fight was absolutely terrible. Inoki went to the canvas the whole time and started kicking Ali's knees, the lower part of the leg. Ali had to go to the hospital because of a blood clot. But that was not a fight really. But after that Ali and I became friends. I wanted him to have a rematch with George Foreman in Las Vegas in 1976. He said, "I will but I already have one or two fights I'm committed to. I will fight George again." But that fight never happened.

Q: After the Antonio Inoki fight, in your opinion, did it hurt his image and were there mixed feelings in the boxing world?
Jose Sulaiman: No, no. It didn't hurt his image because it was

more publicity [for him]. I would say in Japan it was a great, great event. All the other newspapers of the world also went to the fight. Everybody read that it was not a fight at all because Inoki would not stand up with Ali. He went to the canvas and started kicking Ali. So it was not an attractive fight. But I believe that Ali, at the time, could get involved in many things because he was so popular.

Q: The fight materialized when some Japanese promoters thought it would make a lot of money. Was this the prime reason behind this fight?

Jose Sulaiman: Yes. Absolutely and positively it was only money. And I think that they did make a lot of money because in Japan it was a big event and a big success. But it's one of those things like when many, many fighters in life pursue something else. I remember another boxer participating in a wrestling match, so did Joe Louis. But that was at the end of their careers. While the Inoki fight happened when Ali was on top, when he was very, very famous.

Q: Do you feel Muhammad Ali elevated the sport of boxing in terms of popularity and the commerce side of it?

Jose Sulaiman: Let me tell you, Ali has been the greatest happening of the sport of boxing. Many boxers try to imitate his style. Ali has been the greatest for me in the ring and out of the ring. He's been a champion in life as well. I'm profoundly honored to have met him personally and to have him as my friend. He brought a new style in the sport of boxing and made it more spectacular. With that stance, rope-a-dope and all those things, which brought a great interest for the boxing fans around the world. Muhammad Ali is the king in the history of boxing.

Q: You have said in the past that the best moment you ever experienced with Muhammad Ali was when he came to your hometown in the mountains of Mexico. Can you please elaborate?

Jose Sulaiman: He came several times to Mexico. The first time was for my re-election in the year of 1980. When he came to Mexico the whole country gave up to him. He was so alive and so young. And with the Spanish-speaking public he was comical, joking and sparring. It was fantastic. Pictures went all over the world. People loved him in Mexico. Then he came again in 1988 for one of the re-elections of mine. And I remember something very, very important that happened. The president of the biggest television company in Mexico was sitting on a table at one of the dinners at the convention with some important people and beautiful ladies. He asked me to come and sit down at the table. At the table there was Mike Tyson and Don King also. I told him, "No, I'm sitting on that table there with Muhammad Ali." Then he said, "You must be crazy! You don't understand that table is the past, this is the present and the future." I answered him, "Look, the past is what has made me and Ali is my superhero of all time." So I went and sat with Muhammad Ali.

There was one other time when he came to Mexico because I wanted him to be seen by a Mexican doctor, who had discovered medicine at a surgery for the Parkinson's disease. And when he came to Mexico he came to my house. The doctor came and saw him and told him that he was a good candidate. Then he asked for a video. So I took him to my study room in my home and put on the video. We watched it and there was some kind of a surgery going on, which takes some kind of a bone from some part of the body. Then that little bone was implanted in the brain. And when he saw this surgery, it is then he looked at me like: hey, you know. It was an evolution of his personality. We took him to a hospital for the termination of the test. He said it's going to be absolutely private and a secret. So I took him in my car and we took him to the hospital. When we got there, I don't think any television station that existed wasn't there. Every television company was there with the cameras waiting at the entrance for Muhammad Ali. So we stopped the car, and he said, "No, no, no. Let's go back home please." He came to my home with his wife Lonnie. They took a flight and they landed in Chicago. The Chicago airport was full of television cameras.

Then he came once again to my little hometown at the center of the Indian miniatures in the mountains. I took him to a party, which was especially organized for him. He cared for the children with so much affection and sincerity, which really touched my heart. And all the people there were unbelievable, totally devoted to him. He went with Howard Bingham, his photographer, and Lonnie, his wife. He had a great time. Those are four visits which I remember of him coming to Mexico. There was one other visit I remember. We went to a television show, which was very famous. And my God, all the television people were mesmerized when he was being interviewed. It was a demonstration of the love and the admiration that the people of Mexico always had for Muhammad Ali.

Q: What impressed Muhammad Ali about Mexico and did he, as always, get a rapturous reception?
Jose Sulaiman: I believe the hospitality, the warmth, the humility and the simplicity of the people. They had no limits, no barriers. He was loved and welcomed. In the United States, in his home country, there was a lot of discrimination and there were a lot of people for him. When he used to fight, half of the people wanted him to lose and the other half wanted him to win. It was after his retirement that he became the one and only hero of all time of all America and the world. But for many years he was discriminated against. In Mexico he found that from the highest authority to the lowest, they all loved him sincerely and authentically.

Q: Can you relate to me the most compelling conversation you shared with him?
Jose Sulaiman: Well, we talked about everything. He told me how respectful he was about the twelve-round rule. He told me that was the greatest rule there had ever been for world championships. He once signed an autograph to me signing 'Muhammad Ali AKA Cassius Clay', and Howard Bingham, who had been very, very close to him all the time, told me he had never seen him sign 'Cassius Clay'. Howard said this is the one and only time in his life

that I have seen him do this. So I keep that glove as a treasure in a little box with a key. Let me tell you, he was very sincere in the Muslim religion, very, very peaceful. He told me once that he came to a different phase to know the time of the earth in the universe because nobody in the world cared about who did anything that exists on earth.

So he went to the desert and he thought of every grain of sand of being one year of the earth in the universe. He said then he knew how small he was. So he took eighty grains of sand and put them in his hands, and he said, "Perhaps God will give me eighty years to live. So I want to please him very brilliantly because I want to leave a very good mark of my passing through life. Those eighty grains I will throw them on my feet until the wind comes and blows them away." This was a fantastic thing that he told me once. I like it very much.

It's true, if anybody comes into life and doesn't do anything, doesn't record any memories of his life . . . but if someone is big and does something good, then future generations will know what he did for the good of society, until the wind in time comes and blows it away. In other words, he said I want to work all my life for the good of society in the world. That, to me, is one of the most extraordinary thoughts that I have ever heard from anybody in my life.

Q: What mark did Muhammad Ali leave in the boxing world?
Jose Sulaiman: He is without a question a great American. He traveled the world. His sign of success is an example to newer generations in the world. In regards to boxing, there's no question that the best agility in boxing was Muhammad Ali's. In boxing in the past there had been heavyweights who usually didn't move around. They boxed power to power. Boxing agility was seldom used. Muhammad Ali came and brought a new style of boxing. Many, many people try to copy him. And one of the greatest boxers came because of Ali – Larry Holmes.

Larry Holmes became a great boxer. He was Muhammad Ali's sparring partner before becoming the champion. And, in fact, in the end of Ali's triumph Larry Holmes fought him in a fight. I really out loud spoke against it because Ali was over the hill. We ordered an extreme medical examination. They took him to a very famous American clinic and he passed the examination. But he passed an examination of a single person, not of an old-aged boxer, which should be different. The fight took place and, obviously, Ali took so much weight out because he was very heavy. He lost about 40 pounds or so. Obviously, Larry Holmes was totally devastated. I'll give you something I have never told anybody in my life. The lights of the eyes of Muhammad Ali went away after his fight with Larry Holmes. Muhammad Ali's eyes were like a fox, very alive, very approaching, very profound and deep, very bright. After that fight that look had gone.

Q: Do you remember when the United States government sent him on peace missions to Moscow?
Jose Sulaiman: No, very briefly. But I can tell you that the three-and-a-half years that he was out of boxing because he didn't want to join the army was the best three-and-a-half years of his life. He was twenty-five years old only. But they banned him from boxing. Then he returned at the age of twenty-eight-and-a-half. So, from twenty-five to twenty-eight – the most outstanding, extraordinary and powerful years of the ban – those were the biggest years of my life also. And they cannot be compared to any other age. And they took Ali out of boxing. That's one of the most revered positions that any government could have taken against an athlete.

Q: Do you feel he transcends the boxing arena?
Jose Sulaiman: Oh, definitely. There are many, many sports fields, but I don't believe that any of them have reached the top of the top – the top of the crème like Muhammad Ali. There have been many, many heroes but I believe Muhammad Ali is the biggest of them all. Remember, there was a poll to see who was the most known face in the world. Muhammad Ali won over the Pope and many other great people of the time. He was the most recognized face in the world.

Q: Anything significant you would like to include that personifies Muhammad Ali's legacy?

Jose Sulaiman: I would say that he is a beloved person. When Muhammad Ali goes to the Middle East, he is like a god. There is not one single person there that doesn't believe Muhammad Ali is some kind of a god. I remember some years ago the president of Lebanon and the Prime Minister Mr. Hariri, who was killed in a car bomb, asked me to try to bring Ali to Lebanon. Then they asked for Mike Tyson. Then they thought Ali is our king. Ali is our beloved hero. But then there was a confrontation between Israel and Lebanon so that project died. He went to many Middle East countries many times. Ali was the type of a person who's a fighter for peace and goodwill. His religion is devoted to peace and goodwill and gives support to all people. His thoughts in the desert clarify what Muhammad Ali's always been.

I would prefer to say that Muhammad Ali has been the greatest boxing fighter that's ever lived. In the ring everybody wanted to fight him and in life everybody wants to meet him. I think he has been the biggest and highest example of a human being working for peace and solidarity and goodwill. If every boxer would be like Muhammad Ali, perhaps he would be an influence to the rivers of blood and hate in wars and confrontations. We are in the sport of boxing, which is considered by many to be a violent sport, but we are a sport that sets an example. After a fight you must see both boxers go to the center of the ring and they hug each other, even after the tremendous violence. And I hope that was an example Muhammad Ali also gave and I hope that he will be noticed by all the leaders of politics of the world.

LEON GAST

Documentary film director, producer, cinematographer and editor Leon Gast is widely known for his seminal and acclaimed documentary *When We Were Kings*. A native of New York, Gast has received numerous awards for his depiction of the iconic heavyweight bout Rumble in the Jungle between Muhammad Ali and George Foreman. Gast continues to work on documentary projects.

Q: When did you first come into contact with Muhammad Ali and what was the experience like?
Leon Gast: It was in the spring of 1974, probably around May 1974. It was right before the fight [Foreman–Ali] had been signed. I'm not sure of the exact date, but the fight was being planned and negotiated with Foreman. I met Don King, Stewart Levine and Hugh Masekela and I went down to Muhammad Ali's camp at Deer Lake, Pennsylvania, where I met him for the first time. I had been a huge Muhammad Ali fan. When I met him he was in real good spirits. At that time, he was with Belinda, who was his wife who later became Khalilah, and the twin daughters were there. We walked around the camp and he showed me his gym and the place he would stay at, which was a large cabin. He had to pump the water. He told me that before a fight he likes to live in this rusted cabin, which he had right near his beautiful house at Deer Lake. We sat outside and we talked for a few minutes.

I noticed something then but I couldn't put it into words until I read Norman Mailer's great book *The Fight*. In the first chapter, I think even the first paragraph of the book, Norman Mailer describes Ali and says – and I'm paraphrasing even though I don't have the book in front of me – "When Muhammad Ali is in good spirits, he has a golden aura about him, a golden look." Those are Norman Mailer's words. And he said, "But when he's in a foul mood, he has a greenish tint skin." When you read that you think that Norman Mailer's just been literary. But that day with him, it was really golden. It really was. We were outdoors and the sun was shining, it was late May.

Then I had an experience with him once where he wasn't in a too good mood. He said, "What are you, the new Howard Cosell!?" He was very nasty. Not very nasty, but he wasn't in a talkative mood. I don't know, maybe I asked him bad questions. But years later after we had shot the film, actually into the 1990s, we had been contacted by a couple of companies that were going to do Ali commercials. One of them was Adidas. They said everybody here looked at a whole lot of material and they all seem to refer to the footage you shot down at Deer Lake, and then outdoors of him running in Zaire, as the golden footage. Because he just has this golden aura about him.

To even go a little bit further, we started shooting in probably June. We spent some time down there just walking around with him, going on runs with him, going into the gym, working out with Larry Holmes who was his sparring partner. I think Larry Holmes was nineteen years old. Bossman Jones was another one of his sparring partners. A third one was another heavyweight whose name I can't remember. But it had a feeling, they weren't just sparring partners, they were almost like, I don't know if I can say this, but it was like a family. It was very different when I got to meet George Foreman in Africa – the relationship with his sparring partners. Ali opened up his world to me. I mean, any documentary filmmaker or a journalist will tell you that it's all about access – when you can get access to your subject. And I had complete access to Ali.

We were once in Deer Lake, he invited us into the house and we shot him with his wife and the cook. He just opened up. He wasn't somebody that had camera consciousness. He wasn't like most of the athletes of today who will give you the tagline: I'm gonna fight a good fight. Ali was very, very natural and he opened up everything. Then another time we're leaving to go to Africa. I had one of my crew members who had been out in San Francisco training with George Foreman. Me and two crew members had been following Ali from Deer Lake and into New York, and press conferences with Don King, then leaving to go on the plane. So I stopped them outside. We were going from LaGuardia airport to Logan airport, Boston, and to Paris and from there to Kinshasa. I'm there with the camera. I said. "We're going to be going . . ." and he was a little nasty. He said, "OK. Just don't get in my way. Just don't get in my way." It was kind of totally out of character. I thought maybe he didn't have a good morning or whatever.

We got to Africa and we spent time out in where he trained. We'd go out there every day and sit out in front of his house, which was by the Zaire River. He would always make mistakes! He'd say, "We're sitting here in front of the Congo River. Isn't it beautiful?" Mobutu had security people, hostesses and there were a lot of people around. Every time Ali would say, "We're sitting out here in the Congo River," somebody would say, "Ali, no. Zaire, Zaire." He had almost the same response every time. He'd say, "Have no fear, everybody knows it's called Zaire, by the Zaire River." He kept on slipping into calling it what it was known as in the colonial days – Congo. So after that first incident from when we were getting on the plane and when we changed planes, we shot footage along the way and he was fine. Then when we got there, a couple of days later we actually talked.

I shot him doing workouts and he told me, "If you want to get a really beautiful scene, I run in the morning. I run down around here and if you set up the cameras right there, I start running between 5 and 5.30 in the morning. The sun is coming up behind me so you'll get this beautiful shot." He was almost, I can't say directing the film, I may have said that in the past, but he was telling me what he thought would be good scenes to shoot. When he was working out in the gym, he'd see us and he'd always come over to see us where we were. As I started out to say: he was the perfect subject to do a film. It started out to be just a film about that fight, but it turned out to me more of a character study of Ali.

Q: How did the concept of the documentary come about, and what exactly were you trying to achieve with the film?

Leon Gast: The concept initially was: this is a championship fight and Ali is fighting his toughest, and everybody says his most difficult, fight ever. There were people in his camp who were really frightened he was going to get hurt because he was thirty-two years old then. He was fighting three guys who had given him a tremendous amount of trouble – Joe Frazier, George Foreman and Ken Norton. George Foreman had annihilated Joe Frazier in their last fight and he had done the same thing to Kenny Norton. And both those fighters always gave Ali trouble. All of the people in his corner were really concerned he was going to get very hurt, especially Dr. Pacheco, who was really concerned. They all were, Bundini and Angelo, all his entourage were concerned. We had the footage, which I don't think we used in *When We Were Kings*, and I don't think Jeff did in *Soul Power*, where Angelo Dundee is standing next to him, and he says, "Look at him. Look at the shape he's in. This is the best shape this guy's been in years. He's gonna knock George Foreman out." And he said it to me. I don't know why we never used it in the film.

First, it was going to be a trip to Africa and about 240 musicians and their entourage, mostly family and friends, were all going over. Bundini came up with 'From the Root to the Flute'. Then Don King picked up on that. It was all these champions returning home. Not only Ali and Foreman and their people for the fight, but all of these musicians – James Brown; BB King; The Pointer Sisters; The Spinners; The Crusaders, all going back to the motherland, to the roots. So the fight was going to be the wraparound, but the emphasis was going to be the music and the festival. And it was going to be the music which was always going to drive the fight.

The way it was scheduled, it was the music festival that was going to be on, I believe, the date which was September 21, 22 and 23. And then the fight was going to happen on 25 or 26. I'm just looking trying to find some of my old research stuff so I can give you the exact dates. The music concert was going to be September

20, 21 and 22, and the fight was going to happen on 23 or 24 after the music festival. We were in the gym with Ali when he was training when he got cut. The musicians hadn't come over yet. They were leaving the next day. I called the office in New York and told them about the cut.

There was going to be a press conference. Everybody's saying that there's no way those guys are going to fight. Everybody said there's no way this fight was going to come off with the cut. The fight was delayed, which gave us more of a chance to spend time with Ali and get so much more personal stuff with him, while he was waiting for the fight to come off. Eventually, the focus of the film changed and Taylor Hackford got involved. He had seen a rough cut of it and it was Taylor who said, "I loved your film. It's the best material." I think, unquestionably, we had some of the most intimate stuff about Ali that anybody shot during his career. It all had to do with the access. So, we met at my partner, David Sonenberg's, office. And Taylor said – and I'm jumping ahead twenty years because we were . . . should I back track?

What happened was we started to edit the film. The first thing that happened was, as soon as we got back Don King came by the editing room. Along with Hank Shwartz' partner and his film specialist – whoever that was, some TV guy he had working with him – and I showed them the film material, which was in its rough state. I showed them stuff of Ali running. And the guy, who was DK's expert, according to feedback I got from someone who worked for King, said, "Oh, they're not really interested in it." So we were hit with the problem of how the project was being financed if they didn't like it.

Mobutu was putting up the money for the fighters – $5 million for each fighter. And however that $5 million was broken in with Herbert Muhammad, his manager, his trainer, Bundini, I don't know. I heard the contract had two-and-a-half million dollars for Don King. I also heard that it wasn't that much, it was more like a million and he had a backhand deal. But Mobutu put up that money unquestionably. Now, the film. Where are we going to get the money to make the film? The David Wahlberg organization was very interested in getting involved in it. Then enter Hugh Masekela, who is a great musician. He's still around and he had just gotten divorced from Miriam Makeba, who he had been married to for a short time. He settled in Nigeria and he had become friends with the ruling family of Nigeria. They agreed.

I met with their representative in New York City. They represented a company, which was – it gets complex here – a fishing company. They wanted to see a budget. I put a budget together and my budget included everything in it originally. It included the stage, which was going to be built, and included the travel. It was less than a million dollars. I'm not sure of these numbers. So, I met up with their representative and we worked out a deal. They loved the idea. So, now it's getting into July, August, this is 1974. We've got a deal. I've got a film contract with them. We had no money at all. We signed the crew.

I knew I wanted at least six film crews because I wanted to shoot a lot of background stuff. I wanted to be able to shoot all the musicians in their rehearsals, performances, etc, and still shoot Ali and Foreman. And have this material put together and make a film with the emphasis which is really pretty much about the return of all these African-American musicians and athletes. Don King came up with something along the lines of 'From Slave Ships to Championships'. That was like his thing. And I think it may have been on some of the posters. So we wait. We'd actually signed contracts with people. And then finally we got a check from Africa. They put it in one of the New York City banks. I think we hired a total of eighty-something people, including stage people. We had seven camera crews. I wanted each camera crew to be autonomous. So each one of them had a sound guy and an assistant cameraman and a grip who would carry equipment and set up lights.

The headquarters for this whole thing was in Manhattan on 55th Street. It was with Video Techniques – that was the company. Hank Schwartz was in charge of it and Don King was the vice president and he wound up being a partner after that fight, but that's a whole new story. Anyway, Don sees people coming in and we're making deals. Don says, "I don't see many black faces coming in here to work on this. I wanna see a lot more black faces on this crew." I mean, Don King had taken over. But I was the director and the producer. And we talked. Don King said, "I'm in a position now where I could do something for my people." He said it just like that. I mean, great aura that he is and the philosopher that he is. "I have the opportunity now. If I didn't see that there were as many blacks on your crew as whites, I would be embarrassed!" He spoke so eloquently. And this was 1974. I said, "Don, I don't know forty blacks to hire for the crew." There just weren't that many that were working in TV and film at that time in New York City. His response was, "I think if you look hard enough you'll find them."

So we hired a crew from California. We had gotten good feedback on the team what we were looking to do, and then by just asking around. I knew a guy who did commercials – I'm sorry, I'm not good with names – a local guy from New York City. He said I know so and so who worked on the first Joe Frazier–Muhammad Ali fight at Madison Square Garden. This guy was a cameraman. I met him and we hired him. He had a sound guy who he worked with who we actually put together so that the crew was 50 percent white and 50 percent black. Don was really happy about that.

Unfortunately, for me, people I had worked with before such as Kevin Keaton, Paul Goldsmith and Albert Maysles, I knew them. I knew the quality of the material. I knew these guys were excellent cameramen. So there was a little bit of hassle because if we were going to shoot something, I want Albert to be the guy in BB's dressing room, or with Ali when I was going up to his place to shoot something. But Don King had said I'm not seeing enough black people. He was constantly on my case wanting the black crew to be more prominent. I give him credit for that because he was on my case all the time.

There were a bunch of people who really got their, I wouldn't say, start but I'd say it helped them with their film career. We shot the film. We had it all in the lab being processed. First thing that happens is Don King sues. Don King gets an injunction against the whole process claiming he's owed $150,000. He actually got an injunction on the lab that had the material and the place that had all the sound recordings, that music festival – thank God we recorded everything. The people involved with the fight said, "Oh, it will be a waste. What do you need to shoot everything for? You're only going to use two songs from each. So talk to their managers and find out which are the better ones." But I wanted to shoot everything and we wound up shooting everything. I'm happy that we did because Soul Power came out of that. Don King sued. Hank Schwartz from Video Techniques sued.

Then there are problems going on in Monrovia, Liberia, political problems where the Tolbert regime is being threatened. I'm doing business with Steve Tolbert, who is the finance minister, the brother of the president of Liberia. Other than the first check, we're not getting any more money. The labs are owed money, everybody's owed money. Besides, I've got the suit going on with Don King, who's hired one of the most prestigious law firms in the city. Anyway, finally it's heard in a Federal Court in New York City Southern District. They hear those complaints about Don King and we have a court date. I have two lawyers and Don's lawyer gets up and speaks to the judge. The judge happens to be an African-American woman, the first African-American woman in the whole American justice system. There were no blacks until Constant Motley. His lawyer gets up and he opens up with, "Your Honor, I'm sure you're aware of the fight which took place in Africa a couple of years ago." And he didn't even get to finish and she just leaned forward and said, "Don't you assume I know anything about Africa or anything about Muhammad Ali." His litigators are starting out trying to play some kind of a racial card to a black judge who really got upset about it.

Anyway, it went on for half a day and the judge ruled in our favor, that the money Don King was owed had nothing at all to do with it. Actually, King's contract stated that he was to receive $150,000 from the gate receipts of the concert. Because the fight had been postponed and the concert went off on 21 and 22, and people who were there were going to come to Africa to watch the fight didn't show up once they knew the fight was off. The plan was: this fight would happen the day after the three-day music festival.

Whoever priced the tickets priced them $15 apiece. Nobody found out until we got there that the average Zaire person made about $15 a month. There was no way they could afford the tickets. And then another thing that happened, which really screwed things up, was that the tickets were printed in the United States and shipped over and they spelt Mobutu's name wrong on the tickets. People were freaking out! This Mobutu dictator! So those tickets all had to be destroyed. I wish I had one because one of those would be like the stamp where they spelt someone's name wrong. The tickets were destroyed and they got to get someone to reprint the tickets. I'm not sure where, Masekela knows where.

The concert went off and there were very, very few people left. There were mostly embassy people. They sent somebody to reserve the tickets. The guy from the American embassy, not the ambassador, said, "We can't pay for the tickets. How can you not give us tickets?" There were about twenty-six of them. Then from the British embassy. And every embassy wanted free tickets. So there were almost no gate receipts the first and the second day of the concert. I'm complaining to Don King and Mubula – who was Mobutu's main guy who was dealing with the concert and the fight – that this was going to make it look terrible.

We have an empty stadium and we had no people in any of the shots that are looking out towards the crowds – nobody there, just really embassy people. So I along with Lloyd Price and a couple of other people were able to convince Mubula that they've got to talk to Mobutu about making this a free concert. And the big problem is to let people know. And this is a day before. They have to make it a free concert. Next day it was going to be James Brown. Anyway, they used their helicopters and they went all around and all over dropping little leaflets. And on the radio they announced that the festival in Kinshasa is now free. We had up to 80,000 people there.

So there was a crowd. So at least I had crowd shots from the music. So, when you see the film, you see people jumping in front of the stage. That was all done in a one-day shoot.

It got hung up in court. Then it was released to me in my name because I had not been paid either, and they owed me a considerable amount. It took another two years before it was heard and the injunction was released. Then we went back in court, and all the rights and properties of the group that owned it. It was a front for the Liberians called International Films and Records. The money went from Liberia to Switzerland to the Bahamas, then to me. So they never put up any more money. I got all their rights. There was no money. At one point, one of the stage managers, Barrie Singer, who died recently, I got a phone call from him. And I'm telling everybody we're getting the money. They've already put up about $900,000, certainly finish financing it. We're waiting for the money. I went to Liberia, but they wound up not even being there. They invited me to Liberia. I went back and waited for days on end in Monrovia to meet with somebody.

Then I got a call from Barry, who asked, "Have you seen *Newsweek* magazine?" I said no. He said, "There's a picture and people are tied to a pole and it's a three-panel shot. There's been a coup there. The country's been taken over and there's a shot of these guys tied to a post with the firing squad. I guess we're not getting any money from Liberia." David Sonenberg then agreed to finance it. As time goes on, I do a rough cut and edit. It was about three hours at the time. It's got a lot of music in it. I was able to get a good copy of the fight.

I knew Bill Cayton, the guy who ran Big Fights. This was going to be very expensive. It's going to cost about $120,000. He asked me what I was looking for. Well, I want highlights of the fight. I would like round one. I would like definitely round five where Ali really starts to turn the tide, and then the last round with the knockout. "Oh, that's going to cost you a lot of money. That'll be, off the top of my head, $120,000," Bill told me. And I said, "Bill, my budget for all of the archive stuff is less than half of that." He said, "Well, you've got to figure out something." I knew Tom Hauser, who eventually wrote the book *The Life and Times of Muhammad Ali*, and he's actually in the film. So Tom says what you have to do with Bill Cayton is you have to get it on a personal level. Get out of his office, tell him you want to talk about it and you want to have lunch.

I called him and said I'd love to meet you for lunch, where do you want to go? There was this really expensive restaurant right around the corner from where his office was and Cayton's offices Big Fights. Big Fights owned everything. I don't know if you're familiar with it, but Big Fights was a company started by Jimmy Jacobs and Bill Cayton. They just started buying anything and everything that was out there, including Jack Johnson's fights going all the way back to the beginning when they were shooting fights. It was kind of crude but they covered a lot of those fights. And also all of the Dempsey fights and Joe Louis', Rocky Marciano's, Sugar Ray Robinson's fights. They owned everything right up through Zaire.

So I took him to lunch and I said without this footage there is no film. So he said, "How much do you have to spend?" I replied, "About $25,000." He said, "That's ridiculous, we can't." I said, "Bill, I have to license this," and mentioned all the other material we were licensing. He owned every one of the Ali fights. He owned Cassius Clay fights. Those early fights in the United Kingdom with Henry Cooper. We made a deal for $30,000 right on the spot. He said, "OK! $30,000! Before we do anything give me a check. Once it clears I'll give you access to what you want."

So I went back to David Sonenberg and he wrote a check and got him this check immediately. Actually, a kid who was working for me was there. I was going to run it to David but he said no, let Terry bring it over. So just like the messenger, he walks in. Terry told me, "I put my hand out to shake hands with him and all he did was put out the other hand to grab the check." They took the check, the check cashed and we got access to the footage. The company was bought by Disney, and now ESPN Classics owns all of that fight stuff. If you want to do any kind of business, archival fight footage, you have to deal with ESPN Classics, which is all part of the Disney umbrella. It is so expensive.

People call me and try to license from me. I can't license any of it. The Ali training and Ali saying, "I'm beautiful, I'm bad, I knocked out Henry Cooper in the fifth round," all those fabulous rants that he would do from 1964-'65 all those years. We were able to make the deal. I got about seven or eight minutes of the material I needed. A lot of that is in the seventh or eighth minute.

Once I got it, I was able to go through his archives. The fight material we have in the fight is actually made from the exact same tape that was taping in the truck when they were shooting the fight, which then went up to a satellite broadcasting, which you could only get going to a theater in the United States by buying tickets. It was live. Everything I got was the best quality Bill had. Now Taylor gets involved. Anyway, at one point we were going to make a deal with Universal. The acquisition guy from Universal came to the editing room where I was working, and he said we want this. We're going to release this as a feature film. We're going to do bla, bla, bla.

It moved so slowly. A year went by and nothing had happened. It was like, *Oh, we're going to make a deal but these things have to be done first.* So anyway, it didn't happen. I got involved in another project. It was actually sitting in my apartment, everything including negatives. Once the injunction was lifted, I got everything out. All the work prints and all the original negatives. And I had it stored in my apartment. Then I started sharing space and had another place and I moved it down there.

Eventually, we put it in a storage place. That's where we got the material transferred and digitized it all with the help of Jeffrey Levy-Hinte, and made that incredible film *Soul Power*. I don't know if you've seen it, but he did a fabulous job. He had been an editor on *When We Were Kings*, so Jeffrey was familiar with all that material. He always said there's another film here, altogether another film out of the music. And initially my main focus was going to be the music festival, and Ali was there and Ali would come to the music festival and George Foreman didn't.

A West Coast filmmaker somehow sees it. I guess from his friend at Universal. He sees a rough cut of it. It pretty much was a cut, but it was long and it was over two and three hours. He sees it and we set up a meeting. He's got a company. He loved it! He said I want to be involved in it. I have a friend who is a big Muhammad Ali fan and I'd love you to meet him. The friend comes in. The friend is Taylor Hackford. Now we're talking twenty years later. This material has been sitting.

Along the way every now and then something would pop up. And I hear from somebody they want to do a BB King show. HBO Home Entertainment will pay X amount of dollars. So I give BB King's material in Africa to HBO. So, Taylor Hackford comes in and we have the meeting. He said I love the material and there's one thing I would do if I get involved in it. I feel it would bring it into the 1990s – this was 1995. He said you have to find some people who were there that can analyze and offer commentaries. I immediately said that Taylor, Jerry – Jerry is another producer I worked with – and David has been saying all along why don't you do interviews? If you do interviews . . . I said, "No! I strongly believe in direct cinema. It doesn't need a narrator of any kind. A film should work on its own and tell the story." So I didn't want to do interviews. I had become friends with George Plimpton. I was friends with a lot of people.

So, during this first meeting Taylor suggests, suppose you could get an African-American, somebody who was maybe a kid, they were influenced by Ali. And if you had your choice of anybody who would you pick? Denzel Washington was really hot at the time, or just started to emerge. I said Denzel Washington. I think he would be great. He's from New York. Taylor said Spike Lee would be better. Spike has more street credibility and he would be great. I said yes, Spike would be great. Who else? I said immediately Norman Mailer. Have you ever read the book *The Fight*? Taylor hadn't, so I said let me send you this book. He loves Ali. OK, who else? George Plimpton! He was at the fight. He's a buddy of mine. I worked with him on another project. Now we had those three guys and David's working out the deal with Taylor. So we're going to do interviews with those three, two or three months later.

In the meantime, Taylor and I meet privately. Taylor says, "I'd like to see everything that you have, which you think is really good that's not in your cut." I said, "We have so much material. We shot so much. I have so much of Ali and much less of Foreman. But I have Ali, hours and hours of it." So he asked if I could just put it together on VHS or any kind of format and come out to Los Angeles and we'll spend some time together. We had 280,000 feet of film. I went through all the copies of the interviews, the whole thing. So I made probably forty or fifty VHS tapes. Each one was an hour long of Ali. And I gave it to Taylor and hung out with him a couple of days. He went through it all. He said he loved it and came back and we had several conversations. I was living in New York. I had a house up in the country, which I was renting, but I would go back and forth to. I decided that I would move up here full-time.

Another good friend of mine, who passed away, who actually introduced me to Tom Hauser, was a journalist named Jack Newfield – a great writer and a supporter of boxing. He loved Ali. Whenever I had any kind of a cut, I would screen it down at Jack's. Jack would look at it and say I like this or I don't like that. And Thomas Hauser says, "It's driving me crazy. There's too much African stuff. If I see a woman with a basket on her head or another chucking corn, or whatever it is. There should be more Ali, more Ali." And Jack said the same thing. "You've got to make it more Ali. The music is OK, but I want to see more Ali." And Taylor felt the exact same way. So we got all the interviews done and we put it together. I screened it for Jack and he had already cut the negatives. Jack was then writing for *The New York Post* or *The News*. He said, "I have a still in our files. I have to look for it. But I remember it's a shot of George Plimpton and Norman Mailer sitting together at ringside in the third row." He found it and the next day I went to his office and picked it up. We shot it ourselves with a 16mm camera on the wall and got the negative back the next day. We actually physically took the negative and cut that shot into the negative. I think if Sonenberg or Hackford knew what we were doing they would've went crazy because we could have screwed up the negative. But we cut it in and it really looks good. When Foreman goes down it cuts to that still, you can see Mailer and Plimpton with their mouths open. They seem to be reacting to what's happened in the ring before anybody else around them is aware that this is a knockout and he's not getting up.

Q: What's the most intriguing conversation you had with Muhammad Ali, which captivated your attention?

Leon Gast: There were a few of them. One time, in Africa where he was talking about the injustice and the United States and how the black man has been victimized for so many years. And I said, "Aren't we all brothers and sisters?" He went into a rant! "No! We ain't brothers and sisters! Brothers and sisters don't hang one another." 'Lynch' is the word he used. "A brother don't cut off another brother's private parts." There were so many really good moments with him, going back to when he did have a really prominent voice. After the Olympics when he won a gold medal, the story about how he threw it in the river is untrue – it's just become a legend. He would predict the round he was going to win by a knockout. He turns pro after the 1960 Olympics. I'm not sure the year, each one of the fights he had, he would say, "I'm going to knock him out in the fourth round." He was called the Louisville Lip. He would predict [when he was going to knock out his opponents]. Before there was such a thing called Rap or Hip Hop, Ali did it. Rhythmic, it just came out of his mouth and it rhymed. He really was a poet.

He became extremely outspoken and the civil rights movement was happening in this country. It was beginning to change. Change was coming about very, very slowly but there were very few people who sided with Ali and what he was doing. Mostly educated professional African-Americans were very much against him. They all believed that change was coming and it's going to be slow and litigious, but they felt that Ali was too brash and was throwing it in everybody's face. There were people who I thought would've supported him that didn't support him. He was Cassius Clay after the first Sonny Liston fight, but he changed his name to Muhammad Ali. He really didn't have the support of the elite black people.

Q: Can you relate the incident at the press conference in Zaire when Muhammad Ali got frustrated with Don King?

Leon Gast: Oh, yes. That's on film. That was a press conference where King is sitting in the middle, to King's left is Dick Sadler, to his right is Angelo Dundee and Bundini Brown. Bundini Brown was always feeding Ali lines – clever things to say. Ali would not even listen to some of them; some of them he'd use immediately. It was Bundini who came out with 'float like a butterfly, sting like a bee'. And a lot of these things became part of Ali's jargon, which came through Bundini. Bundini leaned over whoever was sitting next to him – I wish I had the film in front of me and I could look at it right now – he whispered something to Ali on the other side of King. I know what it was: tell him to watch the bus stations. Because Ali was saying, "George Foreman, he wants to get out of this fight, so watch all the airports, watch the docks and the ships."

Then Bundini wanted him to say watch the bus stations. Angelo was there, Angelo said something along the lines of, "What did you say?" Bundini just kind of annoyed him. And King said something to Angelo, he put him down. He said, "He's talking to me!" King acted in a gruff manner with Angelo and Ali said, "Don't you ever talk to him like that." Then he didn't let it go and he's pointing his finger at Don King, and he says, "Don't you ever talk to Angelo like that! Don't ever talk to him like that!" It sticks out in my mind because I can remember it at the press conference in Africa, where there was mostly Africans but American press was there, too. Ali stood up for Angelo and got right into Don King saying never disrespect him like you're doing. We have that in the film. That's one of the great scenes.

Q: What was Don King's relationship like with Muhammad Ali? Don King seemed to have problems with many people.

Leon Gast: Because Don King was looking out for Don King, Don King wanted a piece of everything – of everything! I don't know how much I want to go public with this, but Don King was a businessman. He was really a businessman. The way Don King would deal with you is, "No, my brother, shake hands, everything's fine." He'd say to me, "You're going to be a millionaire. One day you're going to be a millionaire!" But when it gets to the deal, unless you have a lawyer poring over everything you wind up with nothing, very little.

Many fighters told me because people knew I had been close with King and that we'd been working together. I would talk to them. I worked on a film with Robert Coppell. I was an editor on a film called *Mike Tyson: Fallen Champ* and I got to speak to a lot of fighters and always talked to them about Don King. Fighters would tell me, "I don't care whatever you say. I don't care how much more money Don King got than I should've got. All I can tell you is before Don King, the most money I ever made for a fight was $12,000. Since Don King's managed me, I made ten times that amount per fight. I don't care what Don King's making, whatever he's doing he's making more money for me than I ever made before." He was a very shrewd businessman, very clever guy.

Q: Muhammad Ali went on to upset the odds by knocking out George Foreman in the eighth round. Whenever he conversed with you did he express any elements of post-fight fear?

Leon Gast: Only confidence. It was only confidence whenever he talked about him, but sometimes that confidence is to fortify him. Not that it was a false confidence, but he always showed confidence he could beat George. We spent a lot of time together, me talking to him, him talking back to me. This is at his place on a favorite bench he had by the river where we'd sit. I know Jeff used a lot of stuff in *Soul Power*. We would usually have two or three cameras.

One time, we start talking about the fight. I'm not a sports journalist, like you are or like a lot of other guys. I mention what everybody does: that Foreman just beat Joe Frazier. He's talking and he's banging his fist. Imagine he's got his right hand up and he's punching the right hand. I'm sitting on the floor and he's talking about why he's going to beat George Foreman. "George Foreman ain't nothing." He's talking, it's almost like he's doing a self-hypnotic thing where the punch into his hand is becoming more and more powerful. Eventually, we used one little piece in the film where he gets up right after that in *When We Were Kings*. He says, "I've got God on my side." That's what he's talking about, when we're talking it seems like this guy's becoming another . . . It's self-hypnosis. Like convincing himself he's going to beat this guy. I noted it and afterwards I said to the crew when we went outside, "He said so much that the whole room was shaking." This was him talking and punching his fist and saying why he was going to beat George Foreman.

The thirty-day delay, without a question, worked so much in Ali's favor and it worked so much against George Foreman. George trained and he was at his peak. He was annihilating his sparring partners to the point he's working in the ring. He'd work with three guys, three rounds with each round. In one of the sessions his trainers were Archie Moore and Dick Sadler. Sadly, Sadler was there also with them. And Sadler would say, "OK, that's enough." He'd go a round-and-a-half with one of the sparring partners. He was so sharp that he was hurting his sparring partners. Sadler would mercifully say, "OK, that's enough!" They'd stop and the next guy would come in. George was in tremendous shape. And Sandy and Archie Moore were shown teaching him about cutting off the ring, trying to get Ali. Actually, Ali came up with that rope-a-dope thing, so he didn't have to cut him off. Ali just waited there on the ropes and let Foreman keep whaling away with the left and right hand, and eventually tired Foreman out. In the eighth round he knocked him out.

Q: Your film came out in 1996?
Leon Gast: The first time he saw the film was when I was making

cuts. As I was making edits, I was sending him VHS of just sections, wherever he was living, mostly in Deer Lake and Michigan. I would send him copies of it. He loves to look at that. I made a phone call one morning, "Hello. Hello," I said, "Champ! Do you remember me!?" He said, "Yeah, you're the skinny ugly guy that was running around chasing me in Africa." We talked and we had an opening and Ali was sitting two rows in front of me. He was with a young man. I could see he kept on poking him as he was sitting at the big screening with a big smile on his face. Then the party afterwards and going out and the whole thing with the Academy Awards. I think we screened it in January at Radio City. We won the Academy Award in 1997 for '96. But we got it in 1997, but the film was released in 1996. I'm looking at the Oscar right now. It says 'Academy Awards'.

Q: When was the last time you interacted with him?
Leon Gast: Three months ago. I got a phone call from Lonnie, his wife, and they're living now in Arizona and Louisville. They have a house in both places. A couple of stories I want to tell you. One, I get a phone call. I had seen Lonnie at Norman Mailer's funeral but Ali wasn't there. Lonnie called and said, "Ali, he loves to look at material of himself. But he doesn't like to look at the fight stuff so much. He likes to look at just him doing things or talking. Do you have any material that wasn't in the film with just Ali sitting around talking or talking to friends?" I said I have a bunch of it, let me go through it and I'll put it on a CD. Now everything is digitized. So I said I'll put it all on a DVD and I'll send it to you. She gave me their address in Arizona and I sent them the DVD.

She called about a month later, and she said, "I'm sorry I haven't called you sooner, we've been so busy. Ali looks at it over and over again. His eyes are like as big as quarters. He just looks and he stops and he rewinds it." This is the material I told you about, which we shot in Deer Lake, in Africa, outdoors walking. He just loves looking at that material. "Do you have any more?" she asks. I called up Jeff Levy-Hinte, who was the director of *Soul Power*, and told him about it. I said, "Here's his address, do not give it to anybody. Can you please just dump all the material onto a DVD, everything you have on Ali. Some of it may be the same as what I sent already." We sent it again. That was a couple of weeks ago.

Another Don King story that happened in Zaire. We get over there. I think there were eighty-two or eighty-seven people in my crew. Someone comes over to me. I'm down at the bar with George Plimpton at the hotel. Somebody says there's a meeting going on at Don King's suite at the Intercontinental. Somebody says, "They're having a meeting like there's a mutiny!" I run up to Don King's suite, knock on his door and someone opens up the door. I see, I would say, 80 percent of the black crew that had been hired. King says, "Here he is! You tell him to his face!" So I walk into the room, and one of the guys there, their spokesman, said, "We don't believe that a white man has the sensitivity to do this film about Africans in Africa. We feel the film should be directed by a black person." This is the mouthpiece and self-appointed leader of this group. And King says, "What do you suggest, Leon?" I'm shocked from the top of my head. I'm babbling on and I said, "So what you're saying is because I'm white I can't make a film about Africa?" "No, we just don't feel you have the sensitivity," comes the reply.

I think it had a lot to do with, as I told you earlier, I relied on mostly the three cameramen I had worked with before. I know these guys are going to get great footage, which will be shot properly. And although I know some of these African-Americans had good reputations, but Paul Goldsmith, Kevin Keating and Albert Maysles have just gone on to illustrious careers and are great cameramen. I think this was part of it and it ended with, I came up with, "So, if we were making a film about murder would I have to be a murderer to make a film?" It worked! It ended there. After our first screening at Sundance, everybody was there including Michael Kuhn, who at that time was the CEO of Polygram out of the United Kingdom. So Gramercy Pictures was very much interested in it. And at Sundance, except for the people who were in the business, there were very few minority people there in 1997.

There was one woman I had seen in front of the theater and she was the only black person I had noticed in the crowd. Michael Kuhn had come up and we were talking, and we shook hands. She came up and said, "Excuse me. I just wanted to say something to you, Mr. Gast. Never did I think that a white person, in the hands of a white person, could make a film about the black experience." She said exactly what these guys said twenty years earlier. And Michael Kuhn heard it. Anyway, we finalized our deal. We submitted the film to one festival, Sundance, that's where we wanted to go. We got into the competition and it did very well. We made a deal with HBO and Magnolia Films and I wound up winning the Best Director for the documentary.

Q: Muhammad Ali was idolized by so many, and continues to be, can you reflect on any significant incidents back when your film was screened?

Leon Gast: Yes. It started out with that night. After we won the award we go backstage and it's crazy. They've got it set up where there's one room. Somebody from the Academy said these are the animals, they're going to keep on shouting at you. Turn this way! Turn that way! Just ignore them. Get on the platform. You'll be there for a minute or two. So I went with David Sonenberg, George Foreman and Muhammad Ali and we posed in that room. Then we went into another room and Ali was hungry as can be. I want to tell you another Ali story. Ali was trying to eat and people just kept on coming up to him. "Muhammad, you've been my idol since I was a boy," and shake his hands. George Foreman placed himself in front of Ali with his back to him because Ali was filling up a plate with fruits and vegetables. He wouldn't let anyone get to Ali until he finished eating. It was like he was his bodyguard. All these years later, George says, "I still can't believe it. I still can't believe that he beat me."

We won another award. A week before the Academy Awards, there's another thing called The Independent Awards and we won Best Documentary. Anyway, I was at a table – a Polygram table –

Fargo won that year so the Coen Brothers were there, and we're all sitting on the table. As soon as there's a break, everybody went not for the door but Ali. He sat at that table and they lined up with their programs. As he just sat there he signed their programs, every single person that was on that line until the hall emptied out. He just sat there and he signed.

He had told me earlier there was a similar situation where he was just signing. He said when I was a kid and I won the Olympic gold medal and I came back from Rome. He wanted to know where Sugar Ray Robinson's place was – that was in Harlem on 125th Street. He walks up from 4th Street to 125th Street in Harlem. He's waiting in front of the place, which is closed. Sugar Ray owned a nightclub called Sugar Ray's, which was very famous back then. This is 1960. Sugar Ray had a pink Cadillac convertible. He's waiting and Sugar Ray arrives, gets out of the car, and Ali says, "Excuse me. I just came back from the Olympics and you're my hero." Sugar Ray says to him, "I'm very busy. I have to get into the place. Sorry, another time." He gave Cassius Clay the brush-off. And Ali said to himself, *From that time on I swore to myself I will never deny anybody an autograph who want it from me.* I saw it. Everybody who wanted it, he signed it. Sometimes not with the eye-to-eye affection, sometimes he would be looking where he was signing and sign it, but he had respect.

BUTCH LEWIS

Butch Lewis, born in New Jersey, was a boxing promoter and the manager behind the success of many champions, including Muhammad Ali and Joe Frazier, the Spinks brothers – Leon and Michael, and later Mike Tyson. He became one of the most prominent promoters in the business before moving into producing sports and entertainment projects from New York.

Q: Butch, how did you drift into promoting boxing and promoting Muhammad Ali?
Butch Lewis: Having loved the sport growing up, when Joe Frazier came out of the Olympics winning the gold medal in 1964, they started a company known as Clover-lay. And my dad was one of the original investors in Clover-lay that underwrote the management of Frazier. Through that relationship, I then became very friendly with Joe. My family were in the automobile business. As our relationship grew, being close to Joe, I started to travel with him a lot and meet a lot of people inside the world of boxing. Eventually, having met so many people, I started to learn and understand the business being somewhat on the inside. There would be meetings that I was not actually a part of, but I would be in the room. And I would see them try to make decisions on Frazier's career as he moved forward. Just like anything else, I would sit in the room on the other side of the room. And just in my own mind think what I would do and suggest if I was on that table, how Frazier's career could best be handled and things like that.

As it would turn out a lot of the times the real decisions that they made, the decisions that I was making in my own mind would be better decisions than the ones they were actually making at that table. Not that it really, in most cases, affected Frazier's career because he went on to be one of the greatest fighters ever in the history of boxing. But nevertheless I guess I started to see myself in my mind what I was able to do. I said to myself that this is something I can do. And because I knew all the major players in the sport, having traveled around with Joe and becoming like his best friend, we were like best of friends. It wasn't like I was doing that and being paid; I was doing it as a friend. We traveled around together and there were certain things I would handle for him to see that things were done, and done the right way for him. I was in Kuala Lumpur in Malaysia. Joe and I had gone there to watch Ali fight Joe Bugner because there was the talk about the fight that Ali would beat Bugner, and they were going to go to the third rubber match with Ali and Frazier classic fights.

A group of German boxing promoters and financier guys approached me because they had seen me all around the world and everywhere. They thought that I actually was a promoter in boxing. They took me to be that. They always saw me with Frazier. I even started to be with Ali who constantly had me accompany him. He used to say, "You're too smart to be with Frazier, Lewis. You need to be with me." But I was never officially in the game. My father just happened to be one of the investors in Frazier. But nevertheless I went ahead and led them to believe that I was in boxing, that I was capable of putting together a deal if the right deal was brought to my attention for Frazier after the Ali fight. So when I went back after leaving that trip, there was a lot of communication between me and the promoters. And I was running a business. At the time, we had three automobile places and I was running all three.

So I approached my father and said, "You know what, I could do this. I can leave the automobile business and become a promoter in boxing." At the time, I was young but I was making $150,000 a year. I was only in my early twenties. So I guess you would compare that in the late 1960s and early 1970s as a young guy making millions, really. That's what I was doing. My Pops says, "Are you nuts? You're making close to $200,000 a year, you're in your twenties. What are you crazy talking about becoming a boxing promoter?" Actually, I didn't know anything about being a boxing promoter. I mean, I knew all the boxers and I had a great relationship with all the top guys in boxing, but I didn't know what it takes and how to make a deal and put a major fight on. I had never promoted a fight in my life. I had never promoted anything – zero. I had never promoted a fight in a schoolyard. It went on and on. The [German] promoters would fax me and call me and we'd be talking. They flew to New York to meet me a couple of times and we met when the fight was finally on in Manila. During the time from the Bugner fight until the fight in Manila, it was constant, constant communications and trying to negotiate for me to bring Joe Frazier to Germany to defend the title.

Now, in the meantime I'm saying to Joe, "Listen, I can do this. When you beat Ali in the third fight I just want you to give me a chance." He would say to me, "Blue, man, you don't know nothing about no boxing. You don't know about promotion!" I said, "Man, I've got the guys from Germany with the money." In my mind I really thought I could. I thought I could figure it out with the help of some people I knew in boxing. I was really kind of conducting myself as though I was a guy who knew his way around in boxing.

Q: Before the first classic Joe Frazier fight with Muhammad Ali, you went into Muhammad Ali's dressing room before the fight. What was the atmosphere in there like?

Butch Lewis: In the 1971 fight? I can't even explain the atmosphere of the fight. It was not a fight; it was the biggest event, I can say, that actually happened in the history of the planet in my time. If you recall, there was an agreement of sort that the Vietnam War would stop so that the soldiers could listen to the fight on the radios on ships around the world. It's the first time ever I've actually witnessed New York City shut down that day for anything, and that would include the president of the United States when they come to New York. I've never seen the city shut down like that. I can't even explain.

Nevertheless, I was in Joe's dressing room. I had a good relationship with Ali so often times they – meaning Frazier – would send me when they wanted something from Ali. I was the guy who would sometimes go to his training camp, go out to Chicago to get some things and sort it out for the promotion when they were trying to get the promotion in order. So when it was time to wrap hands, everybody informed the other dressing room they were ready to exchange the handlers in each dressing room to watch the hands being wrapped. So I being the guy – the Ali camp liked me – I was the guy my camp sent to go down to tell him that we're ready to exchange handlers and start to get the hands wrapped. And you've got to imagine this is exciting. This is a fight that was an event the world had been waiting for – I don't know how many years – to happen. Here it is, it's finally happening.

The atmosphere behind the scenes was incredible. I was like a nervous wreck. I go to Ali's dressing room and the security outside see me. They say, "Butch, what do you want?" I told them what I was coming for so they let me in. Ali is lying on his rubdown table. He's got his trunks and boxing shoes on, but he's laying on this table. I don't know if you remember, but the guy who Ali would have with him all the time, who was like a masseuse. I forget his name, a Cuban guy . . .

Q: Luis Sierra?
Butch Lewis: Yeah, I think that's his name. He was like rubbing Ali down. Now, Ali sees me. Ali's dressing room is packed. It's crazy in there. And Ali's lying on the table and the Cuban guy is rubbing him down. So, when Ali sees me he sits up. He called me 'Lew Smoke' – like Smokin' Joe Frazier. He says, "Lew Smoke! What you doing out here? What you doing out here?" I'm like looking at him and I was... the event was so overwhelming. I finally get it out and say why I was here. And Ali being Ali, he swings around on the rubdown table with hands on the floor. He said, "Butch, is Frazier ready?" I'm just looking at him. I don't know what I did, whether I shook my head, I don't know. I'm overwhelmed right now. Then he says, "If he ain't, tell him get ready. Frazier can't beat me." He's saying all this to me! Then, as you know, Ali would have a full length mirror to work out in his dressing room before he would fight.

He said, "OK, listen. This is what I want you to do. Come here." He goes over to the mirror and I walk over to where the mirror is. He starts shadowboxing and saying to me, "Frazier can't take this." Pa, pa, pa, pa! "He won't be able to handle this, take this back to him." Pa, pa, pa, pa, pa. I'm standing there, and then Ali does his shuffle. Pa, pa, pa, pa, pa! "Now take this back to him. Tell Frazier he can't handle this. He should quit right now." I'm like, *Holy shit.* I was about to pass out just by the overwhelming of the whole thing. I'm like in a zone somewhere. So, I walk out of the dressing room and I'm like numb. Ali's laughing and shit. He says, "You should stay down here with me. I'm going to be the winner! You don't need to be with Frazier, you're too smart to be with Frazier!" I'm like, *Oh shit.* So I come back to see the trainers in Joe's dressing room to tell them that I got to Ali and that they're ready. I said that the guy is going to be here in a couple of minutes and then we can send our guy out there.

So, when I come back in Joe's dressing room, Joe was warming up in front of the mirror, too, shadowboxing. He looks at me. I guess I had a kind of a flush look on my face. he said, "Butch, what's wrong, did they fuck with you or something?" I said, "Nah. I'm good." Joe said, "What was he doing?" I said he was just lying on the table getting a rubdown. I didn't tell him what happened. I didn't tell him what Ali said to me and all that shit. I just said he was lying on the table and then he started to warm up. They had all the cameras in Joe's dressing room. Joe didn't worry about having people. There were a lot of people, but a lot of it was pertaining to closed-circuit cameras showing him in the dressing rooms and shit like that before going to the ring.

So, Joe says to me, "OK, the shit is on. Tell these motherfuckers to get the fuck out of here with their cameras. Leave the people who are with us. I'm like, *OK.* Now over here I'm becoming like the bad guy telling them, "You gotta go. This is it. Fuck it. You can't get no more, it's over." It was like that kind of shit happening. And there are couple of guys trying to hang around with a couple guys from the camera crew. Joe looked at me, and he said, "Didn't I tell you to get these motherfuckers out of here!?" Now I'm pushing guys, pushing these motherfuckers out of there. It was that kind of shit happening as they started to get their hands wrapped. I'm there till Joe gets his hands wrapped, and then I just touch his hands. Then I head out to the arena because they're going to be a while before they come out to fight. So I head out to the arena to take my seat because it's all chaotic out there. People had heart attacks. Fights are breaking out – all kind of shit. That was a moment for me that certainly I will never ever forget.

Q: When they fought the second time, what did you think of the performance of both of the fighters?

Butch Lewis: The second fight when there was no title on the line? Certainly, it could not match up what went on in the first fight. Ali, he went in that ring and nearly got knocked out by Joe. He fought a much smarter fight. The referee was Tony Perez. And the problem in that fight, if you reflect back on the fight, was that Ali would hold Joe close to him on the back of his neck so Joe would have no leverage and not be able to punch. That was basically what Ali would do: stick and move. He didn't make the mistakes he made in the first fight because he had learned from that and fought a much smarter fight. Joe kind of chased him all night trying to catch up to him. Ali won the decision. The decision could've gone either way, but Ali in my mind had done just enough to frustrate Joe and to time and win a decision.

Q: Why do you think the third fight took place? Was it because it was one win for each, and this would be a platform to decide who would prevail in a third and final match, in addition to making the event another financial success?

Butch Lewis: Why was there a third fight? One, in the mind of the world, and when I say this I don't mean the boxing fans, I mean this was an event, this wasn't [just] a fight. You had two of the greatest athletes to ever be in any sport and take a sport to that level, and to take it out of a sport and make it into an event. Here you have one winning the first fight, and the other winning the second fight, which wasn't for a title and not as crowd-pleasing. But there was enough left to say, "We gotta do this one more time to determine the winner of these classic matches," to break the rubber match. I mean, it was, again, an event the world was still yearning for, particularly with Ali coming off the Foreman fight which everyone thought big George was going to destroy Ali. Ali ended up knocking George Foreman out. I mean, the stage was set. It was the most money ever paid guaranteed to any athlete in any sport. It just had and said it all. You didn't even have to promote the fight. There wasn't really a promotion needed; just to announce it was enough. It was what the world was waiting for.

Q: Having worked with Muhammad Ali and Mike Tyson, can you please compare these two great fighters from a promoter's perspective?

Butch Lewis: Having dealt with so many promoters and so many champions in my life, I've been blessed. Going back, my first fight, it was with Ali. As it turned out Joe did not win in Manila and I ended up convincing Ali to give me my first professional fight – first professional promotion. I never did anything else. My first fight was Ali–Richard Dunn. That was my first effort. I did about seven Ali fights, and I guess I did about a total of four or five Tyson fights.

The difference was this: it was a total different atmosphere in the person and I became, of course, very, very friendly with Ali. I mean, never losing my friendship with Joe or Ali to this day. But I became very close to Ali and, of course, doing business with him. With Tyson, it was a situation. People don't know but Tyson used to come up to some of my training camps that I would set up for some of my boxers up near where he lived for a while with Cus. He was still a kid about fourteen or fifteen. He would come down to our camp and watch. In fact, in the summer I had a camp up there. And he had a good relationship with my son, who I had working up at the camp with the boxers in the summer, which he still has today with Mike.

Nevertheless, Mike on the other hand was unlike what people's real perception is – he was never that person. Only he was that person but he was like Jekyll and Hyde. He thought he had to be that kind of tough guy outside the ring as well as inside. When we talk about Ali, Ali was just the greatest promoter that you didn't even need to promote him. Ali was the promoter and he promoted whereever he went. He promoted it for you. You just needed to put the tickets on sale and that was it, really. He would do all the promotion. So, in dealing with Herbert Muhammad, he was very tough in a lot of ways, and he should've been. I mean, he helped me. Once Herbert got done with you, if you can make any money at all after negotiating you were a lucky man. I learned really early about the game of how you could lose a ton of money. It may look like a great promotion, but nobody's making money but Ali. So you'd be losing money. And people would ask, "How could you be losing money?" I'd be like, "Well, because they took it all."

But I learned a lot and I later enjoyed it. I mean, once I understood and I actually really learned the business, then it was like I could do it in my sleep. And with Tyson's situation, initially Jim Jacobs and Bill Clayton, they were more like kind of . . . Jim was a boxing historian and Bill Clayton would try to ring every dollar out of you, again, to where there would be no money left on the table for me. Even to make any of my money back, which would be like ridiculous. I'm like, "No, no. I've already learned that game. I do all this work and lose all that money. No, no, no." So there was a whole different atmosphere. I understand better now than back then, but they kept Tyson almost like a gladiator hostage where they would do nothing but let him come out to fight. Then take him back out of society and put him in the training camp ready to fight again kind of thing. Whereas, Ali was more of a personality who turned boxing into entertainment. So it was a lot more fun with Ali certainly.

Q: Some people feel Herbert Muhammad diminished Muhammad Ali's potential in terms of making even more

money for him by securing better deals. What's your opinion?
Butch Lewis: Did they explain or give an example of it? My point of view is Herbert certainly could not hinder Ali's career. And when you look at Ali's career, except during the time of him being banned from boxing, Herbert would have had Ali boxing every thirty days if he could. He was never shy in trying to figure out how to get all the money. So I don't know how he would hinder. From my point of view, if it was left up to Herbert, Ali could've fought every thirty days.

Q: How did Don King fit in the picture with Herbert Muhammad and Muhammad Ali? Was he trying to make it big back then, do you feel these two men helped shape the direction of his career?
Butch Lewis: Well, of course, he was trying to make it big. Actually, initially when I really got in the game the main guys who did the big fights were the Madison Square Garden, Top Rank and then King came into the picture and Arum retired. Arum actually left boxing because King came in and convinced Herbert to no longer do business with Arum. So Bob Arum just retired and went back to practicing law. Because initially King came in with Foreman doing the Foreman–Ali fight, Rumble in the Jungle, through Hank Schwartz who was basically with a closed-circuit company. They did all the closed-circuit and King went into partnership with them. And they got Foreman and they were expecting, like most people, Foreman was going to destroy Ali. But, of course, Ali turned all that shit around and knocked Foreman out. Don being Don, he just walked across Foreman's body, went over to the other side and was trying to talk to Ali to work out exclusive promotional arrangements, which Herbert would not do. Herbert never did, it was always a fight-by-fight contract. But if you performed well and you were Herbert's favorite at the time, then you would always get the next fight. He'd work it out while you came up with the money.

So when I broke that chain, I was like an unknown guy. I mean, they knew me around but not in the game. So when I had Ali to do the Dunn fight everybody looked at me like an upstart. They really didn't pay me any attention, but that was a good thing. But I was working behind the scenes on my own doing whatever I thought I could do. Ali liked me so much he helped convince Herbert Muhammad to give me a chance because Herbert said to him, "What are you nuts!? The kid's never even promoted a fight in the schoolyard! How the hell is he going to promote a fight for us?" So they gave me a contract, a ninety-day contract. I don't know how I got it myself, man, I'm telling you that. But I got a contract from them to deliver a fight in ninety days.

I don't know the first thing about the shit, so I first go to King and I say to him, "King, listen to this. I've got the contract. Everybody is saying Herbert's crazy giving it to Butch Lewis. Are they losing their minds?" I say to King, "I don't know the game really, but I'm willing to share it with you because you know the business. But we've got to split it 50/50." He says, "Nah, nah, I'll give you a job and you can work for me." I said, "Wait a second, Don. I come from a background where I'm already making in my family business $150,000. I don't need you to give me a job."

As it turns out he kept trying it on. He found out I had ninety days. So in his mind DK had got Herbert Muhammad to say, "If this kid doesn't deliver then DK should get the contract." And Herbert was actually rooting that I didn't come through then he could say to Ali, "Look, we gave the kid a chance, he can't do shit. He's out of here." He had told King if I don't deliver in ninety days they'd give the fight to Don! Ali would be back with Don. So in the meantime, I knew the Garden so I went to the Garden to see if they wanted part of it. Teddy Branham was asking all kinds of questions. And I'm like, wait a minute. I knew Arum had retired, but I said he's the other guy who has worked with Ali. He knows the business. Let me go see if I can get him to partner up with me and come out of retirement. I went to him and we started talking, and Arum didn't really believe I had a contract. He said, "Let me see the contract!" So I had to show him my contract and he recognized Ali and Herbert's signature. He wasn't talking to them because they had kicked him to the curb. They didn't really like Arum.

So we worked it out, but I had to go back and convince Herbert, not so much Ali. Ali didn't give a shit as long as I was the promoter in the deal. Herbert, on the other hand, really didn't care about Arum. I forget what Arum had done to him, but King had poisoned that relationship. I convinced Herbert that you don't have to love him, but you've done business with him over the years, you know he's capable in the business. There's never been a money problem, you got your money. So Herbert agreed. That's how I managed to slip in the maze and have my first professional fight promoting Ali. That's how I went there. I mean, it wasn't that simple. It was a lot of sleepless nights, a lot of threatening, a lot people threatening my life and shit. I'm like, *Oh, this is like a movie here.*

Q: Can we talk about the first Ali–Spinks fight?
Butch Lewis: When I signed Leon and Michael, when I convinced Arum to come out of retirement so to speak, and partner up where I could get the fighters and he understood the business, whereas I had the relationship with all the fighters that we could do this. So I signed up the Spinks brothers. Initially we were just doing a fight-by-fight agreement between Top Rank and myself as a partnership. Then when I signed up the Spinks brothers, that's when I became vice president of Top Rank and I had a partnership with the company. The fight itself, we co-promoted with the Garden because I had gotten in that role with Ali. And they said if we perform they'd give us another fight and so on. So we did Shavers–Ali at the Garden with the Garden. And after that fight Ali was retiring.

So, I'm sitting with Ali, and Ali said he was retiring after the Earnie Shavers fight. Anyway, as soon as a few months passed, Ali's getting ready. He's saying he's retiring, so everybody is talking about different opponents. Actually, I was hoping he'd retire because I cared about him so much because I didn't want to see him get hurt because he was taking a lot more shots. So we're sitting and I said to him, "Listen, if you're going to fight why don't you give my kid Olympic champion Leon a shot?" And he looks at me, because at the time Leon only had five fights, and he says, "Are you nuts? That kid's only had five fights!" But I get him to understand how we can promote this fight and make it happen because I had got Leon in the ratings.

Anyway, I convinced Ali and Herbert. He [Herbert] didn't, again, believe we could deliver the money because he felt it was really an easy fight for Ali. And before the Ali–Spinks fight Leon had to fight somebody else to bring the fight up. Because people were saying you're letting this kid lose, this is ridiculous. Nobody's even going to buy this fight let alone this being a fight, it's going to be embarrassing. So I set up a fight with Scott LeDoux. He was kind of one of the tough white boxers who was in the top ten, a Rocky kind of guy who had a 'name'. So I put together a fight. And hell, we nearly lose the fight. We fight to a draw.

So now it looks like the fight can't happen because I've got an Olympic champion who's just fought Scott LeDoux to a draw. He's only had six professional fights. I'm thinking, *What is this, everyone's looking at me like I'm crazy, including Arum.* He's like, "We can't do this! You're fucking up." I was controlling Leon and Michael. So I said I don't care what you think but this could work. I understood boxing well enough to know where Leon was in his career, and the style of Leon. And if I could get him in top shape – that was the problem: getting Leon to really prepare himself. In the fights he had he probably never really prepared.

Anyway, I convinced everybody we could work it out. And I go to Ali and I say to him, "Listen, I need your help." He says, "What?" I say, "Nobody believes in this fight at all, it's going to be a tough sell. But if you start to talk about how this is your last fight, you don't want this Olympic kid to . . . All kind of stuff, whatever. Just do your thing for me, man." He said, "I don't know that I can really sell this." I said, "You can sell anything." Ali started to do whatever he does and we got ABC, we got a company to buy the live. So I put the shot together. I don't know how, but the rest is history. I took Leon away for three solid months in the camp. I mean, shutting him down. He'd never been in shape like this in his life! The rest is history. You saw what happened. And he really surprised Ali, too. It was like, *Oh shit, he ain't backing down. He's hanging in there.* Nobody had really ever seen Leon in terms of what he could potentially do and the top kind of fighter he was when he was right. They didn't know because he hardly ever trained for any fight before that. But I had him in a condition where he was like a little fighting machine.

I knew his style would give Ali problems. That's a style Ali had a problem with, just like he had with Joe Frazier and Norton. But Leon being the fighter he was, he had a good pair of hands and feet. And we pulled an upset in boxing history. What can I say? It will never be duplicated again. Nobody will win the heavyweight championship of the world like that fight. That won't happen. Not in a real world. That will never happen again in history. And he won and beat the greatest fighter to ever step in the ring.

Q: Can you please talk about the second Ali–Spinks fight?
Butch Lewis: The second fight, Leon probably didn't train until two weeks to the fight. He just went nuts on me. He was all over the place. He was in and out of the clubs. Two weeks before the fight, I'm looking for him! The press was saying, "Butch, man, we can't get to Leon." I told them I had him in a secret training facility. Hell, I didn't have him in a secret training facility. I didn't know where the motherfucker was, myself! I could tell you stories. I'm looking for him, man. He was driving without a license. He didn't have a license. He said he got arrested for having drugs on him. They found half a joint in his handbag. I heard he smoked weed. I mean, I was still young, but I thought I was going to have a heart attack before this fight could happen. The fight was in the Superdome with, I think, over 100,000 seats sold. People forget that fight was free on ABC television and we sold out the Superdome!

Q: Did you get involved with any of the Ken Norton fights with Muhammad Ali?
Butch Lewis: Yeah, we did the fight at the Yankee Stadium. Ken Norton used to be, earlier on, one of Frazier's main sparring

words, they bought the live gate rights from us in Munich and they did not come up with the money. We're in Germany just two weeks away from the fight. This is my first fight. Hell, I don't know what to do. Everything is crazy and they say we might as well pack our bags. No, no, no, we're not packing our bags. I'm not going out like this. I've never . . . This is crazy. Ali's helped me. I'm here and we're two weeks away. Then I was really concerned. I had let Ali down because he had helped me to have his fight. Without him I wouldn't have had the fight.

So I go to him. I'm like hesitant. And then in some kind of way it gets in the newspaper – the local Munich newspaper – about how these promoters didn't come up with the rest of the money and that we're short. We're now short from all the foreign sales money, the TV money, the gate money. I think the number was from $750,000 to a million dollars short. And what we needed to pay to Ali, we had to put up in a credit when he landed in Munich. The credit had to be posted here in the United States at the time. So Herbert Muhammad is calling me every two minutes and saying the fight's off. I think Ali already had a million. I think we paid him $2.5 million for the fight. He already had a million. We can't get it back, now we owe him whatever it was. So Herbert's calling. Herbert hadn't come over yet. Herbert Muhammad would usually come over two or three days before a fight. He wouldn't go over there with all the circus with Ali. So he'd go a couple of days before a fight.

So he called me, he says, "Lewis, we gave you a chance, you failed." I'm like, Oh shit. He says, "I've called Ali and I've told him to pack his bags and get everybody out of there. We're coming home." I said, "Herbert, what are you going to do?" Arum was just going along with it, he was saying, "That's it, we can't do it. Let's just pack the fuck up and go home." That's it, he was going, too. So what I did was I went upstairs to Ali's suite in the hotel... No. He called me and tells me to come up to his suite. He says, "Butch, what's happening?" I said, "Listen, man, I let you down. These German promoters fucked me. They didn't put up with the rest of the money like they told me. They're telling me if I can't come up with it, go on fuck yourself. I'm in Germany and there ain't even a court I could go to – there's nothing." There's hell everywhere and Herbert's saying come home. So Ali says, "How much money are you short?" I told him what the figure was. So he says to me, "If I don't take the million, the rest of the money is OK, and everything can go forward?" I said, "Yes."

He took me into his bedroom and he had his briefcase under his bed. He took the briefcase out. I don't know what's in it. I don't know what he's doing. Herbert had already called him and told him to come home. He'd told him we got over a million dollars, which they can't get back. We don't have to fight. Ali says to me, "I'm not going to let you fail. I'm going to call Herbert Muhammad and tell him I'm willing to forgo the million dollars on my side. I'm willing to forgo the million Butch owes me." I'm like, "What!?" While we're in the bedroom he dials the phone. I'm sitting, me and him only, on the bed. He calls Herbert back in Chicago from Germany. He says to Herbert, "I'm here with Butch and I understand what's happening, but I'm willing to go through with the fight and waive the million dollars. And I know what Herbert's saying, I don't need to hear him. He's saying come home, Ali don't do this, bla, bla, bla. He was telling him don't do it. Ali's saying no, I want to do this. I don't want Butch to fail. Now I'm so taken from this I can't believe this is happening. He's on the phone with Herbert for maybe an hour. Ali's saying he's willing to waive the million and still fight. Herbert tried to convince him.

I guess Herbert was so pissed he never even came to the fight. It may have been the only fight Herbert missed because he was so pissed. Ali hung the phone up and he said OK. Then he gets the briefcase. He opens his briefcase and takes out his check book. And I'm looking at him. He says, "How much are the tickets?" I tell him whatever the price is ringside. I tell him what they are. He says, "How many tickets will $100,000 buy?" I say, "What!?" He says, "I want to buy $100,000 worth of tickets for this fight. How many tickets can I buy?" I told him whatever it would cost and he writes a check, and he says, "Who do I make the check out to?" I told him to make it out to the company Top Rank. He writes a check out for $100,000 from his personal checking account. He gives me the check and says to me there's a large military installation in Munich where the American army is based. He said, "I want you to get those tickets and distribute them throughout all the soldiers so they can come to my fight. And have them all sit at ringside going, 'Ali! Ali! Ali!'" I said OK.

After he told me all this, I had a press conference that the fight was still on and that Ali had donated $100,000 for me to give away to soldiers stationed in Munich, Germany. And the rest is history. I'm telling you this because when he did that, I'm not ashamed to admit it, I broke down in tears. I cried. I couldn't believe what he was doing and he went a step further and bought $100,000 worth of tickets to give away! He did this for me. So there's nothing in the world that I'm not able to do that Ali could ask me, and I would try to make it happen.

ALEX WALLAU

Born in Georgia, raised in the Bronx and Connecticut, Alex Wallau met Muhammad Ali before joining ABC and eventually becoming the president of the company. He initially worked in the sports division of the channel, as the two-time Emmy Award-winning producer and director of ABC's sports coverage. He was honored by the Boxing Writers of America as the top TV boxing journalist in his first year as a boxing analyst. Mr. Wallau also serves on the Board of Directors of ESPN.

Q: How did your working relationship with Muhammad Ali start and your involvement with ABC?

Alex Wallau: I actually don't remember the first time I met him. I met him before I was at ABC, but I don't remember where. And I was friends with Angelo [Dundee] and I was friends with Howard Bingham – very good friends with Howard. And when they would come into town, especially Howard, we would get together. I'm not saying it happened a lot, but it happened enough to form a small relationship there. I was there for all of the Cosell–Ali bonding, when Cosell made Ali more famous, and certainly Ali made Cosell more famous. So, that was all ABC primetime fights. I think they realized that they had helped each other and were grateful for that. Without Cosell Ali wouldn't have been as big as he was, and certainly without Ali Cosell wouldn't have been as big as he was. And I think they both knew it. As you saw them later in their lives, when they got together they still had a lot of fun together.

Q: Can we talk about the Jimmy Ellis fight? He knew and worked with Muhammad Ali from the early days. They both hailed from the same town?

Alex Wallau: Jimmy had been a sparring partner of Frazier. He was not at that point . . . In terms of their relationship, I'm not sure about that. I wasn't part of Ali's entourage at that time. We were doing Ali's fights. I know more about the fight than his background. The atmosphere was very much that it would be an easy win for Ali, everyone knew that. Ali was considered to be so superior that it was not even essential to compare the fight.

Q: Can you tell me about the fight, please?
Alex Wallau: He would talk about his opponent and try to get under his skin, and this was no exception. Jimmy was Jimmy. Ali was not up to his best, which was a case for a lot of his lesser opponents. He didn't 'get up' for the lesser opponents, which is the case for almost all the champions. They find it hard to get motivated for people they know are less competitive to them. About that time, Ali was so much superior to other fighters, so preparation and training wasn't on his high list of priorities.

Q: Any social or humorous incidents that come to mind?
Alex Wallau: I wish I could give you that, but for that particular fight I flew in late and flew back right after. So I don't have any great funny anecdotes to tell you at the training camp for the fight, aside from Ali doing his magic tricks and that sort of thing. It was business as usual at the training camp.

Q: There were a lot of exploiters around Muhammad Ali who were part of the entourage. What's your opinion on this matter?
Alex Wallau: There were different levels of people: there were the fight people – Angelo was the number one and Ferdie Pacheco. And then there were the Muslims. And then there were the hangers-on – Bundini and Gene Kilroy and people like that. Hangers-on is not fair; they were part of his entourage. Bundini didn't know anything about boxing. He was a sort of a friend, a cheerleader Ali liked to have around. Ali liked having him in the corner because he liked his cheerleading. He played no role in terms of the boxing part.

Q: When you visited Muhammad Ali's house on one occasion, he had Persian rugs and wonderful art. What was he like as a

person away from the cameras and the public?

Alex Wallau: I went to a number of his houses. The one that had the art and Persian rugs was the house in Hancock Park in Los Angeles, which is a wealthy gated community. In my opinion, none of that was Ali's taste, it was Veronica's taste. She did all the selection of buying all of that. I don't think Ali cared less. Mostly there was a camera. Certainly when I was around him there was a camera. Other times he was not putting on his act and he was a dear person. Most of the times – in the Frazier part of his career – I felt he didn't behave well in terms of what he said about Frazier. I thought it was very insensitive, and to talk about his nose and all that. I don't think it was pleasant to be around during that time. But in the later years, after the Holmes fight, I would say that he was a lot calmer. And when he finally retired and I visited him at his home in Michigan, Bern Springs, he was more of a sweetheart. He had a lot of trouble speaking. He was both funny and smart.

Q: How do you feel he changed boxing?

Alex Wallau: He absolutely transcended boxing. He became much bigger, not just than boxing, but he became much bigger than sports. I've seen videos of him visiting places. I don't think there's ever been a professional boxing match, it wasn't back then . . . There are videos of him going around in cities in India and thousands and thousands of people following him all around the cities – extraordinary. He was popular in that generation and still is the most famous man in the world, and boxing was the springboard for that. But his personality and the chaos of the 1960s, not just Muslims but Black Muslims – that particular sect – brought tons of controversy and tons of electricity around him as a person. He really was unique.

Q: In the 1970s, there were business deals Herbert Muhammad embarked on, some were bad and some good, what business interests did Muhammad Ali have outside of boxing?

Alex Wallau: The first role Herbert played was he just took a percentage of his purse. So that never had anything to do with other business investments or anything else. My understanding is Herbert took a piece of his purse. I heard it was around the region of 30 percent. I don't have independent knowledge of that. But that was his first involvement. The next involvement was getting invested in businesses, none of which to my knowledge were ever successful. I think that the relationship with the Black Muslims changed after Elijah Muhammad died. Elijah's son was Herbert who took over and was more of a spiritual man and less of a man involved with commerce of Ali's career.

Q: It's common knowledge people stole from Muhammad Ali.
Alex Wallau: If you put Ali's name and anyone else's name, you know he's a rich boxer, it's going to happen. Unfortunately, it comes with the territory.

Q: Do you think some of the people, who were around him and an integral part of his entourage, gave him the wrong advice far too often?
Alex Wallau: I don't like to speak about things I don't know for sure, and I don't have first-hand knowledge of any of the specific business activities which were done by Ali or on Ali's behalf. So I prefer not to comment.

Q: What would be the most compelling conversation you ever had with Muhammad Ali?
Alex Wallau: It was definitely in Bern Springs when he was retired. That was when he was the most real. And he wasn't putting on the public Ali face; he was putting on the private Ali face. It was much more a real conversation rather than him being a performer. He talked about his religion, about what things were important to him at that time. He led a very simple life, even though it was a beautiful horse farm. He seemed to be very content. He was definitely past that [his career] and he had definitely moved on to the life of the main portion of which was doing charity stuff, and that totally

dominated his life. He would still make fun references and jokes, but never talked about the Frazier fight, or the Foreman fight. It just didn't interest him anymore.

Q: What was his most outstanding attribute in the ring?
Alex Wallau: From the fight standpoint, I always felt that the most impressive thing about him was his speed. He was the fastest heavyweight of that size I ever saw. To me, the most impressive thing I thought was his heart. He had an unbelievable chin, unbelievable guts. I've seen his fights many times, the tenth round in the first Frazier fight, the fifteenth round when he got up right after that left hook in the Frazier fight. Every time Ali was knocked out with a punch that hit him, he was back conscious by the time he hit the floor. He had just an unbelievable chin to recover and get back in the fight, so other people would've had no chance. I think it came to hurt him in the Holmes fight and other fights, but at his peak that was always the most impressive thing about him. From a personal standpoint, as I say, almost all the time when I saw the public Ali, the person promoting fights, promoting himself, and that actually sort of tired out after a while. And during his career, especially at his peak, he didn't really reflect or talk about his feelings, fears and his hopes and all of the things that I'm sure were part of his inner thoughts. He was never much into that, which is why I always found it interesting after he retired.

Q: Earnie Shavers, who was one of the hardest hitters in the heavyweight division history, fought Muhammad Ali.
Alex Wallau: I know Earnie very well. The fight came about. I think he gave Earnie a shot. The fight was in Madison Square Garden. A friend of mine named Dean Chance managed Shavers. I think he found out that Earnie still had a punch, and after that he fought very carefully. It wasn't particularly an exciting fight. But Ali always had trouble with punchers. And if you didn't have a punch, then he would be fine.

Let me put it this way: if Ali fought Foreman ten times, he'd win ten times. If Ali fought Frazier ten times – I'm talking about in their prime. I'm not talking about Manila. I'm talking about the first fight – Frazier would win the majority of times. If Frazier fought Foreman ten times, Frazier would get knocked out ten times. Style makes fights in this era and Ali could fight anybody who didn't have a punch. But if you had a punch and you could take a punch, and you had heart and kept coming in like Frazier did, like Ken Norton did, that would always give Ali trouble.

Q: After he retired did you see any changes in him as a person?
Alex Wallau: I saw him once or twice a year. I think he became much more religious. I think he became devoted to Islam. I mean, that was the primary change. And his marriage with Lonnie, she's been a fantastic partner for him and takes unbelievable care of him, especially since his deterioration. I often wonder if twenty-somethings have the same intensity of feeling for Ali. I really don't know. I know anybody in their forties does. But I'm not sure how the young ones do. You saw the reception when he lit the Olympic torch in Atlanta. He's just a symbol of a time when the world was changing in a radical way and he's a symbol of that. He's also a talented athlete and also a compelling figure just as a personality.

Q: Anything you'd like to conclude with pertaining to your friendship with Muhammad Ali over the decades?
Alex Wallau: I don't want to overstate my personal relationship with him, to be honest with you. I was a Frazier guy. I found Joe Frazier to be... He had no personality but was one hell of a fighter. I very much resented what Ali said about him. The issue was with Frazier and I thought . . . Joe Frazier is, if you want to talk about a black man, Joe Frazier is a black man. I mean, Muhammad Ali evidently has white blood in him. Frazier would always say, "He can't dance!" And Ali couldn't dance by the way. If he gets on the dance floor he can't dance at all. But the things he said to Frazier and the hurts it gave Frazier, and also it hurts that he said Frazier was the white

man's champion and Ali was the black man's champion.

Joe Frazier never said or did anything to deserve this. I was very sympathetic to Frazier and I spent time in his camps. I went to his Foreman fight. I went to many of his fights. So I was a Frazier guy. I mean, I really felt Ali should have apologized. Same as like I liked Wilt Chamberlain over Bill Russell. I spent a lot of time in his [Ali's] training camp in Pennsylvania and that was almost always on a professional basis. I would come in with a camera crew. We would set up and do an interview, film at the training camp and we would attend his training sessions. But there wasn't a lot of time just hanging around. I mean, I had dinner there, Betty Shabazz was there. When he was training it was fun, but there's a serious aspect to it. To me, he didn't tell anybody of him as a person.

Q: Would I be correct in saying that you were there when Howard Cosell had Muhammad Ali and Joe Frazier on the show and it almost came to blows?

Alex Wallau: I was there. Ali was joking but Frazier was not. At one point he realized Frazier wasn't joking. And the reason he could tell Frazier wasn't joking is that as he got madder and madder about what Ali was saying to him, Frazier took off his ring. I believe it's in the clip. I actually saw him do that from the studio, but I'm not sure if the camera's on Frazier at that particular moment. But he did take his ring off. Joe was very serious, very serious. Ali was not. But Joe jumps up and stood up first. You see Ali hug him just trying to neutralize the situation. This whole thing was not a prearranged event. Ali was taunting him. I'm sure he knew he was going to do the taunting before he went on. Joe's reaction was definitely a real reaction.

MURAD MUHAMMAD

A native of Newark, New Jersey, Murad Muhammad's introduction to the boxing world was at the age of sixteen through traveling with Muhammad Ali as his personal bodyguard. This role lasted ten years, after which he became a boxing promoter and worked with many champions including Tim Witherspoon, Larry Holmes, James 'Bonecrusher' Smith, Donovan 'Razor' Ruddock and Manny Pacquiao.

Q: How did you get involved with working as a bodyguard for Muhammad Ali when you were only sixteen?
Murad Muhammad: They called a martial arts school. I was one that was picked to go over and take care of Muhammad Ali. Of course, he was a household name among us and we were very fond of him. I had the privilege and honor to be with him. I remember our first fight, when he fought Zora Folley in Madison Square Garden. When he was walking down the street he wore a gorilla mask. No one knew who he was behind the mask. And he would stop at certain places, like the paper stand, and he would scare the guy and then take off the mask. And the guy would say, "Oh, my God, this is Muhammad Ali!" He did that all the way to the Garden. When we got to the Garden, he walked through the gate with Bundini Brown, Dr. Ferdie Pacheco, one of his trainers, Gene Kilroy, one of his controllers and others that had been with him for years. When I got to the gate, they stopped me. They said, "I'm sorry, you can't come in." I said, "I'm with Muhammad Ali." They said he had all of his complimentary tickets already and he's used them. At the time, I didn't know what that meant.

Dr. Pacheco or Bundini Brown did not come back for me. The person who came back was Muhammad. When he came back for me I was shocked and amazed that he even recognized that I was missing. That's when I realized that he doesn't care how small you are or how large you are, he did not forget his entourage. He said to the gentleman, "He's with me!" And they said, "Ali, you have all your complimentary tickets." He said, "You mean he can't come in?" They said, "Yes, he cannot come in." He said, "OK, there will be no fight." He started walking out. They then shouted, "OK! OK!" And that's how I got in. That was the beginning of meeting Muhammad Ali.

Q: How did his security arrangements work and were there any intricacies involved?
Murad Muhammad: Well, it was all to do with observing and making sure no one came to harm him. You did what he asked you to do. I remember after the fight he was very tired. I was in the bedroom. He took off his clothes and he got into bed. And he asked me not to open the door for anyone. About fifteen minutes later, there was a bang on the door, "I made you! I made you! Open the door! I made you!" I looked out the peephole, and I said, "Who is it!?" "This is Howard Cosell!" came the reply. I didn't even know what that meant. I went to the room and said, "Ali, there's a man banging on the door." He said, "Who?" I said, "He's a white man." He said, "What's his name?" I said, "Someone named Howard Cosell." He said, "Oh, OK. Let him in!" That's how I met Howard Cosell. He came in and sat down. Him and Ali were very close. So, they sat and talked for about fifteen or twenty minutes. That was my introduction to Howard Cosell, who I went on to become very good friends with.

Q: Did you travel with Muhammad Ali abroad and can you recall any interesting incidents?
Murad Muhammad: Yes, there were a few times. I'll see if I can narrow it down to maybe three. I remember when we were in New York. Across the street there was an advertisement of a homeless shelter that was being closed down. He asked Gene Kilroy if he could get the number. And Gene gave him the number. He asked, "Where is this?" Gene told him where it was. So he said, "Come on, let's go there." Gene said, "Ali, that's about an hour away." Ali said, "No problem."

So we jumped in a cab and we went up there. They were speaking a different language when we got there. He asked Gene what kind of language that was. He told him it was Jewish. He said someone should be able to speak English here. A gentleman who owned the place shouted, "Muhammad! Muhammad Ali!" Ali said, "You know me?" The man said, "Who doesn't know you!" Ali asked what kind of place this was. He said it's a Jewish place for orphans and they come from Israel. Ali said, "Well, what do you do with them?" He said, "We place them in various different homes and parents who would take care of them." Ali said, "Well, why are you closing down?" The man replied, "It's money." Ali said, "Well, what are you going to do with the people?" The man replied, "We're going to close the place and try to send them back to Israel."

Then Ali said, "Well, what do you need?" The man said it was money! "How much money?" Ali asked. The man replied, "About $150,000." He said to Gene Kilroy, "Gene, write a check for $150,000." So he wrote a check for $150,000. And Ali said, "Will this help you?" The man grabbed Ali and hugged him. Ali said, "Don't put this in the bank right away. What you do is hold it for ten days, by that time I'll be back home and I'll put the money in the bank." He said, "Oh, Muhammad, thank you so much on behalf of the orphans. I know they would love to thank you." Ali said no problem. Then when he gets in the cab, which was waiting for him, Gene says, "Ali, lean over! You know what you just did? You gave away $150,000!" He said, "Gene, lean over," Gene leaned over, "money that I gave them, I can't take it with me. But what I did for them, I can take it with me hereafter." That just touched my heart. Ali was a religious man of the people.

The other situation was when we were in Germany when he fought Richard Dunn. Ali knocked him down with what he called an accu-punch. He hit him and three, four seconds later he realized. When in Germany, we walked through the Jewish camp and saw the ovens. This touched Muhammad and he saw how the Jews were put in the ovens. He was fascinated over that. But when we had a press conference, we were on the stage and the whole stage caved in. I had a job to do. I only weighed 160 pounds, but I could press 450 pounds or more. I was able to straddle that hole and catch Ali between his two arms and hold him up. And I helped him up. It was either him or Bundini Brown. Without Ali there would be no fight. I thought that was the right choice on my behalf.

And the other one that comes to my mind is when he fought Kenny Norton in Madison Square Garden. We wanted a rematch. What happened was I was standing there in the ring. If you go back and look at the tape, I was handing him the comb because he liked to comb his hair. And then there was a riot because at the time the police officers were on strike. People were throwing chairs, there was a big fight. They thought Kenny had won. A lot of people thought Ali had won so it was a controversial decision. He didn't look at anybody else but he looked at me and said, "Can we get past that crowd?" I said, "Yes, we can." He put his arms on my shoulders and I walked him through that hostile crowd. I thought that was unique: a young man who does martial arts protecting Muhammad who has to rely on me to come through that crowd. Those three things stand out.

One more that comes to my mind is when we were in Tokyo when he fought the guy called Inoki. Muhammad was going around scaring all of them. And these guys could take telephone books and rip them in half. And they could break bricks. And they were wrestlers. They were big strong wrestlers, but they were scared of Ali. It was like he was going to hit them. They would run back and he got a kick out of it. So the promoter there said why don't you make it winner takes all? Ali said, "OK. Winner will take all. Because I'm going to whoop him and then knock him out in the fight in the fifth round."

His manager, Herbert Muhammad, said to the promoter that he couldn't do that. Ali doesn't sign any agreement. The promoter said, "Well, he signed this one and he's going to live up to it." Herbert said, "Well, you supposed to put five million in the bank in America." He only had two million in the bank in America. The promoter said, "Well, let me tell you this, Mr. Muhammad, this is not America. We've got a signed agreement winner takes all. We're not going to put any more money in your account in America. We believe Inoki is going to win the fight." Herbert said OK, so we walked out. And he turned to me and said, "Make sure you tell everybody to be downstairs in one hour."

We packed and were ready to go. There was about seventy of us. Sure enough we all came downstairs packed, the promoter says, "What are you doing, Mr. Muhammad!? What are you doing!?" He said, "My contract means nothing over here so I'm going home where it means something." The promoter ripped up the contract and said, "OK! OK! OK! The money will be in the bank tomorrow." It was a good thing he did so because the wrestler, as you know, lay on the ground for fifteen rounds kicking Ali on the shins. The fight was a draw, but we got paid, of course. The money was in the bank. We did go to Korea from there. Everybody said Ali is not going. His leg was injured but he still went over to Korea to keep his commitment. When we got to Seoul, Korea, my God, there were millions of people from the airport all the way to the hotel. They were shouting, "Long live Muhammad! Long live Muhammad!" It was just unbelievable. Those are some of my highlights with Muhammad Ali.

Q: You, of course, went around with him as his personal bodyguard, any interesting stories pertaining to fans?
Murad Muhammad: Well, the people loved him. He used to have all kinds of groups ranging from senior citizens to boy scouts. They would all come up to the camp to be with him. They had a great love for him. One day that stands out as very interesting was at the time of his exile. He was living in New Jersey. His chauffeur was driving him, it was pouring down with rain. Someone was standing on the corner looking for a ride. Ali pulled over and said, "Where are you going?" He said he was going to New York. He said, "You're long away from New York. Get in." He didn't know it was Muhammad. So he got in. Muhammad took him home and told him he could spend the night. Now, that was a tough job for

me because you not only had to stay up all night looking at the stranger thinking, *Is he going to do anything to Muhammad?* So, the next day he took the stranger to the airport and put him on a plane so he could fly to New York.

About ten or fifteen years later – I'm a promoter now, and Ali traveled with me everywhere – we were on the plane and he got up to go to the bathroom. As he came back a senior citizen, who looked about seventy years old, said, "Hi Muhammad, you know me?" He said, "Oh, yes. We know you? Have you seen my fights?" The man replied, "No, we haven't seen much fights of you, but we know of you." He said, "Well, how do you know me?" The man said, "Years ago you picked up a man and brought him to your home and fed him and put him on the plane." Ali said, "Ah, yes. I remember that!" But between you and me, he don't remember things like that. But he likes to make people feel good. When he asked, "How do you know me?" they said that man was their son. I just thought that was amazing.

Let me give you a story which a lot of people will not know unless you write it. I was doing a fight. I had one of my fighters fighting Steve Collins from Ireland. What made that fight so unique is because there was a reason . . . The state asked me would I put on a fight at the Pink Elephant at the arena. A lot of people called me because as a boxing promoter, I did things which were unique which people have not done before. Like taking Roy Jones Jr. from three million to seventeen million; taking Roy Jones Jr. from the middleweight to the heavyweight championship of the world and win. It hadn't been done in over 106 years. Going on the Radio City Music Hall.

The Garden kept begging me to bring Roy out of Mississippi. I said I'm not leaving that place where we promote a monthly bout in a sold-out crowd. I didn't believe Roy could sell out the Garden. They kept begging me. I said give me Radio City Music Hall. They said, "OK. You got it." In two weeks I sold it out. We had two rappers who I didn't know because I wasn't too much into rapping. Roy likes the rapping so we brought them in. I was heading around the corner as they came around. Ninety percent of the crowd were Caucasian. When the rappers came out, people were jumping in their seats and standing up and waving their hands. I thought, *Oh, my God*. I walked from behind the curtain and I said to myself, *I did it*.

Then to get into *Sports Illustrated* for my outstanding achievements, it was a miracle. I should never be in *Sports Illustrated* – I don't play any sport. So that was a first. Then to go to and do a show from behind prison walls, that was original, never been done before. I got a call from Ross Greenberg, the president of HBO. He said do yourself a favor, you like to do things that no one else does. I went behind the prison walls. Don King and Bob Arum were the only two major promoters at that time, and they couldn't go behind my back because I had an exclusivity of the whole institution of the state of New Jersey, which is unheard of. Don was able to find a kid named James Scott. They were paying me to watch a fight at Rahway State Prison. James Scott did a most outstanding job in beating a guy named Eddie Gregory. I sold that to HBO, not Arum or Don King. I brought live boxing to HBO, that's my record, my history. So if you go check my record, they call me the 'Miracle Worker'. I made miracles happen.

When Oscar De La Hoya came out as a kid, I told him I was going to make him a millionaire. He never made over $200,000 in all of his career [at that point]. I told his manager to sign on the dotted line and I'm going to make you a millionaire. He said how could you do that? I said to him I make miracles happen. He signed on the dotted line. I got Oscar through and introduced Oscar to a guy named Jerry Pacheco, shook his hand and we co-promoted Oscar coming out of retirement fighting for the junior-middleweight championship of the world. I made both the manager as well as the boxer millionaires. I was able to get millions out of that deal.

On the undercard there was an African boxer who wasn't my fighter. It was a fight HBO wanted to put on. He had six title defenses and he was the number-one contender and he dropped out! So prior to that, I started a kid named Manny Pacquiao, who nobody wanted. He was making 5,000 a fight. I gave the kid 10,000 to be on that card. His manager said, "I've been in America for two years, why would I go with you?" I said, "I make miracles." He liked that and signed for 10,000. I had him sign exclusively. He signed on a Saturday and on Wednesday I called him, and I said, "How would you guys like to fight for the world title?" He said, "You've gotta be kidding! You do pull miracles." I put him on the card.

He, of course, knocked the champion out and became the world champion. That was the beginning of the success of making Manny Pacquiao a phenomenon in America and in his own country. That's another story. So these are the stories which are unique from the rest of them. It's because of my honesty and integrity in the boxing world, but Muhammad Ali taught me that. Muhammad told me if you do anything transparent, keep everything on the table, it will be the greatest asset you'll have. So, when they began to tell the world after the FBI investigated boxers for fourteen years, the FBI tried to take boxing down when fifteen guys admitted to fraud. I was the only one who came out clean. They didn't have to investigate me. Muhammad used to say, "Did they spell your name correctly? Keep in line."

Muhammad traveled everywhere I went. Once when he went with me to the arena, which we sold out, whilst he was there, I told my security guys – now I've got my own security – to watch out for Muhammad. We walked into the suite and I said, "Muhammad, you take my room?" He said, "Nah, hah, you're a big shot now. I'll take the little one with the two beds." So, he wanted to stay out. My security guy would sit there with him and Ali dozed off and began to talk in his sleep. "I'm gonna kill you! I'm gonna kill you." So he was talking like that in his sleep. When he woke up he asked the security guy to tell him what he was saying in his sleep. The name of the security man was Keith Ali. He had the same last name as Muhammad Ali. Ali asked, "Was I talking in my sleep?" The security man said yeah. "So my wife was telling the truth. She took me to the hospital and the doctors examined me and they said

I talked in my sleep! But you can't touch me because if you do, I could have a heart attack in my sleep," Ali told him. So Keith said, "OK, Ali, no problem." Ali then said, "Come on, you sleep in my room!" He said, "Nah, nah." He said, "I've got two beds in there." That was an honor for the security guard.

Ali got back to bed and the security guard didn't feel like going to sleep so he turned the little light on to read. Later, it started again. "I'm gonna kill you! I'm gonna kill you!" Then he turned around on his knees like he was punching Joe Frazier. "I'm gonna kill you! I'm gonna kill you!" Then he stopped, got out of bed and he started walking like a mummy with his hands like he was going to choke somebody. "I'm gonna kill you! I'm gonna kill you!" He went outside the door and the security guy said, "Oh, my God. I can't touch him!" He remembered what Ali told him – he would have a heart attack. Later, Ali comes back and he kept getting closer and closer. The security guard didn't know what to do. The security guard finally backed off, and Ali says, "April Fools!"

Q: He is seen with great reverence by so many of the elite stars from the sports and entertainment worlds. Can you recall any interesting anecdotes?

Murad Muhammad: Oh, my God, The Beatles loved him! The Beatles used to come over and play with him and roll over the floor. He loved The Beatles. The Beatles loved him. Another star made a diamond robe just like he made one for himself. Elvis Presley loved him. Ali and Elvis Presley were close. Sammy Davis Jr. used to come over and tap dance before he would go out to fight and he loved him. He was loved by all the celebrities. We would walk into the party and the music would be playing, the celebrities lined up to get his autograph. Cher, Diana Ross, Sylvester Stallone, all of them lined up to get Ali's autograph. He was the life of the party.

And these types of people came around to the camp. He was just that kind of a person. They loved him and he loved them. Sam Cooke used to see him all the time. He used to bring Sam Cooke in the ring. The great artist Leroy Neiman, his paintings don't go less than 100,000 in America, he used to stand there and draw Ali. So these people had love for Ali, who gravitated to him. Great people came to Muhammad, and Muhammad was not an idol seeker. He enjoyed them but he didn't chase after anyone.

And he was the kind of a guy when he went to the store to buy things, he would buy six-pack trousers, six-pack shirts, and that was his attire. If he needed a suit, we had to take him into a store and buy it. Then, we wouldn't know what to do with that suit because he never carried suits with him. Yes, they made him the best dressed person in the world. It was amazing that they say here are the three most outstanding dressed people in the entire world. They put Muhammad Ali number one. I just thought that was an outstanding accomplishment. You know, Christians believe in Jesus, Muslims believe in him, too. The entire world knows Muhammad Ali. I've been into countries and it's unbelievable we were going to fight Kenny Norton the very first time in Turkey. The people in Turkey said if Norton won he would never make it home. So Ali never fought Kenny Norton in Turkey. That was just too strong, you couldn't beat him in that country. So these are the things I witnessed and upgrade my mind and made me understand what the world was about, why I became a phenomenon in the sports world. Everywhere I promoted in my early career, Ali was sat next to me.

Q: You mentioned Sylvester Stallone earlier.
Murad Muhammad: Ali liked the idea that Sylvester Stallone made the movie *Rocky*. He liked people who came from nowhere and could create things like Sylvester did. Sylvester created his own way into Hollywood. A guy from Philadelphia that was trying to make it, he became very large with *Rocky I, II, III*. James Brown sang one of his songs in *Rocky*. I think it was *Rocky III*. Ali and James Brown were really close. He had love for James Brown, so that's one of the reasons he liked the movie. Ali got James Brown that part because Ali knew Sylvester well and he knew James Brown. And James did a wonderful job. Ali would give up things. Once he was out of

the country and when he came home, he had Rolex watches and he gave them away to all his staff members. He didn't care about jewelry. He loved cars, of course. He didn't care about anything of material substance.

I'll tell you another story. It was in the latter part of me being around him as a security man. Me and him were watching Joe Frazier and George Foreman fight over and over again. He memorized the fight so well, he could tell you on the day I was sitting in the third row with what suit on. That's how well he remembered the fight. It's quite different now with remote controls, but he had to get up and rewind the tape. When George Foreman knocked out Joe Frazier, he told me to replay it. So we replayed it. I couldn't understand why he kept telling me to replay it when he's watched it a hundred times prior.

He said, "Look at George, he's tired. He's got his hands on the ropes . . . I've got it! I'm going to get him to use up all his energy, his stamina." I said, "Well, how are you going to do that?" He said, "I'm going to make him throw punches. When he throws his punches, I'm going to lay up on the ropes. Round one, he's going to come a hundred miles per hour. Round four, he's going to come a hundred miles per hour. Round six, he's going to come fifty miles per hour. Round seven, they're going to be coming thirty." Then he said, "Round nine or round ten, that's when I'm gonna knock him out." He said, "I've got to play the rope. I've got it!" I asked him what. He said, "Rope-a-dope. I've got to make a dope out of him." That's how he created the rope-a-dope out of that.

Q: How did Muhammad Ali spend his time on the road, how did he make use of his free time?
Murad Muhammad: He studied the Quran. He used to study one o'clock or two o'clock in the morning. So did I while I was a student of the Quran. I watched him study and he made me study. And he studied scriptures. That's why today he's such a sound and devoted Muslim. He can't speak but he hands out cards with "God is one". He loved giving cards and as a Muslim he took his religion

serious. He followed the Honorable Elijah Muhammad when he was younger, then he followed his son in 1975. That's when he became strong in his study. He did that later. I encouraged him because I was always around and a couple of other people. Today, if he's not doing anything he likes to do tricks, magic tricks. He didn't want people to believe in magic. Every time he did a trick, he would then tell people how he did it. He liked cards. So he enjoyed playing with people, entertaining people with his little tricks and cards.

Q: Can you tell me about the movie *The Greatest*?
Murad Muhammad: Well, someone asked me if that was the truth. I said no. It was fabrication, the movie didn't tell the truth. The movie lied. The photographer talked back at Herbert Muhammad in the movie. Herbert Muhammad was one of the most powerful men in boxing. He didn't want any publicity. He never wanted any recordings of him because he didn't like the cameras. But he was powerful. He was so powerful that he created Don King, who was a felon from jail, and Bob Arum, who used to walk around – that's another story. He created a kid named Butch Lewis, who joined Bob Arum at Top Rank. And he created Murad Muhammad. All four were successful. King had fighters from lightweight to heavyweight; Arum was known for fighters from lightweight to heavyweight; I was known for fighters from lightweight to heavyweight and world champions and world contenders.

I had many fights on ABC, NBC, CBS, HBO, ESPN, pay-per-view and closed-circuit. Arum, King and I have done all of that. Butch Lewis ended up with a kid named Leon Spinks when he left Bob Arum, and he's known for Michael Spinks, Michael Spinks, Michael Spinks. Butch was phenomenal! Butch made the first $11 million for the kid who probably wouldn't have made that amount if he fought – when Michael fought Mike Tyson. Butch decided to leave the sports world. Herbert Muhammad was a powerful man. Ali used to respect him. They used to call him 'Judge'. No one disrespected him, not even the Mob. The Mob was fearful of him because he had the whole Nation of Islam behind him. But in the movie they portrayed Herbert the way the photographer wanted to do in his subconscious mind. Then they said Herbert didn't help Ali when he was in exile. When someone said, "Well, Murad, do you approve of the movie?" I said, "I suggest they can do something where my great, great grandchildren will know Muhammad Ali." Sometimes you've got to overlook something which is not true to get the reality because they want to give a perception of something which was more than what it was and take the reality out of the movie.

The reality is that my brother Herbert Muhammad was not only the most powerful man in America in boxing, but in all of the sports. Because no athlete ever, whether they played basketball, football, baseball, whether they were Caucasian, African-American, Latin, no athlete ever received a million dollars for their performing until Madison Square Garden offered Ali with Frazier a million dollars. Ali called the manager of Joe Frazier and said let me handle this. He said no problem, you do it. So when they offered Herbert a million for both fighters, he walked out with his lawyer, the same and very prestigious law firm that Obama's wife went to when she came out of school.

There was a guy named Charlie Lopez. He's deceased now. Charlie walked outside and Herbert said, "What do you think, Charlie?" He said, "What do you think!? Herbert, there's no athlete who makes a million dollars an hour. Do you think the guy is going to give you more? No way! That's a lot of money!" He said OK. They went back inside and they all stood up. There was about five of them from the Garden. They said, "We've got a deal?" They shook each one of their hands, and Herbert said, "Call me when you get up to five million," and walked out. Charlie said, "Herbert, you know what you have just done!?" He said, "Sure, I know what I'm doing."

Sure enough, they got five million – two-and-a-half million apiece for the fight. That's what raised the money in boxing. They did it over and over till the point basketball players started asking for more money, the football players started asking for more money and so on and so on. Everybody in the sports world was trying to follow behind Muhammad Ali. Herbert opened the door. They didn't tell that kind of story, but I lived it so I know it and I know that occurred when it came to the great Muhammad Ali. When you walked up to him, "Muhammad, I've got a deal." He would sit down at the table and while you talked to him he would play like he's asleep – snoring. We would be laughing because you couldn't come to him and try to do business. You had to go through his manager. It didn't make him unintelligent or uneducated; it made him wise to know that this man is going to look out for my wealth, this man knows how to get what we want.

So, all my athletes, they became millionaires or I made more millions for them. I have a club, I call it 'The Millionaire Club'. I learned how to do that by being around Muhammad Ali. Can you imagine Ali fighting in this day at twenty-one years old? Ali would break the record! If you think Mayweather and Oscar could do 150 million, you think that Mayweather and Pacquiao could do 200 million, just multiply that by three and that's what Ali would do in this day. He was phenomenal! He was a promoter's dream. He didn't cry about things saying, "Oh, I have to go to this press conference." He would stand on 42nd Street and stop the traffic and let everyone know that he was fighting this week. He'd get on the train, whatever kind of train it was and wherever it went, he would go from beginning to the end and talk on that train telling people. He would talk with people and not just kings and queens, but bus drivers and cab drivers, the young man who carries your bags to your room, the pimps, the hustlers. Even the prostitutes came out and they all dressed up in their fine clothes.

So when people say, "How great is Muhammad Ali?" They don't know what they are talking about because Muhammad was not just great in the ring, he's a great man outside the ring. These boxers today give nothing back to their community. They don't do anything about people starving. They will not stand up for something they might not get good publicity for. Look what

Muhammad went against: the draft. He said I'm not going to no Vietnam. There's no Vietcong ever called me Nigger. Why would I go over there and kill them because you say they need to be killed? All these people were against him. The people who loved the war were against him.

Today, he's respected for his stand because the Vietnam War was the worst war we could ever have. There are two wars that you don't want: a guerrilla war and a holy war. Today, he can't speak beyond a whisper. Today, his mind cannot tell his body what to do. If you put George Foreman; Mayweather; Pacquiao; Roy Jones Jr.; Evander Holyfield; Joe Frazier and any other boxer all on one side of the street, they are all walking together. And if you put Muhammad alone on the other side, across the street, people will cross the street and go to Muhammad because they know Muhammad, from the old to the new. The young might not have seen him, but their parents speak about The Greatest of All Time. And that's my humble opinion.

SUGAR RAY LEONARD

Sugar Ray Leonard is widely regarded as one of the best boxers of all time, and was the first to earn more than $100 million in purses. Leonard first entered boxing in 1969 and won Olympic gold in 1976 before going on to win world titles in five weight divisions. He fought some of the most ferocious champions of all time, including Marvin Hagler, Thomas Hearns and Roberto Duran. He was coached for much of his career by Ali's trainer Angelo Dundee. Leonard was also the co-host (along with Sylvester Stallone) of the successful TV show *The Contender*.

Q: As a kid, can you recall watching Muhammad Ali?
Sugar Ray Leonard: The first time I saw Ali, I was maybe fifteen, sixteen. And I was blown away by the fact he was so different to the other big guys, the heavyweights, in that he boxed and moved around like he was a lightweight. And he was so smooth. He was so fast and he talked trash. It was more of an entertainment than anything when you watched Muhammad, which drew me towards him being one of my idols.

Q: What made Muhammad Ali different to all the other heavyweights, and what elements did you take from him?
Sugar Ray Leonard: His style of boxing was more scientific than the others. The other guys were a bit more methodical, but Ali was a thing of beauty. It was his artistry that captured my eye. It was his performing that captured my eye. It was just his movement and fluidity that captured my eye. And no one could trash-talk like Ali, but I didn't do that part.

Q: When Muhammad Ali was training at Deer Lake, did you start training there later?
Sugar Ray Leonard: I had a chance to go to Deer Lake and watch him. And I was blown away by that. First of all, I had never seen so

many people in a training camp – fans in the training camp – and he was always in control, even in the gym. And he was relaxed. I found that to be one of the factors in my success, of being relaxed.

Q: He used to joke around a lot. Can you relate any humorous situations?

Sugar Ray Leonard: Well, one thing I do remember is when you were not looking, he would use his hands to make this kind of cricket sound. He would rub his thumb and finger together, which made me jump. I was startled because I thought there was a bug in my ear. Another time was when I met Ali at this black-tie affair. I hadn't seen so many utensils in front of my plate in my life. Because all we used were forks or a spoon. And I waited for Ali because I thought he knew how to properly eat food in a formal affair. He grabbed his bread and his roll and just dumped it in the gravy. So I did the same thing. That was one of the funny moments I remember.

Q: From all the conversations you have had with him, what sticks out the most?

Sugar Ray Leonard: One thing he told me, he said always control your destiny. And he said about being in control of your destiny. I understood it right away because there have been thousands of boxers, maybe more, that made a lot of money, but at the end of the day they had nothing to show for it. And he always told me to control my own destiny.

Q: You were on *The Arsenio Hall Show* with Mike Tyson and Muhammad Ali!

Sugar Ray Leonard: Well, I just felt so overshadowed by Ali and Mike Tyson – two big guys. Without a question Ali was a living legend and Mike Tyson was the most dominant heavyweight in the world. So it was a special moment being on *The Arsenio Hall Show*. That's been considered one of the greatest episodes of all Arsenio Hall's talk shows. It [Parkinson's] wasn't as debilitating as it has become. That disease had gradual progression. But he wasn't as bad. He was very responsive of whatever was asked of him. But he wasn't totally the same. But it was a great, great experience.

Q: Would I be right in saying you modeled some of your style after Muhammad Ali?
Sugar Ray Leonard: No one could duplicate Muhammad Ali. But I picked up as much as I can from him and I picked up things from Sugar Ray Robinson. I picked up things from Bruce Lee. I picked up things from Jersey Joe Walcott. I picked up things from various incredible fighters.

Q: What is your favorite Muhammad Ali fight and why?
Sugar Ray Leonard: Muhammad Ali and Joe Frazier – all three. When Ali fought it was magic, it was his payment.

Q: He reached a level of global idolization, which is matched by very few. How much of an impact and influence has he had on the world?
Sugar Ray Leonard: For me, Ali was bigger than boxing. He was boxing. His legacy will extend forever, for eternity. He stood up for what he believed in by not joining the army because of his religion, and to do that back then, when he was up against heavy opposition, for him to stand forward, and he even sacrificed his career, spoke volumes for the character of the man – Ali the man.

EVANDER HOLYFIELD

Evander Holyfield is the only boxer to capture the world heavyweight championship four times. A multiple world champion in the heavyweight and cruiserweight divisions, he fought some of the top boxers of his era, including Larry Holmes, Riddick Bowe and George Foreman, and fought in classic fights against Mike Tyson and Lennox Lewis. He currently resides in Atlanta.

Q: What are your memories of watching Muhammad Ali on TV when you were growing up?
Evander Holyfield: I watched his fights, fights that he fought with Leon Spinks. And they showed a lot on TV when he beat Sonny Liston, when he won the title the first time. They showed this the most because that's when he was an underdog and looked like he wasn't going to win the fight, but he did. They showed Ali who he was, very confident, and he'd tell people what he was going to do and he'd go out and do it. They [Ali–Frazier fights] were definitely great fights. They were legendary fighters, both had confidence in themselves and the ability to win. Ali won two and Frazier won one. But all these fights were important.

Q: What did you think of Muhammad Ali's boxing style – speed seemed to be one of his strongest attributes – what are your views on his fighting style?
Evander Holyfield: He was a smart fighter. He had good hand speed. He had average power, but because of his hand speed he was able to counter-punch because he had great speed. Also, when it came to power punches he was able to beat people.

Q: Do you think he elevated the sport of boxing because of the way he utilized his personality?
Evander Holyfield: Realistically, other than being a good fighter he was a good communicator. He was a good motivator. So people

came to be entertained and he was able to show a person that you can box, but also show a person you can communicate and inspire people – people to be like you. He was a very confident man.

Q: You were born in Alabama, how hard was it in the 1960s for black people in that part of the country to overcome racism?
Evander Holyfield: It's what Ali did for people: someone has to stand up for a cause. He was in the right position at the right time. When he refused the draft, he said he wasn't going to go fighting [in the army] to show people that: why should I go to war to fight somebody who I don't know when people that I do know hate me here? So it was something that was strong. He said we could stand up. We had Martin Luther King and we had other people who were fighting for us to be treated as human beings. I think all of these things add up to that legacy of black freedom. He played a huge role in that.

Q: When was the first time you actually met Muhammad Ali?
Evander Holyfield: The first time I met Ali was in 1984 at the Olympics. The great thing is Ali had been a light-heavyweight champion in the Olympics and I was, too. So, all these fans kind of allowed me to know that I was going to be a heavyweight, too. Even when I was a kid I was told that I could be the heavyweight champion of the world like Ali. That's where my inspiration came from. When I was eight years old I was told I could be like Muhammad Ali. And I was able to accomplish the same thing he accomplished and was able to take it to another level.

Q: Did you go to any charity or social event?
Evander Holyfield: Yes, I have. He had this thing for Parkinson's disease and I went about five or six times. It was in the 1990s. I was there for the support. At some point in time, you respect the man for all that he's accomplished and you realize and hope the best for him. Parkinson's disease is something that we need to find a cure for. I know he's a man who is always trying to bring people

together for the best. The first time I got to talk to him, I was the heavyweight champion of the world.

Q: Final words on Muhammad Ali?
Evander Holyfield: I think things are made to get better. His generation brought something to the table and Ali definitely was a trailblazer. When he came in he set a standard, which was so high, and no one ever reached it until I reached it. And that has to be endured. Floyd Patterson was actually the first person who said he's the first person that will never be the heavyweight champion the second time. Of course, Ali was the first person to do it three times and I'm the first person to do it the fourth time.

JIMMY WALKER

Jimmy Walker is the founder and chairman of Muhammad Ali's Celebrity Fight Night, which drew a plethora of A-list names from the sports and entertainment worlds to support the Barrow Neurological Foundation and several other charities. To date, with the help of the greatest sportsman, Celebrity Fight Night has raised more than $90 million for Parkinson's sufferers.

Q: What are your recollections when you first got together with Muhammad and Lonnie Ali to discuss having him join forces with Celebrity Fight Night?

Jimmy Walker: The first meeting when was in Phoenix when Muhammad came to the Barrow Neurological Institute for his treatment for Parkinson's. I was a board member of the hospital. I had started Celebrity Fight Night in 1994 and at the time I was a limited partner at the Phoenix Suns basketball team. I called Charles Barkley and asked Charles if he would put on large oversize boxing gloves and box other celebrities in a comedic manner – basketball star Phil Jackson, NFL star Joe Montana, boxing legend Sugar Ray Leonard. And sometime afterwards Muhammad came to Phoenix and I met him agai and I explained that we could attach his name and his involvement to the event to raise money and create the Muhammad Ali Parkinson's Center. He and Lonnie really liked the idea. For twenty years before Muhammad passed away he attended every one of the events. We have actually given $90 million through Celebrity Fight Night – with the lead beneficiary being the Muhammad Ali Parkinson's Center. He's obviously greatly missed. We are still raising money to help those who have Parkinson's.

Q: What do you vividly remember at the first event he attended?

Jimmy Walker: It was in 1996. I remember the people in awe of Muhammad Ali being in the room. And his presence was just electrifying. Muhammad would get on the stage as well as he could with his Parkinson's disease and he was able to speak. And as time went on he really lost his voice, but he still would go onstage and he would present the Muhammad Ali Awards. I may add that in Phoenix in our community I would take Muhammad many places, such as a basketball game. And there I would walk with Muhammad in front of 18,000 people and he would get a standing ovation from practically the entire crowd. We would sit down and players from both teams would come up to him, many of them just wanted to shake his hands. When we would leave the game he would get another standing ovation. I could take him to a Friday game and then take him again the next night and he'd still get a standing ovation. And I've had sitting with me – and I say this with respect – Tiger Woods and Michael Jordan. I mean, people in the crowd know that these icons are there, but not like Muhammad Ali. Only Muhammad would get that ovation because he was so special.

I might add that he had enormous love in his life. Muhammad used to tell me that the greatest religion in the world is the religion of love. And even the Scripture says that among faith love is the important thing. And Muhammad Ali embodied that. Muhammad had no hatred in his life. He loved Joe Frazier, even though Joe previously didn't like Muhammad that much. Muhammad was all about people. Just for the record, there never will be another Muhammad Ali. They don't make people like him anymore.

Q: When Muhammad could still talk, what is the most thought-provoking conversation you both had that left an everlasting impression on you?

Jimmy Walker: The visit I will never forget is when I first met him. It was at an LA Lakers basketball game. The owner of the team, Jerry Duckworth, and Sammy Davis Jr. were present with Muhammad. I was at another table so I went up and I introduced myself to him. I just couldn't get him to say much. So I repeated myself. I still couldn't get much out of him. He could talk at that time. I said, "Muhammad, you and I have a mutual friend in Earnie Shavers." And he kind of looked at me. I said, "Muhammad, Earnie really loves you a lot." And Muhammad said, "If he loves me so much, why did he hit me so hard?" Earnie went fifteen rounds with him in Madison Square Garden. And Muhammad said to me that Earnie had hit him harder than anyone. That's a moment I will never forget. This was probably 1987. Years later when I heard Muhammad was in Phoenix I made a point to meet him and Lonnie. After that we spent a lot of time together as we were together for 20 years. I remember once I took him to a baseball game. He loved to look outside the window of a car. This was typical of Muhammad. And people would be driving their cars and almost drive off the road staring at Muhammad, and he'd smile. This particular time he was waving to people to follow us after this baseball game. We had about twenty cars behind us and we got to the house where Muhammad lived. All these people behind us got out of their cars – twenty people walking into the house and Muhammad waving all these people to come inside the house. And Lonnie asked him, "Muhammad, who are all these people?" She said, "Muhammad, those are strangers, you don't even know them." Muhammad said, "Lonnie, those are my friends." He had all these people in the house. That was Muhammad: such kindness, love and warmth, everybody was his friend.

Q: Can you reveal any anecdote in relation to A-list celebrities attending Celebrity Fight Night?
Jimmy Walker: Three people come to my mind immediately. One of them is Billy Crystal. Billy got his start impersonating Muhammad Ali. They both had such a connection it was really amazing. They were close. Thick or thin, whatever it took, Billy would do anything for Muhammad. The first time I attended the Muhammad Ali Museum in Louisville, Angelina Jolie and Brad Pitt were there. And I met them. President Clinton was there. Again, you have to understand that Muhammad could draw any kind of crowd. People loved to be around him.

At one event Celine Dion was singing and her husband Rene, who has now passed away, was sitting next to Muhammad.

Muhammad is right in front of her. She stops singing in the middle of the song, and she says, "Rene, you know who you're sitting next to? You're sitting next to Muhammad Ali, the Greatest of All Time." She then starts singing, finishes her song and Rene had tears coming out of his eyes. It was the biggest thrill of his life. Robin Williams was always saying funny things. I remember Halle Berry said something once. She got her award onstage and in front of 1,300 people she said to Muhammad, "You know, Muhammad, I married all these other men. I should've married you." And Lonnie Ali jokingly said, "Well, Halle, there he is. You can take him. He's all yours." Muhammad couldn't talk so he took his finger and rolled it around his ear as to say, *You're crazy.* We always had a lot of fun with our celebrities.

Oh, my God, each one of them had something special, including Andrea Bocelli, one of the greatest singers in the world. I'm in the Ritz Carlton in New York and I'm in the lobby. I see Andrea. I go to the elevator and I stop the elevator. I introduce myself. I let Andrea know that I do a charity event with David Foster because David produced Andrea's music. But he didn't say much. Then I said, "I do this with Muhammad Ali." Andrea said, "You know Muhammad Ali?" I said, "Yes, I do this event with him every year." He said, "He's my hero. All my life I wanted to meet him." I said, "Andrea, I know you're coming to Phoenix for a concert next week. When you're in town, would you like to meet with Muhammad? We could go to his house." So the next week my wife and I picked up Andrea and some Italian conductors from the Ritz Carlton in Phoenix and we go over to Muhammad Ali's home. Walking up to the door I mentioned to Andrea that it was Lonnie's birthday and told him that she's Muhammad's wife. She opens the door and Andrea immediately sings happy birthday to Lonnie. We're walking into the house and I'm making the introduction leading a blind man to a man who can't speak. They sit next to each other. Andrea kisses him several times on the cheeks. He's down on his knees and says to Muhammad, "I'm humbled. I'm honored. It's a great thrill of my life and I'm very nervous. I always wanted to meet you."

He then got up and Muhammad whispered to him, "Would you sing to me?" Bocelli sang him an Italian opera song. It was pretty special. Then next night we're in the Coliseum in front of 20,000 people at the concert. Lonnie and I, my wife and Muhammad are sitting in the front row. And Andrea Bocelli comes out with boxing gloves on and he's punching. He said to the audience, "I had the biggest thrill of my life last night when I met Muhammad Ali. I went to his home."

Q: Muhammad's health deteriorated with Parkinson's, in the last several years of his life how would he spend time at home?
Jimmy Walker: A good question. Muhammad, during the day, liked to watch a lot of boxing movies. He'd watch fights that he fought Joe Frazier, Earnie Shavers, Ken Norton. He loved magic so he would sit and do magic tricks. I remember I took Billy Crystal to his home and he would do tricks for Billy. And Puff Daddy, I took him to Muhammad's home. Once I picked him up and took him to his house. It would be so easy to ask any celebrity, "Would you like to go to Muhammad Ali's home and spend some time with him?" And the answer would be yes. They'd stop everything they'd be doing and go. That's easy because Lonnie is so hospitable she would invite anybody in. I remember on Denzel Washington's 50th birthday we did a video for him at Muhammad's house. Muhammad always loved people stopping by the house. He would get in the car and they'd drive around. He liked to go to the games. It was very unfortunate that Parkinson's robbed him of his voice. He had such a great way of talking. He is so well known for the things he said, but he lost his voice so couldn't speak anymore. Early in the morning the daughters would call and he could get a few words out, but it was very difficult. But Lonnie is a superstar wife and really loved Muhammad. I think she fell in love with him when she was in grade school and he was Cassius Clay. They grew up in Louisville. She was an amazing wife who did everything to help Muhammad. They would keep him busy and he'd do some stretching exercises. He would do whatever he could. He had

tremors and he'd take his medication for it. Dr Lieberman would practically go see him every Sunday. So he had the support of a lot of good people around him.

Q: What legacy has this great iconic figure left?
Jimmy Walker: I think the legacy left, personally for me, is the love he had for people and the sense of humor. I mean, you're talking about the most recognized person in the world at one time. He could go anywhere and he was so highly recognized. Much of it started when he carried that torch in 1996 at the Atlanta Olympic Games. The funeral was at Louisville basketball team arena with 14,000 people there. There were people all over the streets and when the car carried Muhammad's body people in the streets threw flowers, it was very special love and appreciation. He loved crowds. I heard Muhammad wanted his funeral in the Yankee Stadium. Lonnie asked him, "Why?" Because Muhammad wanted a big crowd. Once I took him through Yankee Stadium. We were in a cart and we went around before the game started. The 50,000 people in attendance gave Muhammad a standing ovation. Then all the players came out, about fifty baseball players, to shake his hand although only three or so were supposed to come over to receive an award from him. There are so many memories with him. The legacy is the respect he had for people and how much people loved him. He just changed a lot of lives with his influence. I do know this: with the problems we are having in this world, if Muhammad had a voice he would go to these countries without a bodyguard and he would talk peace. And he represented peace. Just like Vietnam, he didn't want to go there nor kill anybody. He was a man of peace. If he had his voice he would have gone into these troubled countries. Nobody would hurt Muhammad. He didn't have a bodyguard. He didn't need one. He was Muhammad Ali.

APPENDIX

MUHAMMAD ALI TIMELINE

January 17, 1942. Born in Louisville General Hospital in Louisville, Kentucky. Attended Virginia Avenue Elementary School.

1954. At the age of twelve, starts boxing after police officer and boxing coach Joe Martin directs him to boxing trainer Fred Stoner.

Between 1954 and 1960. Wins six Kentucky Golden Gloves titles, two national Golden Gloves titles and two AAU titles.

Completes 9th grade at Du Valle Junior High School.

September 4, 1957. Enters Central High School.

March 31, 1958. Voluntarily withdraws from Central High School.

1959. First time hears about the Nation of Islam.

1960. Wins Olympic gold medal in the light-heavyweight division at the Rome Olympics.

1960. Signs with the Louisville Sponsoring Group and turns professional.

October 29, 1960. Has his first professional fight and beats Tunney Hunskar in Louisville, Kentucky.

November, 1960. Is sent to California to train with Archie Moore.

December 19, 1960. Begins training with Angelo Dundee at the famous 5th Street Gym in Miami, Florida.

December 27, 1960. Fights and beats Herb Siler in Miami Beach, Florida. The first fight cornered by famous trainer Angelo Dundee.

November 15, 1962. Fights and beats former trainer Archie Moore in Los Angeles.

June 18, 1963. Fights and beats Henry Cooper in London, England.

1964. Joins the Nation of Islam.

February 25, 1964. Wins the heavyweight title in Miami, Florida, after Sonny Liston fails to answer the bell for the seventh round.

March 6, 1964. Elijah Muhammad gives him his new name Muhammad Ali.

August 14, 1964. Marries Sonji Roi in Gary, Indiana.

May 25, 1965. Knocks out Sonny Liston in the first round in the rematch in Lewiston, Maine.

November 22, 1965. Defeats Floyd Patterson via a technical knockout in the twelfth round.

January 10, 1966. Divorces first wife Sonji Roi.

1966. Classified A-1 making him eligible for service in the United States Armed Forces. Makes the famous 'Vietcong' remark.

May 21, 1966. Beats Henry Cooper for the second time in London, England.

November 14, 1966. Beats Cleveland Williams at the Astrodome in Houston.

February 6, 1967. Beats Ernie Terrell in Houston, Texas.

March 22, 1967. Final fight with Zora Folley before Ali's stripped of his title and his license is revoked.

April 1967. Refuses induction into the United States Armed Forces.

June 1967. Prominent African-American athletes and Ali have the historical meeting in Cleveland.

June 20, 1967. Court finds him guilty of draft evasion and fines him $10,000 and sentences him to five years in prison.

August 17, 1967. Marries Belinda Boyd.

April 14, 1969. Nation of Islam officially suspend him and take away his Muslim name.

October 26, 1970. Returns to the ring in Atlanta, Georgia, defeating Jerry Quarry in three rounds.

March 8, 1971. Fight of the Century, Ali fights Joe Frazier in Madison Square Garden in New York. Ali loses in a unanimous decision.

June 28, 1971. The Supreme Court rules in Ali's favor, reversing the 1967 draft-evasion conviction.

July 26, 1971. Beats Jimmy Ellis in Houston, Texas.

January 1972. Performs pilgrimage in Mecca.

June 27, 1972. Beats Jerry Quarry for the second time in Las Vegas.

September 20, 1972. Beats Floyd Patterson for the second time in New York City.

February 14, 1973. Beats Joe Bugner via decision in Las Vegas.

March 31, 1973. Loses to Ken Norton via decision in San Diego.

September 10, 1973. In the rematch with Ken Norton in Inglewood, California, Ali wins a decision.

January 28, 1974. Fights Joe Frazier for the second time in New York and wins via unanimous decision.

October 30, 1974. Fights George Foreman in Kinshasa, Zaire, in Rumble in the Jungle knocking Foreman out in the eighth round.

June 30, 1975. Beats Joe Bugner via decision in Kuala Lumpur, Malaysia.

March 24, 1975. Beats Chuck Wepner. The fight inspires Sylvester Stallone to churn out the script for the *Rocky* movie.

October 1, 1975. Frazier–Ali III – Thrilla in Manila – takes place in Quezon City, Philippines. Ali retains the heavyweight title after Frazier's corner stop the fight just before the fifteenth round.

1975. Converts to Sunni Muslim after the death of Elijah Muhammad.

June 26, 1976. Fights wrestler Antonio Inoki to a draw in a mixed martial arts fight in Tokyo, Japan.

September 1976. Fights Ken Norton for the third and final time at the Yankee Stadium in New York. Ali wins in a unanimous fifteen-round decision.

January 1977. Divorces second wife Belinda Boyd.

1977. Marries Veronica Porche.

September 29, 1977. Beats Earnie Shavers in New York City.

February 15, 1978. Loses a split decision to Leon Spinks in Las Vegas.

September 15, 1978. Beats Leon Spinks in a rematch in New Orleans, winning the title back.

1979. Moves to Los Angeles.

June 27, 1979. Announces his retirement.

October 10, 1980. Comes out of retirement, losing to Larry Holmes in the eleventh round in Las Vegas.

December 11, 1981. Has his final fight, which takes place in Nassau, Bahamas. Loses to Trevor Berbick.

1984. Is diagnosed with Parkinson's disease.

1986. Divorces third wife Veronica Porche.

November 19, 1986. Marries fourth wife Yolanda Williams then later moves to Michigan.

1990. Travels to Iraq to meet Saddam Hussein to negotiate the release of American hostages.

1996. Carries the Olympic torch at the Olympics in Atlanta.

1996. Joins forces with Jimmy Walker to lend his name to annual charity event Celebrity Fight Night.

1999. Is crowned Sports Personality of the Century by the BBC and *Sports Illustrated* names him Sportsman of the Century.

November 17, 2002. Goes to Afghanistan as a guest of the United Nations.

2005. Muhammad Ali Center opens up in Louisville, Kentucky.

November 9, 2005. Is presented Medal of Freedom at a White House ceremony.

October 3, 2013. Attends the first Muhammad Ali Humanitarian Awards in Louisville.

April 9, 2016. Attends for the last time Celebrity Fight Night in Phoenix.

June 3, 2016. Passes away in hospital in Scottsdale, Phoenix, aged 74.

June 9, 2016. Funeral takes place at Freedom Hall in Louisville.

ABOUT THE AUTHOR

FIAZ RAFIQ is a professional sports and entertainment contributing writer for more than half a dozen prominent national newspapers including *The Sun*. For fifteen years, he was a chief columnist for a bestselling combat sports magazine *MAI*, and also contributed to *MMA Uncaged, Fighters Only* (the world's biggest MMA magazine), *Men's Fitness, Muscle & Fitness* and *Impact: The Global Action Movie Magazine*. His work has appeared in publications around the world. He has interviewed many famous personalities including some of the greatest boxing, UFC and bodybuilding champions, countless Hollywood actors, producers and directors.

An acclaimed biographer of some of the most iconic figures in sport and Hollywood, he is the author of three oral biographies, *Bruce Lee: The Life of a Legend, Muhammad Ali: The Life of a Legend*, and *Arnold Schwarzenegger: The Life of a Legend*. Fiaz co-authored the critically acclaimed *My Brother, Muhammad Ali: The Definitive Biography* with Muhammad Ali's only sibling, Rahaman Ali, which was 'A *Sunday Times* Book of the Year' in 2019. He contributed to the authorized documentary *How Bruce Lee Changed the World*. He remains close friends with more than one member of Muhammad Ali's family.